D1545718

THE PROUD

Public Library Catalog
10ted 1994

THE PROUD
Inside the Marine Corps

Bernard Halsband Cohen

WILLIAM MORROW AND COMPANY, INC.
NEW YORK

HIGHLAND PARK PUBLIC LIBRARY
494 Laurel Avenue
Highland Park, IL 60035

359.96
C678

Copyright © 1992 by Bernard Halsband Cohen

All rights reserved. No part of this book may be reproduced or utilized in any form or by any means, electronic or mechanical, including photocopying, recording, or by any information storage or retrieval system, without permission in writing from the Publisher. Inquiries should be addressed to Permissions Department, William Morrow and Company, Inc., 1350 Avenue of the Americas, New York, N.Y. 10019.

It is the policy of William Morrow and Company, Inc., and its imprints and affiliates, recognizing the importance of preserving what has been written, to print the books we publish on acid-free paper, and we exert our best efforts to that end.

Library of Congress Cataloging-in-Publication Data

Cohen, Bernard Halsband.
    The proud: inside the Marine Corps / by Bernard Halsband Cohen.
        p.   cm.
    ISBN 0-688-11737-6
    1. United States. Marine Corps—History.   I. Title.
VE23.C64   1992
359.9′6′0973—dc20   92-1299
                                         CIP

Printed in the United States of America

First Edition

1 2 3 4 5 6 7 8 9 10

BOOK DESIGN BY LISA STOKES

For Arthur and Ida

Author's Note

★

When World War II broke out my father attempted to join the Marines and was rejected because he was too short. He was, instead, drafted into the Army, where he spent the entire war on a rifle range in New Jersey. Though he forgave the Corps, he never forgot. Thereafter, the mere hearing of the Marine Corps Hymn would give him goose bumps.

When the Vietnam War began heating up, my father reminded me that I was a couple of inches taller than he was, and so the Marine physical "would be a cinch" for me.

I didn't want to be a Marine. So, like my father, I was drafted into the Army. And, like him, I spent my hitch far away from the action, riding an M-60 tank around central Germany.

In the fullness of time my father passed away and I was asked to undertake a book on the Marines.

In the three years I have worked on this project I have traveled from the sand pits of Parris Island to the swamps of Camp Lejeune to the rolling Mediterranean off Tarquinia to the "PT" courses of Hawaii.

I have flown, sailed, marched, crawled, slept, eaten, and partied with Marines around the world. I have, indeed, found some of the very things my father sought. I have also seen some things that would disappoint him terribly.

I have been privileged, lucky really, to have been witness to all this during three of the most fascinating years in the history of the Corps, three years that mark the transition from the last days of the post-Vietnam "malaise," through a sea change called "warrior training," to a final glory in the vanguard of Desert Storm.

I have seen what it means to be a Marine.

Acknowledgments

———————— ★ ————————

When you research a book over three years, from coast to coast, from Hawaii to Rome, in the air, on the sea, and through the swamps of the Carolinas, you need the help of an awful lot of people.

The officers and men of the various Public Affairs Offices of the United States Marines are among the finest press people with whom this writer has ever worked. I was aided, accompanied, and acculturated by more than thirty of them, but there are a few to whom I must give a special thank you.

To Lieutenant Phillips, who lent me his canteen for a march through Camp Lejeune. To Gunny Nummer, who got me on the strike helo when current events demanded otherwise. And to Major Conway, who not only got me onto the U.S.S. *Guam*, but also got me home again.

I must also acknowledge the heroic and marathon support of Nick Ellison, not a Marine, but my friend and literary agent.

Contents

THE PROUD

The Landing That Wasn't

───────────────────── ★ ─────────────────────

The dust of Desert Storm hadn't yet settled as Gen. Norman Schwarzkopf stepped to the lectern, picked up his pointer, and smiled at the assembled press in the hotel ballroom.

Though the battle was still under way, the outcome was no longer in doubt—if it ever had been. Iraq's Saddam Hussein had loudly predicted that the coming conflict would be the "Mother of All Battles." Instead, the armed forces of the United States, in partnership with a coalition of armed forces from nations of the Persian Gulf and around the world, had swept through, around, and over the vaunted and much-publicized Iraqi defensive line, and had, in less than two days' time, destroyed better than half the Iraqi force and pinned Saddam's crack Hammurabi Division, the jewel of his elite Republican Guard, against the Euphrates River. Now it was all over but the blooding, and the briefing. General Schwarzkopf had a right to be smug.

He began his talk with an account of the subterfuge that preceded his attack. He told about "blinding" Iraq by taking out its air force. He told about movements at night. Then he smacked the pointer against a chart and said, "We continued our heavy operations out in the sea, because we wanted the Iraqis to continue to believe that we were going to conduct a massive amphibious operation in this area."

Heads nodded. Some Marines in the audience shifted uncomfortably in their seats. No one, of course, would admit to such a thing for attribution, but for the United States Marine Corps, Operation Desert Storm, despite its glory, contained some very disappointing moments.

"I think many of you recall"—Schwarzkopf fairly winked at the press—"the number of amphibious rehearsals we had and the maneuver called Imminent Thunder which was written about quite extensively."

The reporters laughed. Imminent Thunder, which took place just days before the actual assault, was heavily reported to be the prelude to war and much of the press coverage centered, quite negatively, on the dangers of an amphibious raid against such heavily fortified positions as the Iraqis had set up on the beaches and shoreline.

Now it was Schwarzkopf's turn to laugh. He had used the press expertly in his campaign against Saddam. "We continued to have those operations because we wanted him to continue to concentrate his forces, which he did." Again, Schwarzkopf smacked the pointer against the chart, this time on the shoreline of Kuwait, where much of the Iraqi personnel and materiel remained uselessly mired for the duration of the conflict.

Imminent Thunder, the eagerly awaited Marine amphibious landing, the first such major undertaking from the sea since Inchon, in Korea, had proved nothing but a decoy.

"I don't want to characterize Imminent Thunder as being only a deception, because it wasn't," the Army general said with a scowl. "We had every intention of conducting amphibious operations if they were necessary."

But they weren't necessary, and that stuck in a lot of Marine craws that remembered Tarawa and Saipan and Iwo Jima. If amphibious maneuverings were a thing of the past, they wondered, could the Marines themselves be next to go? Absent the need for a strong amphibious assault in the American military overview, was there really a role for the Marines? Proud as they may be, the Marines often think like this. The nightmare scenario of the Corps' disbandment is not an unthinkable thought in the ranks.

Many remember that the end of Vietnam brought with it dark rumblings of a phasing out, of decommission, of an end to the Corps, or, at best, its incorporation into the Army, and this was not the first time the Corps had faced its demise. It may come as a surprise that the Marine Corps, arguably the most famous of all military units, has had to fight for its political life several times in its history. Even after World War II, surely the Marines' greatest glory, it took an act of Congress to keep President Harry S Truman from doing them in.

The post-Vietnam rumors of disbandment blew threw the ranks of the jungle-fatigued Corps like a yang wind. In the bicentennial year of 1976 they exploded in the devastating Brookings Institution report, *Where Do the Marines Go from Here?*

"There is growing evidence," said the report, "that administration officials and legislators alike are beginning to take a hard look at the Corps. It is no secret that . . . studies commissioned by the Secretary of Defense, James R. Schlesinger . . . included an examination of the question: why a Marine Corps."

Noted briefly were the great World War II successes in the Pacific. "U.S. Marines," the report admitted, "carried out most of these landings. But they did not . . . participate in any of the great amphibious assaults in the European theatre: the seaborne invasions of North Africa, Sicily, Salerno, Anzio and Normandy were undertaken by Army units. . . . "

Truth was, even in the war with Japan, the Marine Corps' amphibious monopoly was not complete. Many landing operations in the southwestern Pacific were Army shows under the command of General Douglas MacArthur.

But even granting the Corps the franchise for beach operations, Secretary Schlesinger himself had questioned "the need for an amphibious assault force which has not seen anything more demanding than essentially unopposed landings for over 20 years, and which would have grave difficulty in accomplishing its mission of over-the-beach and flanking operations in a high threat environment."

The report enthusiastically agreed and pointed out that "the Corps remains organized, equipped, trained and deployed *mainly* . . . on the amphibious mission, which stems from a variety of military, political and institutional factors . . . a distinctively tailored 'light' infantry force—a force that in order to be readily deployable and adapted to helicopter and amphibious ship operations, conspicuously lacks armored fighting vehicles and heavy weapons."

The authors of the Brookings report were convinced that the full-scale amphibious assault was a romantic relic of the past.

"In all the ten long years of battle in Vietnam, a sea coast country criss-crossed by a lattice of rivers, there was not a single raid from the sea and the lion's share of the riverine operations were undertaken by the Army and the Navy."

To add insult to injury, the Brookings report offered statistical evidence that the once proud Corps, now reduced to a "romantic relic" of itself, was in serious trouble with regard to its own troop discipline.

The percentage of high school graduates in the ranks was the lowest of the four services, while courts-martial were the highest, running at three times the rate of the Army. Desertions were four times as high!

Citing America's declining post-Vietnam appetite for military "intervention"; the inability, even supposing such intervention, of the Navy to get the Marines to the beaches in a timely and sufficient fashion; the inability of the Marines, once there, to fight effectively in the brave new "electronic battles environment"; and the terrible effect this "negativity" was having on the esprit de corps; the report suggested that the Marine Corps of today "cannot remain as it is, structured for past rather than likely future contingencies."

Was amphibious warfare, Marine style, to be consigned to the mothball yard of history? Would there be no more glorious island campaigns? And no more Inchons?

In fact, there had been a sea change in weaponry since 1915, advances going far beyond the advent of rapid-firing weapons. This time it was not just the efficacy but the very core philosophy of amphibious warfare that was being put to the fire.

Amphibious assault depended on speed, but air was quicker. It relied on stealth, but how do you hide troop transports on an ocean that is increasingly becoming the photo subject of a flock of spy satellites? It relied on mass-on-point, but how do you dare mass men when missiles and precision-guided "smart" munitions of sure lethality strike so quickly and so silently and with such merciless effect? What do the thousands of men on the beach do when the defenders "go nuclear"?

The Brookings report concluded that, if the battlefield of the future were to preclude the amphibious assault, "how useful Marine infantry forces—short in firepower and battlefield mobility—would be in non-amphibious contingencies against technologically sophisticated enemies is in serious doubt." It proposed four alternative options for the Marines; all involved cutting them roughly in half.

The new, smaller, more armored, more heavily gunned and less uniquely leathernecked Marines would either a) continue the present role afloat, b) join NATO as a second small army in Europe, c) become an army for strictly Asian operations, or d) take on the role of an airborne division.

Those recommendations had the effect of grapeshot in the rigging. Marine Corps lobbyists went to work. The Congress went to work. The recommendations were rejected. The Corps, again, was saved, and immediately it set about the job of reinventing itself in its own image.

Recruiting standards were raised. Training increased and focused on self-discipline. Maneuver warfare, the idea that by rapid movement you could defeat an opponent in his mind long before you could attrit his men, began to bubble up as the main Marine fighting doctrine. Unit continuity was strengthened so that fighting men would know each other better, and rely on each other more effectively.

The proud new programs had a slow but positive effect. By 1981, when Senator Gary Hart authored his seminal piece "The Case for Military Reform" in *The Wall Street Journal,* he noted that "traditionally, the [armed] forces were organized on a 'corporative' model. Each officer was inculcated with and worked in every way to advance the overall goals and purposes of his service. Today, only the Marine Corps adheres to this model."

The trend was up. The Marines were regrouping. And then, in 1988, General Al Gray appeared. He was the commandant the Marines felt they would need to make it all the way back.

There was a bit of a fuss attached to General Gray's being piped aboard his "watch." The changing of the Marine Corps commandant usually gathers little notice in the public prints, but Gray's nomination, coming after what *The Washington Post* described as "a real brawl in the Defense Department," was news.

For one thing, Gray was up from the ranks, a one-time sergeant who had kept his striped mentality all the way to the top. This peculiarity was already at work. The Marines have since World War I used the bulldog as a kind of unofficial mascot, but when Gray called himself a "bulldog" all the Marine Corps exchanges and off-post haberdasheries exploded in lines of bulldog T-shirts and hats and dolls. And when it was seen that the new CMC preferred camouflage utilities to dress blues, those same emporia quickly came out with new lines of camouflaged objects that ran from the predictable "sand and spinach" skivvies all the way down to camouflaged shaving cream can covers.

Gray was also news because he was assuming command from a watch that had not gone well for the Corps. Still fresh in the hearts and minds of all U.S. Marines were the 240 Marines who lost their lives in the demolition, by a suicide truck-bomb driver, of the Marine Corps barracks in Beirut, and the consequent sorry retreat from Lebanon.

Too, there was the much-publicized Marine Sergeant Clayton Lonetree, the lovesick security guard of the American embassy in Moscow, and the resultant "sex for secrets" scandal which involved him and several other Marines and raised uncomfortable questions about the job the Corps was doing safeguarding our embassies overseas.

There had also been that operation on the tiny Caribbean island of Grenada, a seaborne raid in which the surprisingly small Marine component covered itself with what glory it could and then grumbled privately that only a few short years ago the whole damn operation would have been a United States Marines show.

There were also some questions about Gray himself, and they were hard ones. Sure, he was a wonderful soldier, a brave warrior, but did he have the polish necessary to handle the delicate Pentagon wars? Could he win the Corps its share of the war-room battles that determine which service gets what and how much?

Senator Sam Nunn, chairman of the Senate Armed Services Committee, had opened Gray's nomination hearing by noting that "some critics of Defense...have claimed its provisions would prevent experienced commanders with [Gray's] mix of skills from rising to the very top military positions. General Gray's selection," he said, "certainly demonstrates that this is not necessarily so."

Still, "some people," said the less charitable *Post*, "believe he lacks the smooth edges you normally see in Washington."

U.S. News and World Report, in a mixed review, called Gray "a gruff individualist known for getting the job done at the expense of bureaucratic niceties." Gray was, it said, "a sharp contrast to [former Commandant General P. X.] Kelley, who was more a manager than a warrior and," in fact, "lobbied against Gray to succeed him."

In his change-of-command speech before 4,500 Marines on a hot June night at Camp Lejeune, Gray had very graciously responded.

"This is General Kelley's night," he said of the former commandant, "... a great American and a great patriot, one who has led, one who has followed, one who has been fearless in combat." Then he paused.

"I mention that tonight"—he smiled here, having discharged a "nicety" and moved on to what he took to be the ceremony's main objective—"because we must from time to time remember that the nation's Corps of Marines... are warriors! We're warriors and people who support warriors, and we must always keep that focus. This great nation loves her Corps of Marines; they pray for us; they support us; they fund us. The nation demands that we teach nothing but winning... and by God, [we're] going to make it happen in the years to come— God bless and Semper Fidelis."

The change in command was brutal, direct, bulldog, and well received the next morning at mess.

"Gray's supporters," *The Washington Post* grudgingly acknowledged, "characterize the... general as having 'credibility inside the Marines as a leader.'"

The question remained: Was there a role for the United States Marines in the modern American defense posture? Gray thought so. But to secure it he would first have to resell America on the mystique of the Marine Corps; and to do that, he would have to resell the mystique to the Corps itself. The Marines were now poised for a return to the fabled gung-ho days of song and story. Commandant Al Gray would begin the process by making "every Marine a rifleman." He would call it "warrior training." He would drive the Marines to glory.

In many ways, Desert Storm was the American military's successful comeback from the disasters of Vietnam. The Marines were looking to come back, too, perhaps more so than any of the other services. And so, three years before Iraq invaded Kuwait, the Marines began the final phase in making themselves ready for whatever role history would bring.

To follow the story of that great and deadly earnest undertaking, you need to know that before there was a Kuwait there was a Carteret.

Good to Go!

★

Major Dan Conway, Paducah, Kentucky, was standing in a narrow, dimly lit hallway rubbing his eyes and smiling. The major has a mischievous little grin, one where the tip of the tongue peeks out from behind clenched teeth, giving him the look of a prep school boy who is perpetually about to play a prank.

Conway had made a career in the military intel field. He was now the senior intelligence officer for the 24th MEU (Marine Expeditionary Unit). When the president says, "Send in the Marines," it is the expeditionary units that go "on float."

The 24th MEU was the one that went to Beirut and got its barracks blown up. But the Marine Corps comeback was now well underway, and Major Conway had new orders in his hand that would speed it along.

He fingered the yellow-and-black-striped file folder with the stenciled TOP SECRET on its face. He peeked inside the folder, then looked up and smiled that little smile again.

"You sure you want to go on *this* one?" he said.

The answer was most affirmative. The contents of the yellow and black folder were then revealed.

The orders were marked "Confidential—Destroy." They began with the admonition that the "situation" was acute. Some

Third World army general named Jean Claude Varsett, a locally charismatic commander, had launched a bloodless coup against the president of Carteret.

This had not been reported in *The New York Times*, or *The Washington Post*, or in any other American newspaper.

"Although the coup attempt failed," the orders said, "the officers and men of the Carteret Air Force (CAF) are still fiercely loyal to their commander. They have been successful in establishing several strongholds in the southern region of the country."

On the fifteenth of May, the situation brief continued, in a second incident which also went unreported on the evening news, ten people were injured when an incendiary device was detonated in a Carteret nightclub known to be frequented by American businessmen. And "threats were being directed toward the American embassy."

It was determined (by what the orders cryptically identified as the "national command authority") that "there was a significant threat to Americans present in Carteret." A response was needed. Groundwork had already been laid.

"The government of Carteret," the orders said, "has assured the U.S. that it would assist U.S. forces in a noncombatant evacuation but insists that any U.S. force that comes ashore does so with the minimum force necessary to accomplish the mission."

Action orders like the one in Major Conway's hand had been quickly dispatched to "all necessary units" because the "national command authority" had decided, as it had decided again and again across the previous 213 years, to send in the Marines.

The idea was to mount a quick and quiet evacuation from the site of the American embassy. But these papers, labeled "MEUEX ORDER 05," contained a stinger. It read as follows.

"Intelligence assets have identified a CP [command post] from which the People's Army for the Liberation of Carteret (PALC) and the rebel Carteret Air Force (CAF) have been co-ordinating their efforts," the brief said. And then this.

"CTF 62 [the 24th MEU's crack landing team] is ordered to *destroy* the joint PALC/CAF HQ. There are approximately 10–15 armed personnel at the site. They are armed with AK-47s [assault rifles], RPKs, RPGs, and SVDs." This is your basic Soviet-supplied rifle-grenade-rocket-launcher force trained in insurrection.

So this is how, on a warm Thursday night a couple of years before the Iraqi invasion of Kuwait, you find yourself sitting next to Lance Corporal John Hess, nineteen, of Buffalo, New York, floating in a small gray motorboat surrounded in all directions by the blackness of approaching midnight, rising and falling on the swells of a quiet and forbidding ocean.

The boat is a "Rigid Raider," a newly operational craft developed as a replacement for the older, slower, and more vulnerable rubber raft of a thousand commando movies. It is designed for quick and silent seaborne "insertion."

The slim Raider is gunwale-to-gunwale with Hess's burly squad of six and a coxswain who stands at the rear commanding its powerful engine bay and lightning-fast rudder.

As the Raider bobs quietly at idle, the cox speaks softly into a radio. He and his fellow coxes are lining up the attack boats in the darkness. A second Raider now slips out of the gloaming and into view on the right. Then another on the left, bobbing up and down on the black velvet swells. There are eleven Raiders in all, six Marines to a boat, sixty-six attackers from the sea.

Hess's squad has drawn the point position in the attack on the rebel command post. They've piled all their weapons, mostly Marine-modified M-16's, M-79 grenade launchers, and a SAW (M-249 Squad Automatic Weapon) light machine gun, in the center of the boat, and have protected them with their packs and their armor vests and the ammo-laden battle suspenders.

"When we crank this thing up," Hess whispers, "hold on real tight to the rails but try to stay loose in your shoulders. This thing hops around like a mother rabbit and it's real wearing on your arms."

Young Hess's voice is thin and reedy, but it carries a note of authority. He is, after all, the basic building block of the Corps. He's the lance corporal. He's on the first rung of command. He's the squad leader.

The cox hears something on his headset, responds almost inaudibly. Water laps quietly against the sides of the boat. Hess cocks his head. "Good to go?" he whispers.

The cox draws a hand across his neck, in effect telling Hess to shut up.

"Just give us a heads-up and light your cans," Hess snaps, more for the squad than for the cox.

There is a matter of honor here. Hess doesn't outrank the cox, but he doesn't want his squad dismissed so curtly by a man of the same rank as his own.

What he's said to the cox is meant to point up the difference between their two jobs: the one in the mud and the blood, the other in the relative safety of the boat. All Marines harbor a little envy of the grunt, the basic jarhead. Therefore the cox is stung. Honor, for Hess's tight little band, is preserved.

The small *frisson* between the cox, who is in charge of the boat, and the squad leader, who is in charge of the men, is the kind of precarious partnership you see everywhere in the military where men are torn between differing loyalties: the larger loyalties like the Corps or country or cause; the smaller personal ones like the equipment for which one is held responsible; and the emotional ones, that tightly woven intimate loyalty to "the outfit"—the squad or the company or the battalion or whatever the command is perceived to be.

In general, Marines lean toward the last. There's no dearth of love of country here, nor disregard for materiel, and love of the Corps is legendary. There's just a simpleminded, romantic belief that if "the outfit" prevails, Corps and country and everything else worth living for will be the prime beneficiaries. Hess may be running a lot of things through his head right now, but most of them have to do with what he sees as "the outfit." In this case, six bunkies.

Hess puts a hand in the water and runs his fingers across his lips. He's a slender guy with a sharp face, no more than five foot six or seven, easily the smallest man in the squad. He says it doesn't bother him. He says, "God made us free but the M-16 makes us equal." Still, he's grown a ratty little mustache which he denies has anything whatever to do with "the height thing."

The greasy black and green slashes of "cami" that crisscross his face don't improve his looks any, but his eyes lase through the darkness. Squad leader eyes. The men like him. Better than that, they trust him.

Though Major Dan Conway's intelligence on the raid is exquisite, the plan is simple enough. According to Hess, the rebel HQ is roughly fifteen miles inland, but a narrow river winds to within about eight miles of the camp. When the command is given, the phalanx of Rigid Raiders will speed across ten miles of ocean to the mouth of the river. They will then proceed more quietly up the river and down a small estuary. There the squads will disembark.

Conway has made maps which show the terrain down to the smallest detail, but the squad leaders will not be carrying them. In the dark the various squiggles and lines would be dangerously unreadable. Instead, the maps have been studied for hours and committed to memory.

Sixty-six men will make their way, in complete silence, up a dirt road to a dense wood, mostly scrub pine and brush. They will then pass through a bramble swamp. "Bet your ass the enemy thinks the swamp's impassable," says Hess. And, hell, maybe it is.

The swamp gives on a meadow. Shorn of cover, the squads will get down in a crawl. If all has gone well, they'll have covered five miles in about five hours.

From the meadow a second dirt road will take them to a clearing. Here the squads will split off. The main group will flank to the left and prepare to lay down a base of fire. At about 0500, an hour before first light, the small force, with Hess's squad in the van, will attack the rebel base across the wide clearing.

There are to be no prisoners taken. When they have dispatched the camp and finished their grisly business, the attackers will make their way from the objective to the far right corner of the clearing, carrying all dead and wounded (the Marines never leave their dead), and there find a third dirt road.

The Rigid Raiders will have continued on up the river to intersect with that road, and this is where the attack will be "extracted."

"That's when we light the cans and blow the hell out of there," says Hess.

There's a possibility that the terrorists' base camp may be supported by armored track vehicles from the rebel Air Force. This is a source of concern to Hess. The squads are traveling ultralight, fine for the terrain and correct for the quiet surprise they have planned, but they have little to throw against an armored attack. "Those things hit us on that last road or at the pickup point," Hess whispers, "and there ain't gonna be no extraction."

The inky sea plays tripling sounds against the sides of the Rigid Raider. Hess puts his hand in the water again. "Feel that?" he whispers. "It's warm."

The men in the boat shift around to look at him. Hess feels the water again. Rubs it on his lips.

"When we're leaving it's gonna be foggy," he tells his squad.

They stare at him, uncomprehending but ready to rectify it with his next word, white eyes appealing from grease-dark faces.

"The air'll cool down overnight but the water'll take longer to cool down, and that's gonna make ground fog all over the river area."

They all nod bovinely as they bob up and down in the dark. Hess smiles back reassuringly from face to face.

The squad man with the radio is also a lance corporal. His name is Hagen. The squad calls him "Hagoid," though no one is really sure why. He joined up a couple of months before Hess. That's sometimes a problem in a squad, when one of the members has more "time in grade" than the leader, but Hess and Hagoid seem to have worked it out. Hagoid is one of Hess's "fire team leaders," which means he, at least, has some small authority over two other men.

One of these is Booker, a big, roundish, naturally muscled type from a bad part of Chicago. Booker is married and has a child. Tonight he has slashed six bright green lines, war paint style, across his prune-black face. Hess likes Booker. "Man smiles lots and says little," says the squad leader. "You know, I think he's just putting in his time and he's gonna get out, but he's a good Marine."

Next to Booker is Sanders, who's been transferred to this

outfit from "barracks duty." Sanders is usually a security guard. He prefers spit-shined boots and sharp creases to the mud and the blood he'll have to go through tonight. This doesn't make him a bad Marine. It just gives him a little attitude. Hess has his eye out for it.

Next to Sanders is Smith, a sleepy-eyed Jamaican hunched down against the gunwale with his hat pulled low. "Good man," says Hess, "but he can sleep standing up." This is by way of explaining private Smith's unfortunate nickname of "Quaalude."

Next to Smith is King, a thin, nervous pfc. with a hard face. "He's okay," says Hess. "He had a little trouble when he first got in. Went UA [unauthorized absence]. But he's got it all together now. He's gonna be a good Marine." If Hess has had some part in that process he is too modest to say.

Even in the dark, these are all recognizably Marines. The camouflaged "utilities" (the combat dress that the Army calls "fatigues") have become as much a symbol of the Corps as the brassy "dress blues," and there are subtler, smaller telltale signs.

The men wear no rank insignia and no unit patches. They don't even wear their names. The Marines call themselves "the few" because they are few. This notion of intimacy is carried down to the smallest units. Each man is supposed to know his fellows.

They wear the flat-topped, somewhat squashed-looking utility cap, not the "baseball" cap worn by the rest of the American services. Many times the Marines have fought off Pentagon attempts to standardize their hat. There's nothing special about the Marine hat, understand, but it too has become a symbol. It is the hat of Tarawa and Inchon, except they don't call it a hat; they call it a "cover." Marines call all hats covers. And covers sit on the "nod," not the head. The "head" is the bathroom. It is not uncommon for lots of job categories to create their own little worlds. The Marine/Navy lexicon of coinages just happens to be a little more colorful than most.

Take a night photo of this boat to any intel man in any service in any foreign country, friend or foe, and he will tell you in an instant—leathernecks. The reputation is at once a boast and a personal challenge to the boaster.

Highland Park Public Library

Gunny (Gunnery Sergeant) Walter Holzworth, a colorful character out of the China Service days of the thirties, once explained the Marines' esprit de corps this way: "First they started out boasting how great they were. Pretty soon they got to believing it themselves. And they have been busy ever since proving they were right in the first place."

The guys in Hess's squad have all reacted in different ways to the seaborne insertion in the little Rigid Raider boat, none happily. Some have taken pills. Some now purse their lips and swallow hard in a kind of ritual meant to ward off the seasickness which they know will come as soon as they let down their guard. It isn't so much the up and down of the boats, or the stygian curtains that surround them, or the thoughts of what lies ahead tonight. It's all of that.

On every one of Hess's men you can read the agonizing realization of the young night raider. Water, and most especially this *much* water, is a hostile environment. But not for Hess.

Hess is a boater. Like a lot of Buffalo boys he spent his teen years on Lake Erie. He loves the water. Most of his last three summers were spent motoring, day and night, about the lake's littoral, happily charging his friends and relatives for fishing expeditions. He knows all about the winds and the tides and the currents and all the different kinds of weather.

When Hess first came into the Corps he trained on the old attack boats. He was a cox. But that was before the advent of the Rigid Raider. Now Hess has heard, "They're starting up a new company of nothing but boat drivers, all Rigid Raiders."

What he hasn't told the squad, or the cox, is that he has submitted paperwork for a transfer to that Rigid Raiders training program. "I'll reenlist for it, if I have to," he says. He wants to be a cox again.

"Hess, heads up," the cox whispers. "Change number four thousand and thirty two."

Hess smiles, waiting for it.

"When you put ashore," the cox continues, "they want to set up a hasty three-sixty defense perimeter right away; protect the boats just in case we fucked up. You'll be all the way to the right on the shoreline, right by the boats. Sergeant Kragar will be to your left."

"Roger that," says Hess.

"And they just got a report from weather," says the cox. "They say it's gonna be really foggy now at the extraction."

"No lie," says Hess.

"You just better ass find us," says the cox.

"You just be there when I get there," says Hess.

"I'll be there," the cox says. "But I ain't gonna be there long."

Hess turns to his men. "Okay, listen up," he says, and he begins to relay the message to his men. They listen as if everything depends on it, and of course, everything does.

He's just about finished when the cox gets another call on his headset. They're "good to go."

"Heads up!" the cox calls out, and he pulls back on the boat's drive stick.

Like a gray sea beast, the Rigid Raider stands up on its haunches with a growl and then leaps at the black and distant shoreline.

Arms pull taut against the railings. Wave tops pound against the bottom of the hull. Spray washes up over the bow and blows like hail against the faces of the men. The Raider begins to buck like a horse.

Hess's squad holds on. Some gear comes loose, a sixty-pound pack. Hess grabs it with his feet. Booker grabs on to the pack, wedges it into the rest of the gear.

The boats are forming a line abreast. Rooster tails of spray rise high in the air. There are two on Hess's right, eight more on the left. The line plows on at fifty knots to shore. The engines are too far out to be heard; the rising wakes too dark to be seen. The coxswains pour it on.

"Turning!" comes the shout from the helm. Everybody grabs something, or someone.

The Raider heaves up out of the water and turns to the right. Fingers tighten on rails. Muscles tighten inside shoulders. It is *very* wearing on the arms.

The attack line forms itself into a vee and cuts across the waves. The black swells roll in off the starboard now and are caught at an angle. The hull continues to buck and pound but now it also rolls from side to side as it skips through the waves.

Hess turns around and smiles. "This is real!" he shouts above the engines.

This *is* real. The starry sky, the crescent moon, the half-dozen luxo-condos that now come into view, rising on the left side of the shoreline.

Carteret, however, is not real. This is a military "maneuver," a training game, a "problem," that very curious kind of adventure that mixes the real and the unreal into nights men talk about for years.

The Rigid Raider

———————————— ★ ————————————

With a grin of anticipation and his eyes on the distant shoreline, Lance Corporal Hess leans into the night breeze as his Rigid Raider sends up its black rooster tail behind him in the night.

There is no rebellion to which he is speeding, and no General Vaisett and no Carteret Air Force. Carteret is the name of the coastal county in North Carolina in which the huge Camp Lejeune Marine Corps Base is located. This is something of a knee-slapping inside joke among the USMC training people who issue the units their battle orders, but perhaps the likening of Camp Lejeune, home of the 2nd Marine Division, to a foreign country is apt.

The approach to Camp Lejeune along U.S. 17 in North Carolina is an unforgettable trip into an ever thickening jungle of honky-tonk bars and pawn shops all specializing in "We Buy Your Dress Blues!" and through a tide of taxicabs that ebb and flow between the camp's main gate and the tiny Jacksonville Airport, which is the Lejeune Marines' port of entry and exit for the rest of the world. Turning all of this into some Third World backwater in the throes of a military rebellion is all part of the unreal.

But there is another Camp Lejeune, one of hard passage

and sore traverse and long stretches of bone-worrying terrain, and across its nasty corporeal presence there is a task for Hess and the Rigid Raider squads to perform, and this task is real.

True, nothing will be "taken" tonight, nothing destroyed. The personnel at the objective are not Third World rebels; they are Marines from another battalion, working as "aggressors."

But the "evaluators" who will hide behind trees to determine the success or failure of the raid, they are real. They will be grading Hess's battalion and that grade is very real.

This is the start of "raid week," a seven-day maneuver in which the 24th MEU will ready itself for "a pump," that is, for sea duty. The MEU's vanguard fighting unit, the BLT (Battalion Landing Team) commanded by Col. Sigurd Jensen III—his men call him "Big Sig"—has provided the men for this first raid, this first test for sea duty.

Sea duty is what you think of when you think of the Marines. In fact, it's what the Marines think of when they think of Marines. It's the basic Corps stuff.

Yes, there's a guy at your local recruiting station in blue pants with red stripes, and sure, there are Marines all over the place doing radio stuff and personnel stuff. That's all part of the job; but it's not "the spirit of the Corps."

Deploying to sea in assault ships like the USS *Guam*, floating around the Atlantic and the Pacific and the "Med," sleeping in narrow bunks sometimes five to the stack, and waiting for that call to Lebanon or Grenada or Nicaragua—*that's* the Corps. Sea duty is the mythos, but it's also the reality, and it's this combining of the mythic and the real that gives the Marines their stouthearted, dewy-eyed self-confidence. Fitting and good, because it is sea duty which will lead the Marines, inexorably, to the Persian Gulf.

In the mid-eighties, when the carefully constructed and highly polished Marine image was dented and darkened by the demolition of the Beirut barracks, the dereliction of a love-starved Marine guard at the Moscow embassy, and the devotion to duty of Colonel Oliver North of the Iran-Contra basement brigade, the quick fix was easy—better sea duty.

Now, in the Marine Corps system of today, a unit may not

deploy to the sea, to its real duty, unless its BLT is SOC (special operations capable). It must be capable of handling special operations like hostage rescue, terrorist control and eradication, and all sorts of micro-unit tactics once thought the purview of semi-irregular commando units. This has become part of the business of the Marines, the real business. It's why they have pressurized exercises like "raid week." It's why they have SOC.

No SOC, no deployment to sea. No deployment to sea and your colonel is SOL (shit out of luck). Down here in the ranks, more real than that you can't get. A quickening sense of purpose has filtered its way through the eleven squads of the assault. "Look around you," Hess shouts, and nods in the general direction of his men, who hold tight to the bucking rails of the Raider. "Every damn swinging dick is motivated and dedicated."

Steve Maier, who used to fly Marine A-4's in 'Nam and now is the CEO of a big film company, likes to say, "The generals and the colonels take the heat, but there is a real feeling in the Corps that Marine units perform only as well as their juniorest members."

This is all on Squad Leader Hess's mind. "I'll tell you, Camp Lejeune's great duty," he yells above the roar of his Raider, "but the damn training games down here can be a bitch."

Fall out of this bucking boat and the sea will drown you. The sea is real; it doesn't know about the war games. It doesn't mark you down. It *takes* you down. The cottonmouths in the swamp don't know about the games either. They are as real as the hills and the streams and the fallen log bridges that Hess's men will traverse tonight. Fail any of them and you'll find yourself going down in the yearly training "statistics," or worse, going home in an LPB (large plastic bag). Death in training is part of the price you pay for realism. The Marines take every precaution to see that training is as safe as they can make it, but they don't stint on the realism. At Camp Lejeune, death is a fact of life.

"How you all doing!?" Hess shouts back as the Raider blasts on into the night.

The squad members nod or grunt. A few don't even look back at him. For twenty minutes they ride their bucking water bronco across the crests and troughs, holding on.

Then the motors cut out with a silent snap and the Raider, as if grabbed from behind, seems to stop in its own length. The gear shifts forward. Hands get tangled in side rails, shins knock against bulkheads. Hess puts his fingers to his lips. They're at the mouth of the river.

A few seconds ago you could hardly hear yourself think; now it's so quiet you think you can hear the fish swimming beneath the boat.

The Raiders are arrayed single file, two ahead of Hess and eight more behind. Hand signals are passed. The cox gets a message on his headset.

With a gurgle at the stern, the Raider slides ahead on its silent motor and, quiet as a snake, the eleven-boat convoy begins to undulate its way up the black ribbon of river.

The gear is checked one last time. Only two hours ago Hess was laying it all out for inspection in his barracks room on the base.

The Marines, like the rest of the armed forces, are moving slowly from the big, open, World War II-vintage barracks to the small three-man dormitory room.

Hess was bunking in a room that has a Bruce Springsteen poster on one wall and a Marine Corps recruiting poster on the other. Booker and Sanders were in there with him.

All their stuff was shiny and clean and "broken down" on their green-blanketed beds, awaiting the perusal of the first sergeant in terms of proper "clothing and equipment display" as set forth in Marine Corps Publication P100.44A (*Essential Subjects*). Each bed displayed the shelter half, the ammo, the M-16, the entrenching tool, the two canteens, the gas mask, the armor vest, the battle suspenders, the ALICE pack (All-Purpose Lightweight Individual Carrying Equipment), the whole "sixty-pound load."

The orders for the raid say "quick, surgical strike," but a strike force never knows what it may run into or how long it may have to stay before it can run back out.

Now, as the boats make their way upriver, and Hess quietly goes over the gear, he isn't checking for neatness. He's checking for battle readiness.

After the barracks inspection, in a frenzy of last-minute

preparation, everything that jiggled was taped down with green or black tape. Everything that shined was greased with green or black cami. Now Hess satisfies himself that nothing in the gear will give them away.

"Aggressors" or "evaluators" may be anywhere. They may be hunkered down in the woods that now peel slowly back in the darkness on either side of the boat. They may be in the trees. They may be listening.

"If you had a base camp up a river," Hess muses, "would you put a listening post down here somewhere? I would."

The squad peers out at the impenetrable banks. Their awful joyride is over. No one embarrassed himself by being sick. All thoughts of that have disappeared so completely that they now seem silly. Now there's a mission, and a real worry. Nobody wants to be the one who gives it away. They must get SOC.

For a half hour the boats make their way up the river. At times the banks are so close that overhanging branches become a threat to unseeing eyes. At other times they are so far off the Raider seems to have plied off the face of the earth.

Suddenly, the motor cuts out. The intel unit says that there are shoals at this point in the river. To snag a boat on one would be to jeopardize the mission before it starts.

The cox throws his legs over the side of the boat and lets himself down slowly into the water. It comes up to his chest. He walks to the front of the boat and pulls a length of tow rope from the bow. Then he hefts it to his shoulder and begins to pull the boat upstream. All eleven coxes are in the water now, pulling the convoy upstream one soggy step at a time. It is slow going, but to jump out and help them would be to risk unwanted noise.

Hess watches his cox strain under the weight of the rope. Okay, so it's not *The Love Boat*. He smiles. That's okay with him. He rubs his hand along the gray gunwale of the Raider. Then he removes his denim utility hat and rubs his fingers through his hair.

Hagoid points silently to Hess's forehead and touches a strip of gleaming white skin at the hairline. It was missed when the squad leader "camied up." Hess understands this immediately and quickly replaces the hat.

The cox climbs back into the boat. Hess gives him a hand and an unobtrusive "high five." They are past the shoals.

"Careful when you get out," the cox whispers directly into Hess's ear, so low that it is almost a hiss. "There are alligators in the water."

Where? There is a splash off to the left, and then another. Something moves in the darkness by the bank but you can't be sure. Is this a joke? Hess shrugs. Just be careful.

The boat bumps against the bank. Hands reach for gear. "Let's go," Hess hisses. "Let's go! Let's go! Let's go!"

The boat has come to rest at some kind of a landing. Just beyond it up the bank, a road leads off to the left. Hess gets a head count of his men and makes a visual check as they slog up the bank. "Form a perimeter," he says. The men comply. Eyes dart everywhere looking for the defense perimeter or the best place to set up and wait; but mostly everyone looks for alligators. There are none, or at least none come out.

Hess has a different problem. His segment of the hasty 360 perimeter defense is down a dark defile which is heavily overgrown. Hess grabs a pair of his people on their way down. "Forget the perimeter," he says. Then he grabs the rest of them and whispers the same thing.

Hess thinks the trees and the overhanging vines are too dense down there, especially in the dark. He's concerned that when the word is given to move out he'll have to spend too much time rounding up his men.

"Line up in a column at the tree line," he says. "Take two steps down into the bush and then get your spacing." The men deploy in a line stretching from the road to the landing, weapons pointed into the trees.

The Marine Corps doctrine of maneuver favors "mission pull" rather than "command push." At each level of command, the facts on the ground must modify the points of the plan. Down on Hess's "juniorest" level, this allows him to decide to abandon his place in the company perimeter for what he feels is a superior position. He'd better be right.

Hagoid gets an order on his radio and passes it along to Hess.

"Okay, let's go! Let's go! Let's go!" Hess says as he pulls

his men bodily out of the line and hurries them up the road.

The landing area has been deemed secured so they are moving up to the head of the line to join the vanguard. You bump into dark shapes all along the way. Then Hess puts his hand up to signal a stop. You can barely see him. You bump into each other and then come to a ragged halt.

At another order from the radio you drop your ALICE packs, leaving only the combat load.

Apparently, intelligence has decided the attack looks good. The packs will be stowed back on the boats and will meet the men at the other end. Then the realization: The other end is still eight miles away!

Colonel Jensen rises up silently behind you. He is six foot three or four and between his helmet and his chin strap, in the space where his face ought to be, there is a scary, goggle-eyed contraption—night vision glasses.

Jensen confers with Hess, who tells him he thought the woods at the landing were too thick for the circular defense perimeter the colonel had ordered. The colonel now agrees. Score one for Hess. It could have gone the other way.

The colonel offers you a peek through the night vision glasses. The line of men which just moments before was nothing but an obstacle course of dark mumbling shapes is now clearly "lit" in an odd, greenish light. You can make out faces, weapons.

"For the price of a single helo you can outfit every grunt in the Corps with a pair of these," says Hess, "and all the soldiers and sailors too." But squad leaders aren't holding their breath.

"The problem," says Hess, "is that the congressmen and the senators get rides in the planes and watch demos of the missiles and such, but very few of them get to take a walk in the swamp at night with us grunts."

It's a little more complicated than that, of course, but not all that much. Yet, the night belongs to the Marine colonel. He lifts his hand and you move out into your night march.

The dirt road is muddy and a little slippery but you can see the guy in front of you and the pace isn't too bad. Then, as soon as you think that eight miles of this is going to be easy, the man up front raises his right hand and you turn off into the blackness of the trees.

There is a footpath but it is on a decline and full of mud puddles that you find only with your feet. You begin to slip and slide in the dark. Hess moves up and back alongside the column whispering "close it up" into every squad member's ear. But you've closed it up already. Truth is, if you fall back more than four paces you lose sight of the man in front and become instantly lost. You squoosh into something wet. Wet toes cause woes.

The path gets narrower and darker and then disappears altogether, but you keep following the man in front and you're okay. Hess continues to move up and back through the line with a kind of skip-hop. He whispers to each man in the squad that every so often they should look back and make sure the guy behind is still there. Good idea.

King turns back as he walks ahead. You can barely make out his eyes. "You back there?" he asks.

"Yeah," you answer. So far.

The men walk this way for about a half-hour, and all the time Hess is moving up and back. Sometimes he whispers to "close it up." Sometimes he gives out a weapons check. The line is supposed to alternate its weapons so that they point right and left in sequence. Guys are tired. They forget.

The line of march is amazingly quiet. The tape-downs really work. When a man in another squad way behind this one opens his canteen to take a sip, you can hear it. Lance Corporal Hess skip-hops around, reminds each man about keeping quiet. The aggressors could be anywhere.

And so you march on into the night. The mud sucks at your heels and climbs over your ankles. The branches of trees snag your suspenders and poke at your eyes. And all the while Hess keeps skip-hopping back and forth whispering things in your ear. Nine out of ten times you can't make out what he's said and can't ask for a repeat because he's gone to the next man. It doesn't matter.

"I just remind people what they already know," he explains. "As long as I'm hopping around and talking to them that motivates them. If I can do it, they can do it."

When Hess skip-hops away again, you try to guess how far you've come, how far you've left to go. It's an hour since you've left the landing area. Maybe you've done two miles, or three.

Your feet say three. Your calves, tensing and relaxing to keep you upright through all the slips and slides, say a hundred years.

But it is two A.M., you've only four more hours to the objective. Win or lose, you're four hours closer to lying down again in the boats. You don't want to think like that but you do. Four hours to go.

Sanders is four hours closer to getting back to his barracks duty and his spit-shined shoes.

King is four hours closer to being a better Marine, whether he wants to or not.

Hagoid is four hours closer to becoming a squad leader himself.

Booker is four hours closer to Chicago, and everybody is four hours closer to Kuwait.

Hess falls in beside Booker. "Boys' night out, big guy?"

Like Booker, Hess is married. He met his wife at a carnival on the nearby Marine air station.

"She's in the Corps," Hess explains. "She's a weapons repairman. But we're getting ready to have a child so she's getting an early out. Because she's a WM [woman marine] she has that option—to get out when she's pregnant."

They've talked it out and decided that Hess will stay in. "We both love it," says Hess. "She'd stay in too but it came down to a matter of priorities. We would both be deploying. There'd be too much day care."

Suddenly the ground plunges into a depression. It's steep and slippery and mushy. Hess goes skip-hopping back and forth. He whispers, "We're in the swamp, close it up, close it up!"

You remember the map; you remember that the swamp was halfway. Halfway is good. But it's cold comfort as you sink into the muck. You slow to a slug's pace. The swamp is full of brambles. They tear at your utilities and knock off your cover and draw blood from your face and hands. This has got to be hell.

Each man moves directly behind the man in front, close enough to drink from his canteen. For an hour you march this way. Silent, slow, stuck. You inhale the rot and the decay.

Strange things pop into your mind to ease the tedium and the pain. Things you normally wouldn't lust after. A yellow,

short-sleeved shirt, fresh off the clothes line. A ride in a con-
vertible. A gin and tonic. You wonder what, and who, is popping
into the minds of the other members of the squad. You wonder
what's moving down around your legs.

There are snakes in the swamp. Some of them are downright
nasty. Makes you want to pick up those feet. But then you
remember there are snakes in the trees too.

An hour later, the ground rises up again and you can breathe
deep. You're climbing up out of the swamp. Okay, you're one
swamp closer to the objective. One swamp closer to the showers.
One shower closer to sleep.

The swamp gives onto a meadow. The meadow is starlit.
The air is sweet again, or maybe it's just not so fetid. No, it is
sweet, and there are crickets here.

Hess comes up alongside. He's got a smile on. He leans
toward your ear. He wants to chat. Tell the truth, he's not a bad
guy to take a walk with in the woods.

He tells you how he was hyperactive in school, "just couldn't sit down." Now he's learned to "channel all that energy
into something important."

"He's a killing machine," Hagoid whispers as he walks past
Hess, overhearing, kibbitzing.

Hess turns thoughtful at this. As he walks on under the
stars he says, "I look at it this way. If I do have to kill, I will.
And while I'm doing it I'll be thinking about my family. My
mother. And, lookit, do I want some raghead Ay-rab dictating
the price of gas she buys or some commie-type hardass coming
over here, ruling her, telling her what to do, and you know,
exploiting her. It's for that you kill. It's for us."

He thinks about it again. "Hell yeah, I'll kill them all. And
not just the communists. It's anybody who's against the United
States. Anybody who wants to say that one man can be a dic-
tatorship and the people don't have anything to say about it.
And he wants to try that on the United States? Well, I'm gonna
kill him with all the vigor I have in my body. That's what it's
all about: preserving our way of life. That's my job."

The column snakes through the meadow and emerges onto
a road. Almost there now. Walking tall. Hard ground. Lap of

luxury. The march forms into two columns. Hess's squad takes the lead on the right.

Hess says he saw all the old John Wayne movies. He admits that was one of the reasons he decided to join the Marines, "right as soon as I finished high school." But "my favorite movie in the whole world that nothing is ever gonna touch is *Scarface*.

"It was realistic," he says. "All the violence was realistic. The cuss words were realistic. Yeah, Scarface was a bad guy and into drugs and all that, but the man is something I admired, I mean, outside that drug stuff. The man said, there's only two things I got in the whole world and that's my heart and my balls and I'm not gonna break 'em for nobody I don't think I wanna break 'em for. That pretty much sums it up for me."

The column stops. Ears prick up. There's a crashing in the woods, close by. Which way? To the right. Over on Hess's side of the road. Those are track vehicles! The orders said the aggressors could be reinforced by three tracks.

"Those ain't tracks," Hess says. "They're tanks!"

A sergeant comes running up the center of the two columns. "Get down! Get down! There are tanks!"

You hunch down at the side of the road. You listen to the crashing in the woods. A thought occurs. What happens if the tanks come crashing out of the woods and cut across the road? What happens to the guys hunched down where the tanks come crashing out? What the hell are they doing?

"Keep your eyes open," Hess says.

No lie.

"Listen!" he says, onto something now. "You still hear the tanks?" Yes you do. They are getting closer. You can hear their hellacious engines churning. "But you don't hear no trees crashing," says Hess. "You don't hear no trees or anything."

No you don't.

"They're coming down the road!" Hess shouts. "Get in the ditch!"

All down the column, squad leaders are picking up the cry. Men are diving right and left into the shallow ditches on either side of the narrow dirt road.

Suddenly the headlights of the lead tank pierce the darkness. The road vibrates. How wide is a tank? How wide is this road? How small a space can you take up in this ditch?

The first tank thunders by, inches from men's faces. Mud flies everywhere. A second tank follows right behind it, and then a third. Heads are buried in the mud. Prayers are mumbled and violent curses hurled silently. The tanks roll by.

When the ground stops shaking, when it is dark again, you get the word to rise.

"Assholes," someone says in the dark. You continue the march.

You've come seven miles in seven hours. Seven miles closer to SOC. Seven hours closer to another day. The lines of men on either side of the dark road now grow ragged. You move up, fall back, then run to catch up. It's the dreaded concertina effect, alternating bunches of men and wide open spaces. Hess moves up and back trying to keep proper spacing.

You turn off the road and onto a path. There is the vaguest hint of brightening in the eastern sky. Are you too late? The column halts; they've been stopped by a "recon" man.

Behind Hess, squads are moving into the woods on the right and left. Ahead, the recon man is conferring with the company commander.

It seems that the bunkers that guard the objective have been moved. They are no longer in Hess's path. They are in Sergeant Kragar's to the left.

Hess gets his orders changed. His squad is to take the right flank of Kragar, lay down a base of fire, and then move off the objective to the road. The assault hasn't been hit by the rebel tracks and there is strong suspicion it will be jumped during the extraction. Hess's squad will be the extraction security team. He will have to clear the road.

"If you run into anything," the commander tells Hess, "just get down and get blazing. While you hold them, we'll be coming up on both flanks. We'll cut them off, wipe them out, and get the hell out of here."

"Aye aye, sir," says Hess. The Marines have switched over from the nautical usage to the Army's less evocative "yes sir," but in instances where a Marine takes a direct combat order, the historical form is much preferred.

You move through the woods to the edge of the second meadow. There is no one behind Hess's little squad now. Booker and Hagoid and Quaalude and King and Smith and Hess are all alone. The enemy cannot be seen, but intelligence says they are just beyond the open meadow, in the trees on the other side. There is nothing to do now but wait for the other units to settle into position.

Hess goes around patting his team on the back. It is a bit of a disappointment not to be the point of the spear, but they have gotten here without incident and that's half the battle.

Kragar's guns suddenly erupt on the left. That's the signal. The men burst from the trees and race across the meadow, guns trained at the tree line, barrels blazing their M-82 blank training cartridges.

Hess lets loose a war whoop he never learned in Buffalo. The rest of the squad picks it up, howling and firing and leaping across the meadow. King howls like a wolf. Booker yips like a lapdog. Somebody yells, "Kill their balls!" but you can't make out who.

You can hear Kragar's point squad whooping it up on the left. And between Hess and the point of attack, the rest of the squads are laying down a murderous raking fire.

Evaluators sit in the trees with white tape on their hats and red flashlights on their clipboards.

Howling like the hounds of hell, you race across the meadow, the yoke of silence thrown off, the shield of invisibility discarded. "Devil Dogs" is what the Marines were called in World War I; they still do call each other that, sometimes, and only partly in jest.

Every eye is on the tree line as the men blaze away, and the dark shapes of the rebel buildings are only now coming into view. At the first sign of a muzzle flash in your direction you'll have to hit the dirt, slow the attack, belly-crawl. So you run as fast as you can. But no one is shooting back. All their fire is directed to the left. Kragar has them by the nose, and the fire support is kicking them in the ass. You run, and you run. How wide is this goddamn meadow!?

"In the dirt!" yells Hess.

At last you hit the opposite tree line and fall in behind

another squad; it's one of the fire support teams. A small miscalculation. Fog of battle. Hess is too far to the left of the attack. They yell at him to "move to the right! Move to the right!"

The squad slides on down the line. Meanwhile Kragar's squad is overrunning the rebel base. It's quite a melee. Actually, training rules state clearly that you're not supposed to fire a blank round within twenty feet of another person, but it's getting pretty close in there.

Hess secures the road point. Everyone is shouting now, the night has turned upside down.

A sergeant comes running by, windmilling his arm at Hess. "Take the road! Take the road! Get the hell out of here!"

You hit the road at a run, three men to the right and three more to the left.

"Don't run!" Hess yells. "This is a patrol!"

Running jogs the eyeballs, and you're supposed to be looking out.

"Just pick up the pace!" Hess shouts.

Ankles ache, calves burn, thighs feel like wood. You mount the "sixty-inch pace." It's a killer. But there is nothing to the right. There's nothing to the left. The boats aren't more than a half-mile down this road. So you pick'm up and lay'm down. And then there are lights, red and white lights, dead ahead.

"Hold it up!" Hess shouts, and then, lower, "That could be an aggressor track."

You stop. You kneel. Someone shouts out of darkness for your password. It happens to be "plastic." The countersign is "television." But Hess puts a finger to his lips. The men draw beads on the lights, though they know their 7.62 NATO standard rounds won't penetrate a track vehicle.

"Wait here," Hess says.

He flips his M-16 onto full automatic and moves ahead down the road. There's a Marine there. Behind him Hess can see that the lights are flashlights, held by two other Marines. There is no track. But Hess still isn't sure it's not a trick.

"What's the password!" shouts the Marine in the middle of the road, aiming his M-16 directly at Hess's belly.

"You know who I am?" Hess asks.

"Yeah, you're John Hess."

"Let's go!" Hess wheels and waves his arm. "Move it! Come on! Move it!"

Inside of ten minutes all eleven squads, all sixty-six dog-tired men, were back in the Rigid Raiders and the coxes were blasting the sleek gray boats back down the river. The sun was coming up into a bright red sky.

Hess lay back and laughed as he explained the little last-minute drama of the extraction.

"I thought it was a trick," he shouted over the motors. "I thought as soon as I gave the password they were going to open up. But you know the game has its limits. You can kind of go outside them and come back in. You see, all the aggressor guys are from the One-four Battalion and I don't know anyone over there. So I asked this guy if he knew me and as soon as he gave my name I knew he was one of our guys and that we were okay."

An hour later the raiders, still being smartly marched by their colonel, "Big Sig" Jensen, showed up for breakfast, cami on their faces, sleep in their eyes, a half hour ahead of morning mess.

"We on alert or something?" a cook shouted to the colonel.

"Hell no, man." The Big Sig smiled. "We're just coming in off a raid. Fire up those eggs."

There was some easy banter as men took their seats at the tables, mostly about alligator sightings. Two were confirmed.

Big Sig walked around the hall giving his troops an off-the-cuff instant analysis of their performance.

"Ambient noise was low," he said, "you drifted in and out a bit but you looked good."

Then he stopped at a table of sergeants and said, "We have to remember to wrap our paddles and make sure our coxes know how to stern-paddle."

Hess was working on several eggs with potatoes and grits and a large slice of French toast. He looked younger in the light and even more slight. He was looking forward to bed but he was still anxious to talk.

The squads had made SOC. They were special operations capable. They were "good to go."

The evaluators had fixed them with only two dead. None of them were Hess's people. The rebel base had been totally pacified.

There was some gentle kidding from the officers about the three tanks that nearly ran the men down. It turned out they were from somebody else's exercise and had only crossed the path of Hess's war game by accident.

"Happens all the time," said Hess. "I told you, the games down here are a bitch."

The squads were rising from the mess tables now, hitting the line for seconds before the regular troops reported in for chow. The kitchen helpers didn't stint.

"Well, this's what it's all about." Hess smiled.

The two "dead guys" were being kidded mercilessly, but in a gentle, clubby way. These guys, too, were definitely good to go.

It made you want to ask for a memento, some token of having been on this raid with them, some colorful item to add to your collection of such things. But the club's too tight.

"You know, in Grenada," Hess said, sensing the request and cutting it off before it could be uttered, "the Army gave out over eight thousand medals. We gave out only two hundred medals. Pass the salt." He paused as he meticulously painted his eggs with an even layer of white crystals. Grenada was before Hess's time, but all Marines get a heavy dose of Corps history in their training.

"That medal thing, that's just the way it is with the United States Marines," Hess continued. "We just don't give a lot of shit away."

As Hess shoveled in the eggs and the potatoes and the toast, this "juniorest" member seemed as totally at ease in speaking for the Corps as if he were the commandant. And that was the most impressive thing of all.

The "Former"

★

The house in Virginia is modest. Swathed in siding faded to a pastel that is either orange or pink or tan depending on your own point of view, it sits among the spruces behind a small Cyclone fence. The gate is held fast by a twisted wire. There is a late-model sedan in the driveway and azalea bushes on the walk.

Inside the house the rooms are bright and colorful and well kept, except for the small one off the kitchen which the woman of the house calls "the junk room," and the man calls "the den."

The den has faded pictures on the walls, and weapons, and plaques, and old dusty flags. On shelves all around is a scattered collection of souvenirs taken from this place and that. One of them is a clear pill vial filled with a coarse black sand.

"That's the volcanic ash of Iwo Jima," says Herbert Newman, sixty-three, a "former." Marines like to point out that soldiers say they are "in" the Army, and sailors say they are "in" the Navy, but people always say of a leatherneck that he "is" a Marine. Therefore, there are no "ex-Marines," only "formers." This former top sergeant was in the 4th Marine Division. He picks the clear plastic vial up off the shelf and holds it out proudly for examination. This piece of Iwo Jima is his, and these are his memories.

When then Secretary of the Navy James Forrestal saw the now legendary flag-raising photograph by Joe Rosenthal of the Associated Press, he said, "The raising of the flag on Mount Suribachi means there'll be a Marine Corps for the next five hundred years."

The flag-raising on Iwo Jima, staged as it was, must be understood as the inarguable zenith in the history of the Corps, with everything before it leading up to the crowning moment, and everything after leading inexorably downward and away.

Newman, whose jowls are now slackening but whose voice retains the motor rumble that used to drive the troops, rubs his forearm where a tattoo of the "eagle, globe, and anchor" is fading to a smudge. A design which has evolved from an old tunic button device, it is the oldest insignia in the armed forces of the United States in continuous service. "Semper Fi," he says, displaying the skin art. "So far, so good."

For Herbert Newman, Marine history began just before Guadalcanal when he quit high school in Turtle Creek, near Pittsburgh, to join up.

He was too young. His father, who had been a Marine corporal in World War I and had gotten gassed, refused to lie on the enlistment papers and so Newman had to either wait it out or join another service. There was no choice but to wait it out. "My father was a Marine, my brother was one, and my sister was one, and *they* both married Marines."

By the time Newman got in, the six-month struggle for Guadalcanal had been won. "But there was still a bit of work left to do."

Marine life began then the same way it starts today, with boot camp. "It was pretty bad." Newman laughs about it now. "I was quite small, about 126 pounds, and I had short legs and I couldn't always keep in step with those big guys and every time I'd fall out of step, why the D.I.'s [drill instructors] they'd crack me on the head with those swagger sticks."

Lessons came early. "We had to be in civilian clothes those first couple of days there, and we'd sit around these potbellied stoves with the D.I.'s and talk about the great history of the Marine Corps and some of the guys thought things were going a little slow for a war, and there was one D.I. who picked up on this and said, 'Hey, anybody here sorry they decided to join the Marines?' And one guy says, 'I could learn this stuff at home,' and the D.I. leaps at this guy and grabs him by the throat and, *wham,* pins him against the wall and says, 'Anybody here wanna go home with this guy?' And after that, we all listened up.''

As every "boot" knows, the United States Marines were "born" on November 10, 1775. Every year, units all around the world celebrate "the birthday," as they call it, with ruffles and flourishes, and robust parties.

The idea of fighting men on sailing ships, however, goes all the way back to Phoenicians, who used "sea infantry" as boarders and raiders. The latter, Newman points out as he takes a book of military woodcuts from a shelf, were not so very unlike our own Marines.

Behind the old top sergeant, on another shelf full of history, is a set of highball glasses painted especially for him by a Marine Corps artist. Each of the glasses depicts Sergeant Newman in a different uniform, from the musket days to the modern. Yes, this is a splendid place to learn about the Marines.

The present-day form probably stems from the British, who in 1664, under Charles II, raised "a Regiment of Royal Marines." The Corps' familiar "dress blues" come from a long association with these units of Royal Marines.

"Their buttons today," says Newman, "show the Eastern Hemisphere, and ours show the Western."

In the 1740s America had three regiments of Colonial Marines; one of them, the one in Virginia, had in its muster a junior officer who was George Washington's half brother.

It was, however, not Washington, who in fact had little interest in such sea fighters, but the Second Continental Congress, meeting three decades later amid the gathering fire storm of the Revolutionary War, which provided for "two battalions of Marines to serve for and during the present war between Great Britain and the colonies."

The Marines' first taste of action was in March of 1776, in the Bahamas. A pair of forts were captured. On their return the men were given new uniforms, green ones with a feather everyone hated and a leather collar—a defense against the odd cutlass slash—which provided the much-loved nickname "leather-neck."

Marines then lit out on a campaign to fight Indians near Lake Michigan; a harassment of British shipping in New Orleans; a less-than-successful attempt to take a British fort in Penobscot, Maine; and finally, in April of 1778, something of a success.

Sailing in John Paul Jones's ship the *Ranger*, Marines took the Revolution directly to the British with two raids on English soil. These had, however, little effect on the general hostilities. There was another long raid, in 1781 on the Isle of Jersey. Then, in 1783 a group of Continental Marines captured the man-of-war *Baille*. A month later the war ended with the Treaty of Paris.

For the Marines, it wasn't exactly stuff for a glorious history, or even much of a beginning. At the very height of the war they never numbered more than 124 officers and 3,000 men. And they didn't fare much better in the peace that followed.

"When the War of Independence ended," says Newman, as he launches into a hoary old Marine tale, "the Army and the Navy looked around to see what was left. All they found were some mules and a company of Marines. They flipped a coin and that's how we Marines got into the Navy. The Army won and took the mules!" He laughs, heartily. The story is apocryphal, but to the point.

In fact, Marine history might have ended right then and there were it not for the Barbary pirates. Sailing from Mediterranean ports in Tunis, Morocco, Algiers, and Tripoli, these pirates preyed on merchant shipping and were ample excuse for each of the "host" countries involved to charge exorbitant fees to, in effect, moderate the predations and thus guarantee safe passage. It was a kind of protection racket.

"Millions for defense but not a penny for tribute." The "top" now shakes a fist, echoing America's thunder. For the first of what would prove to be many, many times, the United States sent in the Marines.

Of course, she had to resurrect them first. Congress quickly passed and President John Adams signed "An Act for Establishing and Organizing a Marine Corps," authorizing 33 officers and

848 men. They got a new uniform again, this time with the now familiar blue trousers trimmed in scarlet.

The campaign against the pirates and their confederates went well. Tripoli, which had gone so far as to declare war on the United States for her refusal to pay the ransom, was the primary target.

Marine Lieutenant Presley O'Bannon led an extraordinary attack. After marching his troops some six hundred miles, O'Bannon, in perfect coordination with a bombardment from three American ships, surprised the defenders and took the city. When O'Bannon raised the American flag from the ramparts, it marked the first time it had flown on foreign soil.

Later, the pasha of Tripoli handed his sword over to O'Bannon. At a ceremony in the 1850s commemorating this moment, it was decreed that the honor of wearing such a sword be extended for Marines down to the rank of sergeant. It remains, to this day, the only situation in the armed forces in which noncommissioned officers may wear what has, by tradition, been reserved as an officer's weapon. In the Marines, every "boot" aspires to the sword.

The War of 1812 came and this time the Marines did rather well. They fought in the defense of Fort McHenry, at which Francis Scott Key wrote "The Star Spangled-Banner."

They fought beside Andrew Jackson at the Battle of New Orleans. Twenty years later Jackson returned the favor by offering to disband the Corps, becoming the first of several presidents to attempt to do so, always in peacetime.

Jackson wanted the Marines to be part of the Army. It angered the Congress, several of whom were now "formers" themselves.

"Congress has always helped the Marines, right from the beginning and right now," says Newman. In response to Jackson, an act was passed "for the better organization of the United States Marine Corps," which actually increased the number of men in blue and scarlet and put them back at the president's disposal.

Jackson sent them off to fight the Seminoles, who had refused to be put on a reservation and had retreated to fighting territory in the Everglades. Though in six years he never did manage to dislodge them, Commandant Archibald Henderson was promoted to general, the first Marine to hold such rank.

Sending in the Marines had, by now, become a routine first response. The Marines fought Cuban and Malay pirates, and broke up a riot at the Massachusetts State Prison. When slavery was made illegal they went ashore in Liberia to crack a slaving ring.

War with Mexico came. A brigade of Marines formed the vanguard of General Winfield Scott's march from Veracruz to Mexico City. They took Chapultepec Castle. Sergeant Newman starts to sing in his comically gravel voice, "From the halls of Montezoo-ooma . . . "

The "Marine Hymn" was written sometime during this campaign by an anonymous leatherneck, and sung by the troops to the tune of Offenbach's then popular operetta, *Geneviève de Brabant*.

Everyone knew about the "shores of Tripoli," but if the troops were confused by the reference to "Montezuma," that was understandable. Apparently the unknown rhymester's grasp of history had been faulty, and he had simply confused Chapultepec Castle with another story he had once heard about the Aztecs. There was not then, nor has there ever been, a serious attempt to put this error right. The hymn, as Newman or any Marine will freely tell you, is perfect.

There was an uprising in Argentina and the Marines went down there to save American lives. There was a holy war in China in 1856 that killed twenty million Chinese and ten Marines who had arrived to show the flag.

Then came the conflict half the Marines call the War Between the States and the other half call the Civil War. At the outset, before Sumter, it was Marines who routed John Brown and his armed slaves at Harper's Ferry, and they were commanded by Robert E. Lee. Later, things got even more confused.

Leathernecks fought on both sides of the war, but the U.S. Marines fought for the Union. They were there at Bull Run, a 350-man unit in the middle of the line. After a day of Rebel cavalry charges the Marines broke ranks and fled with the Army. "That is the only such recorded panic in Marine Corps history," Newman says.

But the rest of the war didn't go all that much better. The low-water mark was the disastrous raid on Fort Fisher, North Carolina. There were 400 Marines in the 3,500-man assault. Three hundred died. Both the Navy and the Army, seeking to avoid responsibility for the failure to take the fort, blamed it on the Marines.

This time it was the House of Representatives that sought, at war's end, to disband the Corps. The commandant went to the Navy for help, "and he went right to the soft spot." Admiral David Porter, whose testimony had skewered the Marines for Fort Fisher, was now faced with loss of the Corps. He admitted to Congress, "A ship without Marines is like a garment without buttons."

The Corps survived, and was strengthened. The Marines had won another important engagement in the halls of their own government. "We were beginning to get good at that," says Newman. It would come in handy.

It comes as some surprise to Newman, as it does to most Marine watchers, that after the long and arduous experience of the Seminole campaign, and the high regard in which the "horse Marines" were held, nobody ever thought to "send in the Marines" against the Indians during the plains wars of the second half of the 1800s.

Instead, the Corps was sent to Uruguay, Japan, Formosa, China, Nicaragua, Chile, Argentina, Panama, and Hawaii (twice). They destroyed illegal whiskey stills in the Irishtown section of Brooklyn, New York. They quelled the violence that erupted in the railroad strike of 1877.

Newman points out that it was about this time that two commandants left an important mark. Charles Grymes McCawley was an "eyewash" man and he standardized the uniform for the first time, eliminating that vaguely semi-irregular look the Corps had borne. He also went to work on the Marine Corps Band, firing its director and hiring another "former" Marine, who turned out to be John Philip Sousa.

Colonel Charles Haywood was more performance oriented. Taking a page out of Navy history (American success in the War of 1812 had been largely attributable to the Navy's strong reliance on gunnery practice), the colonel decided to make every Marine a rifleman. Marksmanship regimens were developed and a new Marine base, at Parris Island, South Carolina, was created to administer the arduous new training—which continues, of course, to this day.

The Navy, perhaps alarmed by all this growth, now attempted to "disband" the Marines by consuming them. The plan was to sharply reduce the Corps in manpower and confine its duties to shipboard operation and shore police work. The Congress threw it out. Then the battleship *Maine* blew up.

The Spanish-American War was a good Marine show. They took Manila Bay in the Philippines, they took Guantánamo Bay in Cuba, and before the guns had cooled they were off to China.

There was a xenophobic rebellion going on in Peking. The faithful who wanted the Westerners heaved out called themselves "The Fist of the Righteous Amity," a flowery handle that cut no ice with the pugnacious American press, who dubbed them the "Boxers."

The "Boxers" had the American embassy under siege. The Marines on guard defended it against incredible odds, and the Marines arriving from Tientsin relieved it.

Theodore Roosevelt became president. He had been the secretary of the Navy when the Marines went to Manila, and the vice president of the United States when the embassy in Peking was saved. It was a bit of surprise, then, when T.R. sided with the Navy in yet another attempt to declaw the Corps.

This time the plan was to take the Marines *off* sea duty and turn them over to the Army. Roosevelt ordered the Corps to disembark at all points. Congress, more disposed to the Marines (and their blossoming popularity) than ever before, refused to grant a Navy appropriation bill unless the order was rescinded. It was.

The Marines went to Nicaragua in 1910 to quell an election riot and then to Haiti to quell another. Then the guns of August boomed. The War to End All Wars had begun.

The Corps' ranks were swelling with new recruits who, like Newman's father, were answering the siren call of the Marines' "First to Fight" poster. Commandant George Barnett was determined that a Marine group be part of the American Expeditionary Force. The War Department said the Army had enough men of their own. The Marines' first battle of World War I was fought in Washington, D.C. They won. President Wilson sent Herbert Newman's father and the 5th Marines with Pershing. "The first time Marines wore steel helmets," says Newman.

They landed in Saint-Nazaire and went into the line at Belleau Wood. They relieved a battered and beaten French contingent whose commander suggested that the Marines fall back to more defensible positions. "Retreat, hell!" roared the Marine commander. "We just got here."

It became a rallying cry. The Marines were outgunned by the Germans, but they had the fire and movement training of Parris Island, and they were sharpshooters. They began to clear the woods. The Germans, requesting reinforcements, referred to these new shock troops they had encountered as *Teufelhunden* or "Devil Dogs." Marines, like Hess and Newman, still call each other that.

"And we took the bulldog symbol from the British in that war," Newman points out. The bulldog is akin to the Army's mule, a mascot of the Corps. "That's how it got started."

The Battle of Belleau Wood, and all the awards and kudos flowing therefrom, put the United States Marines on the world military map as an elite force second to none.

After the one about the mules, the story leathernecks like to tell best is the one about how the Marines were able to pick up the amphibious combat role only because the Army dropped it. This one happens to be true.

The Army thought the lesson of the Allies' costly attack at Gallipoli, in 1915, was that large, seaborne, over-the-beach assaults were no longer feasible in a battle environment that included long-range, high-explosive artillery and the dune-sweeping machine gun.

What the Army didn't credit, according to Newman, was that the long planning and intricate timing and total teamwork needed to pull off an over-the-beach assault in the face of superior firepower could be accomplished but only by "a unit with the esprit de corps to work together, really tightly together, each guy sacrificing for the other, like the Marines."

As Army planning moved further and further away from the notion of amphibious assault, the Marines became, at times unwittingly, more and more versed in it.

The period between the two world wars was a busy one for the Corps, and most of the action, generally in support of big-company assets in sugar and fruit produce, involved shore landings and jungle fighting.

The Marines began working on perfecting their tactics, adapting different flat-hull boat designs for off-loading artillery and heavy materiel on beach sand, then finding track-laying designs for breaching reefs. At first, it was simply to make their present assignments a little more effective, but the implications turned out to be long-range and far-flung.

"If the Battle of Waterloo was won on the playing fields of Eton," said General H. M. Smith, "the Japanese bases in the Pacific were captured on the beaches of the Caribbean." But it was actually Commandant John A. Lejeune who set the Marines on course for Iwo Jima.

Here was Lejeune's problem. The end of World War I showed clearly that defense was best left to massed armies, deeply dug in, and willing to fight a slow war of attrition.

Attack was best left to armor, heavily gunned and supported by artillery, and able to probe the weak links of the line. If another European war was to be fought, and few military men doubted the certainty of this, where was a role for the lightly gunned Corps in this battle plan? There was none.

There was an idea rattling around the Marine officer clubs, however, and it concerned the rising of the Japanese sun. If the Japanese went to war, the thinking went, would it not be prudent of them to reach out into the Pacific to capture naval bases that would provide a defense-in-depth of their new empire?

Lejeune bet everything the Marines had on the Japan card. He backed a report titled *Advance Base Operations in Micronesia*, which became known, when implemented, as the "Orange Plan." Then he restructured Marine Expeditionary Forces into the Fleet Marine Force, and began training and equipping it for amphibious warfare.

Landing exercises were held in Cuba and Puerto Rico. The flat-bottom, drop-gate Higgins boat was developed and Donald

Roebling's tank-tracked Everglades "rescue vehicle" was adapted as the forerunner of the LVT (landing vehicle tank).

As the seventeen-year-old Herbert Newman watched and anxiously waited his turn, the first great Marine Corps victory in the Pacific, the Battle of Guadalcanal, took six months. There were 3,000 Marine casualties, 8,500 cases of malaria.

In the end, the Marines had accomplished much. Though the "landing" was less spectacular than the "staying," the Marines proved that a determined beach assault, borne by fast seaworthy craft, supported by light armor and intensive, ultra-low-level "close air support," could move a much mightier foe out of well-dug-in positions.

Guadalcanal cost the Japanese 25,000 men, 600 planes, and 24 warships. The rising sun had been stopped in its ascent.

"On the troop transport going over," Newman remembers, "we all knew the war was going to be won. It was just a matter of time, and trouble." Thus it was a curious mix of confidence and concern that informed the card games and the gabfests belowdecks.

"Oh, we were tight. We were green. Hardly any of us had seen combat; maybe some of the officers. But we knew what was what. We'd heard all the rumors about the war. We knew what we were getting into.

"But I remember one night, just before we landed in the Marshalls for our first action. They handed us out some shotguns. These were for the snipers that would shoot at you out of the palm trees. Each platoon was supposed to get a shotgun and this sergeant was showing us how to use it and a live round went off and that buckshot hit the steel ceiling above him and all hell broke loose. That loosened us up."

Newman turned eighteen aboard ship. Then they hit the beach in the Marshalls, the tiny twin islands of Roi-Namur. Roi was less than a mile long and almost completely covered by its airport. Namur was even smaller. It took four days; 173 Marines died.

"I picked up this pistol," says Newman. He walks over to a wall where an olive drab pistol hangs. He removes it from its hook and hefts it. It's heavy. "Seven-millimeter," he says. "I picked it up off a dead Jap and carried it through Saipan, Tinian, and Iwo Jima. It's a Nambu. It's good, and very accurate, and there was plenty of ammunition for it; all the dead Japs had some. Funny thing is this safety here." He flips a toggle back and forth. "When I took it off the guy, I couldn't read it to know which was the off and which was on, so I fired it at him and when it went off I flipped the lever the other way and put it in my pocket."

Newman's next port of call was in the Marianas. The Air Force was looking for a spot from which to bomb Japan with the new B-29. This was to be it.

Nine days after D day at Normandy, the Marines stormed ashore at Saipan. "That was rough. There was a reef there and even though the tracks could breach it—some of them— the Higgins boats had to go through a channel, single file. We lost our whole mortar platoon going in. It was pretty close for us, too.

"We landed on the beach and, well, we didn't move too far the first day. See, they had all the high ground. They had Mt. Tapotchau, and we didn't know for a long time that they had a spotter at the top of the smokestack of a sugar cane mill that was right on our flank and he was zeroing in the mortars and artillery all over us.

"The first night was real bad too. We had two-man foxholes where you stand watch a little and then wake up the other guy, or in some places we had one-man holes and you stand watch awhile and throw a stone over to the next guy. We heard motors running all night and we thought maybe the Japs had tanks and we were gonna be overrun by them. But it turned out the next morning the motor noise was coming from our own tracks that made it over the reef all right but got stuck down in the sand and they were trying to get them out all night."

Herbert Newman got a Purple Heart on Saipan. "We were having a tough time taking a small hill, and I mean we were trying everything. Then the order comes down that at a certain signal we were to all stand and march up the hill firing our weapons." He rolls his eyes.

"Well, they gave the order and we all stand up and we start going boom, boom, boom, and I got shot in the arm. I think they took the hill; I don't know. I was back on the ship getting patched up."

After a couple of days of ship duty Newman was looking to get back into it. "What'd I know?" He smiles. "I was young. I was still gung ho." He was also judged unfit for combat. But he was okayed for shore duty, the guys who lift and ship and off-load. "So I took it, and as soon as I got to the beach I took off and found my unit up at the front. This time I got it in the leg," a second Purple Heart in as many days.

Saipan was the HQ for the Japanese Central Pacific Fleet under Vice Admiral Chuichi Nagumo, who had commanded the striking force at Pearl Harbor. The Marines suffered nearly thirteen thousand casualties taking the island from him.

"Here's a picture of the company," Newman says. It's pinned to the wall. Thirty or so men with hollow cheeks and happy smiles and a turmoil of thoughts known only to men who've endeavored in the fields of blood are arranged in rough formation beneath a tattered palm tree. "That's all we had left," says Newman. "Very few guys got through it without some kind of wound."

The bittersweet photograph is not the only sad thing on the wall. Below it and to its right, half covered by a plaque from a division reunion, is a Japanese flag.

"I took this off a dead Jap on Saipan. It's not a trophy, really," says Newman, a bit embarrassed. "We would go through the dead looking for papers or orders or anything that would give up a little intel. But every once in a while you'd come across something like this."

The flag is covered with Japanese writing. Each string of congee figures is quite obviously rendered in a different hand. "I'm going to have it all translated someday," says the old sergeant. But he won't. He knows what the writings say. They are prayers and best wishes from the family of that young Japanese man who gave up his flag in death to the American Marine. Newman doesn't really want to read the writing. The message is clear.

When the island was finally wrested from the Japanese, Premier Hideki Tojo, citing the Battle of the Philippine Sea and the loss of Saipan, submitted his resignation to the Emperor Hirohito.

Newman's leg wound healed in time for Tinian, which when taken became the B-29 base for raids on the "home islands." Their aerial pounding was relentless and effective, but in no time at all the 4th Division was planning to sail again in search of still more advanced basing. It seems that many B-29's returning "hit" or low on fuel were unable to make it all the way to Tinian. They were ditching in the sea. Another amphibious operation was drawn up.

"We knew pretty much about it, this time. We had a lot of briefings on the ship. We didn't have no name for it. That was pretty quiet. We didn't know the name until we were about ready to land." The name was Iwo Jima.

"I thought it was sort of typical. Here we'd taken Tinian so they could take off on their raids. Now we were supposed to take Iwo so they could get back."

He picks up the vial of black sand again, scrutinizes it, rolls it in his palm as if he can feel something. "We had twenty thousand casualties there, but I suppose it was worth it. Of course we didn't appreciate that at the time."

By now Newman was a sergeant; he was responsible for some people. "All good men." He nods. "Our group landed at 'Yellow Beach' and it was pure hell. They were dug in with the high ground and everything zeroed in. We had some tanks with us but the way they were shelling them, right on the money, you didn't want to be anywhere near them. I mean the air raids had hurt them Japs not a bit.

"And there was no cover but the craters made by the bombardment. You couldn't dig a foxhole; the sand was too loose and it'd just keep falling back in."

Newman has a somewhat unique theory about this. He thinks "the loose sand helped us some because it swallowed up a lot of their shells, so that when they exploded they were far enough under it that the frag stuff and shrapnel was muffled. But, hell, it was coming down all around."

On the first day Newman won a Navy Commendation Medal for blowing up a pillbox. Admiral Chester Nimitz would later say that on Iwo Jima, "uncommon valor was a common virtue."

Sergeant Newman puts it this way: "You had a job to do and the job just happened to entail stuff that made you a hero."

William Manchester, in his memoir *Goodbye Darkness*, says of that first day:

> It resembled Doré's illustrations of the *Inferno*. Essential cargo—ammo, rations, water—was piled up in sprawling chaos. And gore, flesh, and bones were lying all about. The deaths on Iwo were extraordinarily violent. There seemed to be no clean wounds; just fragments of corpses. It reminded one battalion medical officer of a Bellevue dissecting room. Often the only way to distinguish between Japanese and Marine dead was by the legs; Marines wore canvas leggings and Nips khaki puttees. Otherwise identification was completely impossible. You tripped over strings of viscera fifteen feet long, over bodies which had been cut in half at the waist. Legs and arms, and heads bearing only necks, lay fifty feet from the closest torsos. As night fell the beachhead reeked with the stench of burning flesh. It was doubtful that a night counterattack by the Japs could be contained.

But there was no counterattack. The Japanese battle plan was to lie in their position and pound the Marines into submission. The next day was more of the bloody same.

On the third day of the attack Newman saw the flag being raised atop Suribachi. "I wasn't in that attack; in fact I was attacking in the other direction, up the rock quarry, *straight* up the rock quarry. But I was dog-tired and for a second I rolled over on my back and I said, 'Damn, they're putting the flag up on the mountain!' I mean you could see it all over the island!"

It was staged for the press and it was way premature. Fighting on Iwo Jima would go on for days, weeks, and before it was over three of the six flag raisers would be dead.

"But it was inspiring," says Newman. "It gave you goose bumps. I flopped over and humped it right up to the top of that quarry." There he got shot, in the leg again, and this time it was bad.

"Well, you know, the third time's the charm; the third

Purple Heart meant a trip back to the States and I was happy about that. But first I had to get down off that quarry.

"Now, you know, in those days the band people also served as the stretcher bearers. So they picked me up and carried me down and it was steep. And shells are coming in all the time. There's hardly a minute without it.

"We make it down and I remember there's an LVT down there and it was full of dead, so they strapped my stretcher with me on my back across the bow of this thing and that was the longest trip of my life.

"I guess the beach was only about seven or maybe eight hundred yards away but it seemed like it took forever. The terrain was all pockmarked and the LVT was rolling this way and that and shells were bursting all around me and here I was, still alive, I knew I wasn't going to die—I didn't know if I was going to have a leg or not—but I'm thinking, 'Here I am, and I've got my ticket back to the States and I'm going to get killed on my way back to the goddamn ship!'

"I'd made it and yet I hadn't," he says, and stretches out the leg that still plagues him from time to time. He made it. "And I still have the leg, too." Which is probably his best Iwo Jima souvenir.

The Second World War was over for Newman; in a few months it would be over for everyone.

About 458,000 Marines fought the war, about 5 percent of the total American forces. They made 26 amphibious assaults and though there were several bad moments here and there, none failed. Nearly 20,000 proud leathernecks died. Hollywood couldn't crank out Marine movies fast enough.

Yet, the year after *Pride of the Marines*, in which John Garfield played a Marine hero blinded on Guadalcanal, President Truman began laying plans to *finally* dismantle the Corps. This time, it nearly happened.

Congress had already put the peacetime strength of the Corps at only 107,000, the secretary of defense had decided that no Marine would serve above the Army corps level, and on the Joint Chiefs of Staff, the body which would now play a key role in determining the character of American defense, there was no representative of the Marines.

Even the Marine Corps birthday was canceled, all official observances of the anniversary to be expunged. Needless to say, the "private" parties were more robust than ever.

When a congressman petitioned the president for better treatment of the Corps, Truman, a one-time Army captain of artillery, fired back a bold salvo.

"For your information," he wrote, the Marine Corps is nothing but "the Navy's police force and as long as I am President, that is what it will remain. They have a propaganda machine that is almost the equal to Stalin's."

There was a public uproar, and quickly, a very public apology from the president. Still the battle for the Corps dragged on.

With the heady victory of World War II receding and the angst of the Cold War not yet begun, the services had commenced scrambling to preserve what they could of a fast diminishing military place in American affairs.

The Army, pointing out that amphibious assault in the new nuclear age was impossible, was hell-bent on taking over all land-based operations.

The Air Force, fresh and ferocious in new blue uniforms, had its eyes on the Marine air role, and in fact, plans were already being circulated that would have *all* air power, including carrier-based naval aviation, under the sway of the USAF.

It was probably this last "outrage" that put an end to the interservice squabbling. Congress intervened, gave each of the services a piece of the pie, and reestablished the Marine Corps— just in time to send it to Korea.

The North Korean People's Army had launched an assault across the 38th Parallel, which had come as something of a surprise to the West, still celebrating the end of World War II and reveling in the resultant economic boom. Seoul was gobbled up almost immediately.

As the diplomats decried and denounced and wrung their hands, the NKPA pushed the South Koreans, and the hastily built-up American military, to a small area in the southeast corner of the peninsula, the Pusan perimeter. This is where the 1st Provisional Marine Brigade landed.

The brigade, supported by the withering Marine "close air support" developed in the Pacific, turned a flank at "No Name

Ridge" and stopped the North Korean advance.

General Douglas MacArthur now turned to the Marines for his masterstroke. With the fighting locked up in the southeast, the 1st Marine Division staged an amphibious assault at Inchon, high up on the western coast, well to the NKPA rear. Seoul was quickly recaptured and a classic "hammer and anvil" campaign caught the NKPA between the Marines in the north and the reinforcements pouring into and out of the Pusan perimeter to the south.

They did so well that China, perhaps fearful of its own borders being penetrated, entered the war in force. It was at least as big a surprise as the original NKPA invasion.

When the Chinese swarmed across the border in their extraordinary numbers, it was the 1st Marine Division that got trapped at the Chosin Reservoir.

Surrounded by a foe that outnumbered them five to one, seared by frostbite in the subfreezing winds, the twenty thousand Marines, under the already legendary Colonel Lewis "Chesty" Puller ("Well, this is just great; it means we can shoot in all directions!"), broke a hole in the bamboo ring, marched sixty miles through mountain terrain, fighting every yard to the safety of Hungnam harbor. They arrived dragging all their war-fighting materiel, and, as has become the Marines' custom, carrying out all their dead.

It is a largely untold story, this American Dunkirk, but it is instructive of the nature of the Korean War that it was a high point.

The rest of the "police action" went even less well. As in World War I, positions became hardened and the ongoing hostilities became a war of attrition, with hills taken and lost for map markers, men's bodies used for artillery scores, and all the while the diplomats talking about peace.

"I was at Bunker Hill," says Newman. It was so named for its dug-in Marine bunkers. "We were close enough to Panmunjom to see the buildings where the peace talks were going on!" He rolls his eyes. "You know? In just the last part of that war, when Marine positions became static, stuck in their sectors of defense, that's when we suffered forty percent of our casualties."

The Marines in Korea were now deployed as the "second

land Army," which neither they, nor the Army, ever wanted them to be. The Air Force had taken control of all the air operations. The leatherneck grunts griped about the lack of their carefully nurtured "close air support," but it was lost amid the babble as the armed services squabbled on and the armistice talks dragged on. Then one day, as with a game grown tiresome, the diplomats decided to return to square one, the 38th Parallel, and it was over.

The war lasted three years, one month, and two days. Over four thousand Marines died. This time, when it might have been most expected, and accepted, there was no call to disband the Corps.

The National Security Act of 1947, provoked by Truman's attack on the Corps, had set Corps levels at three divisions and some two hundred thousand men.

The "Cold War" Congress now passed a bill reaffirming that composition for the peacetime Corps. And this time, a Marine was allowed to sit, as an advisor, on the Joint Chiefs of Staff.

Eisenhower, like most Army men, was no lover of the Corps; nevertheless he sent in the Marines early and often. They evacuated Americans during the Suez crisis, then they evacuated the UN truce team. They rescued by helicopter an American ambassador and an Eisenhower press secretary from an attack by radical demonstrators in Tokyo. They joined the rescue effort for earthquakes and floods in Morocco, Turkey, Greece, Spain, Ceylon, Mexico, and British Honduras.

The Marines landed in Lebanon in 1958 when the murder of King Faisal of Iraq threatened to destabilize the area. They protected American citizens during the Venezuelan coup of the same year.

In 1962, Colonel John Glenn, Jr., became the first American to orbit the Earth. He was a Marine. It was a very high point. Newman got out the next year. "That was a low point." He laughs. Then Vietnam happened.

Fighting in Indochina had been going on, more or less uninterrupted, since the thirties. The names of the combatants and the color of the uniforms changed from time to time, but the long-range goal was always the expulsion of foreigners—the Japanese, the Chinese, the French, and now it was the turn of the Americans.

The Marines were not "first to fight" in Vietnam. There were Marine drill instructors in 'Nam training the ARVN (Army of the Republic of Vietnam) and there were some Marine helos supporting troop transport ops, but the real action, for the Corps, began in March of 1965.

The USAF was already pounding away at the countryside with raids out of Da Nang. When the base began getting heavy rocket attacks from Viet Cong units in the surrounding hills, two Marine battalions were sent in to provide "base security," a traditional Corps task. The job, however, was complicated a bit by an order prohibiting Marines to fire unless fired upon. It meant that ARVN units under fire, in full view of the Marine units, could not count on them for support.

This changed when it became clear that the indigenous Viet Cong was being supported by elements, in fact four whole regiments, of the North Vietnamese Army (NVA).

The American point of view was that the NVA was an invading army (and, technically, it was as much so as the North Korean People's Army was) and President Lyndon Johnson responded (this was, as with Korea, a presidential campaign) by sending in the Marines to "search and destroy." In-country came four Marine regiments with four Marine air groups.

Once again there was an argument over correct usage. The Marines wanted to fire and maneuver. The Army wanted to use them as an Army subcontractor doing Army work in Marine mufti. "I agreed with General Krulak," says Newman.

The somewhat slight but nevertheless pugnacious General Victor Krulak was called "Brute" by his Marines, "but what was special about him," says Newman, "is that he was so smart."

Krulak, who as a young officer had been in the vanguard of the development of the LVT, tried something at Le My that was one of the early successes of Vietnam.

After clearing the village of enemy, he had his Marines work with the people, rebuilding huts, digging new wells, dispensing medical aid and forming a militia. Le My, though shaky, held. It led to "County Fair," a pacification program by which the

Marines intended to win "the hearts and minds" of the Vietnamese one village at a time.

Says Krulak: "This painstaking, exhausting, and sometimes bloody process of bringing peace, prosperity, and health to a gradually expanding area became known as 'the spreading inkblot' formula. It should have been at the heart of the battle for freedom in Indochina." It was rejected.

General William C. Westmoreland thought County Fair too unmilitary considering the military "assets" available for more conventional war fighting, and the secretary of defense, Robert C. McNamara, choosing between these grand strategies, called the "inkblot" formula "a good idea . . . but too slow."

The more Army-like sweep operations which then became the basic battle plan were not without their successes, and the Marines had their share.

Operation Starlite (Chu Lai) was a spectacular success, killing half a 2,000-man Viet Cong force. It was followed by similarly successful sweeps called Blue Marlin, Double Eagle, and Golden Fleece. One hundred fifty clashes in eighteen months left nearly 10,000 VC dead. And the rest of the American military was having similar good fortune.

Whether your politics called the Viet Cong cause a "revolution" or an "invasion," it was unmistakable that it was withering in the heat of battle.

The lunar new year, Tet, of 1968 became the turning point. The Communists, who usually declared a truce of observance at about this time, instead launched a furious attack that took them to the very gates of the American embassy in Saigon.

The Viet Cong were thrown back on almost every front. Their spirit was crushed. Their ranks were broken. But if the light at the end of the tunnel was now lit, it would turn out to be the light of a television set.

The television scenes of Tet, of Viet Cong on the lawn of the embassy with their AK-47's, became the basic evening news fare for a month. This took its toll on the American will. The rally time flowered, the candle burning, the peace song singing, the flag burning. The turning point swung 180 degrees and turned the other way. In defeat, the Communists had unwittingly stumbled into a major victory.

Meanwhile, their one surprising military success had left the Marines pinned down under heavy, continuous fire.

Deployed as an Army group, the leatherneck defenders of Khe Sanh had been trapped, "sitting on their ditty bags," as they had been at Chosin.

It was to be a seventy-one-day siege, a hellacious bombardment, the air alive with shot and shell. Only heroic "close air support" by the Marine Air Group, and Operation Pegasus launched by General Westmoreland specifically to relieve the embattled Marines, saved a very seriously deteriorating situation.

"Colonel Dave Lounds, the guy with the waxed mustache who commanded the troops at Khe Sanh, was my platoon leader on Saipan," says Newman. "He was so distressed he left the service over what happened at Khe Sanh."

When Lounds's Marines returned to base camp they set about making immediate preparations, as ever, to go back into battle. But their new orders were to be for home. It had been decided to Vietnamize the war.

More Marines served in Vietnam than in all of World War II. Thirteen thousand died. All that was left the Corps was to watch and monitor the inexorable defeat of the ARVN.

When it came down to the end, the last days, it was Marine Operation Frequent Wind that helo'd out the last Americans and "friendly nationals" from the roof of the now pathetic embassy.

"Then there was that 'Corps in search of a mission' stuff." Newman laughs, sardonically, remembering the "bad time," as he calls it. *Disbandment* is the word, but the old-timer still cannot bring himself to say it.

"But we were worried about it," he says. "The rumors were not having a good effect on the ranks."

At the time of the Brookings report Newman was active, and still is active, in the various associations of former Marines, an unofficial but very large and effective lobbying force in Congress.

"I was one of the organizers of the Marine Corps Council at about that time. The idea was to coordinate all the different associations to support the commandant and the purposes of the Marine Corps. We're pretty strong. But you know what? I never really had a doubt in my mind. I think no Marine ever really doubts the future of the Corps."

Newman rises from his chair and goes rummaging across his wall for something and he finds it above a series of cartoon caricatures. It is an eight by ten glossy of the former commandant Clifton Cates. A small mother-of-pearl cigarette holder is taped to the photo.

Like Newman's father, Cates had been gassed. The small holders were a concession to his ravaged lungs in lieu of quitting cigarette smoking. The holder had become rather a trademark.

Cates was the Marine most instrumental in beating back Truman's charge against the Corps some three decades before the Brookings report.

"I got this from him at one of our division association reunions," Newman says of the cigarette holder. Somewhere else on the wall there's a nice letter from Cates to Newman congratulating him on "the fine affair" Newman had arranged.

"The general told me a little story that night about the Truman thing," Newman says. "It was rough, he told me, but hell, we knew that a lot of people were working for us, a lot of congressmen; and he told me that when Truman made that dumb crack about propaganda and the Marine Corps, he called up General Cates that very same night."

According to Sergeant Newman, the conversation went like this:

Cates: Cates . . . *[that's how he answered his phone]*
Truman: This is Harry.
Cates: Harry who? I know a lot of Harrys.
Truman: This is Harry your president. I'm going to read you a letter that I'm going to release to the press tomorrow. Let me know what you think. *[And then he read the letter.]* So that's it Clifton, what do you think? Is that enough of an apology?
Cates: It's fine, have another bourbon and go to bed.

Newman laughs at his own story—that gravelly sergeant laugh. "Cates never had a doubt then, and when that stuff happened after Vietnam, *I* didn't!"

There was no real doubt according to Brookings, either. The report simply and brutally concluded that, for quick insertion into a hostile environment, "the Marine Corps confronts a superior competitor in the U.S. Army's 82nd Airborne Division." The Corps was in danger of losing its amphibious role to history.

Indeed, there was no seaborne Marine assault in the Urgent Fury operation, the invasion of Grenada. In fact, the island assault plan, which so clearly presented itself to the Marines as a way to recapture the glories of Tinian and Tarawa, was basically an 82nd Airborne show. More than six thousand paratroops landed on Grenada with missions to take all the main points. The single Marine Battalion Landing Team landed in the northeast corner of the island to capture the tourist-oriented airfield. They found few defenders to fight.

On all of tiny Grenada, at that time, were only about one hundred lightly armed Cuban guards and about seven hundred even more lightly armed Cuban construction workers. Even so, there was bloodshed and mass confusion.

All the services had demanded their piece of the pie on this one and the communication problems were horrendous. A Navy jet strafed Army positions, leaving dead "friendlies" in its wake. Another jet bombed a mental hospital and killed fifteen people.

The Marines, who had been quick about the job of securing the airport, went looking for other targets. They decided to attack Fort Adolphus, which was flying a flag with a device of "an unknown type." The Grenada operation had been precipitated by a left wing coup that had put six hundred American medical students in jeopardy of becoming hostages and had President Reagan ruminating about the possibility of "a Soviet-Cuban colony being readied as a major military bastion to export terror and undermine democracy." The Marine BLT decided to storm the mysterious fort. It is fortunate that the epidemic of communications problems led ultimately to a decision to call off a barrage of artillery meant to soften the Fort Adolphus target. It turned out to be the Venezuelan embassy.

Nineteen Americans died in Urgent Fury. Three of them were Marines. This came in the same week as the bombing of the Marine barracks in Lebanon. There was a low feeling in all the stations of the Corps. Lebanon could be explained; it was a surprise, it was a fluke, it was a single fanatical martyr screaming, "Allah Akbar!" Grenada, the sharp slap in the historical Marine face, was another matter. And Panama was worse.

In Panama it was the Army's Southern Command that did the commanding. And it was the Army that did the chasing of Panamanian dictator Manuel Noriega. No Marines were sent to Panama. None. The Marines who got involved in the scuffle were the garrison troops who were already on station in the isthmus, and their main claim to fame was that they set the roadblock on "The Bridge of the Americas." No Marines came from the sea.

Newman was a lot happier with the results of Desert Storm. "We did a hell of a job in the Persian Gulf," he says. "You heard the Schwartzkopf briefing." Newman was not surprised that there was no amphibious assault. "They went about it just about the way I thought they would," he says.

"The modern tactics are going to involve air drops, taking strategic points, vertical [helo] envelopment, but I think it's like Grenada; that's what the amphibious landing is for. We're not gonna storm Europe; we're too smart for that. We're gonna have to mess around with oil islands off Iran and maybe the banana republics. Small stuff. Hey! But it was *always* small stuff. The biggest thing we ever landed on was Okinawa! Iwo Jima was only five hundred yards across!"

Still, there hasn't been a sea raid since Inchon and the questions of the Brookings report continue to wait for their answers.

The U.S. Marine Corps of Hollywood fact and fable is largely a hard-won myth. The longer history is clear. For a century and a half the Corps was little more than a lean, semi-irregular force sent in to quell disturbances of the smallest scale. It often did a good job, but not always.

It was the sharpshooting at Belleau Wood that brought the Corps its fame, the prescient Orange Plan that brought it a storied role, and one wonderfully custom-tailored war in the Pacific that presented it with the winning streak that even now assures its prominence. Do we really want to freeze the Marines in amber, even at a "peace dividend" reduction of the current force level, for all time?

The Corps remains a force without analog in the armed

services of the world. Yes, there are elite units here and there that practice the amphibious role, but like the British Royal Marines, who number only seven thousand men, they are all small-unit commando outfits.

British Colonel Mark Gosling, a Royal Marine who has undergone extensive training with the U.S. Marines, says, "The difference between your Marines and ours is that we're light, we're small, we specialize, we don't have many tanks and such, or nearly so many men. If we had all that stuff, I think it would be rather difficult to distinguish us from the Army."

Precisely put. With the island-hopping campaign of World War II now safely half a century behind us, the question the Brookings report asked becomes more apt by the year. Is this Marine Corps really necessary?

When, in 1957, General Krulak was asked by Commandant Pate to jot down a few notes on the very same question, he responded in part:

> . . . does the United States need a Marine Corps? . . . she has a fine modern Army, and a vigorous Air Force. . . . Marines claim to have a mystical competence in landing operations but they really don't. . . . If I had to stick to pure and un-qualified military techniques, I would find it most difficult to prove, beyond question, that the United States does truly *need* a Marine Corps.

When Krulak included this letter some years later in a book he wrote for the Naval Institute, he found that the intervening years had not been kind to the Corps' position.

The military buildup under President Ronald Reagan included a "600-ship Navy," several of which vessels were new craft designed specifically for the Marine amphibious role, but nearly every other military development of the last decade had argued, with Brookings, against the Corps.

America had become wary of armed intervention, and when it *had* sent in the Marines the result had too often been vague disappointments like Grenada, or disasters like Lebanon.

The battlefield had become more electrified, the bombs more "smart" than ever, and the promise was of more of the same to come. The traditional U.S. Marine role was becoming increasingly harder and harder to defend in the war-gaming strategies.

Complicating matters was the fact that United States' armed forces, in general, had become something of a relic. For a variety of political and economic reasons, American might had like the fiddler crab "evolved" into a one-clawed monstrosity—that arm flung athwart the forward line of the old Iron Curtain. Though the Marines had carved out a small niche for themselves in this line, it was hardly a role to justify a three-division Corps. And what about this old Iron Curtain? With walls coming down all over Eastern Europe, and the dissolution of the old USSR, and the curtain going up on democratic movements everywhere in the NATO theater, armed force was becoming more and more difficult to justify.

But suppose Uncle Sam's defense posture were one day to move dramatically, or even substantially, away from NATO (and preparation for a third "great war" which few seem to think will ever happen) and gravitate instead toward a more far-flung "brush-fire" force that might have to operate in many places at the same time? Then a small, elite "second army," well versed in amphibious attack skills, might not be too shabby a thing for him to find in his kit.

When Iraq invaded Kuwait, it was the Marines who went, 45,000 strong in a week, to sit in the desert like some foreign legion waiting to spill their blood against the fruit of Islam. No, it was not a classic amphibious maneuver, but it was in many ways a seaborne insertion. It utilized the prepositioned ships and supplies for which the Marines had lobbied hard. It used the "floats" that had "pumped" out for training and now found themselves on the front line. It was the first "go" job of any real military size in the post–Cold War era, and the Marines got the call. But the question lingers: Did those riflemen sitting in the dunes *have* to be highly trained "amphibious" Marine Corps troops?

The very change of their most basic nomenclature, from "Marine Expeditionary Force" to "Marine Amphibious Force" and back again in a period of a dozen or so years, seems itself a sign of the Corps' own strategic schizophrenia on the question.

If they can't figure it out, how can the Joint Chiefs? Or the Congress? Or the American people?

Does the United States Marine Corps really have a role to play in the modern American defense structure? That is a very good question.

The Commandant

--------------------★--------------------

At seven A.M. on a brightly chilly winter morning, a big green C-20 is sitting on the tarmac at Andrews AFB with its jet engines idling. It is a basic corporate jet, but in its military application it boasts a lot more power, a mess of high-wiz electronic equipment, and a plug ugly coat of flat olive paint.

Its interior is divided, as in most corporate jets, into several rooms. In the main room, a young galley sergeant is serving coffee at a collapsible table, around which sit a crisp and spit-shined sergeant major, two retired Marine colonels in business suits, and the balding, smiling Colonel Barney Barnham in his dress khakis.

Barnham, secretary to the Marine Corps commandant, Al Gray, rolls his early morning cigar around his lips and explains that this is going to be "another ceremony day."

"The commandant likes to get out among the men as much as he can," says Barney Barnham, "and this is one of the ways he does it. Okay! Here he comes!" Barney Barnham quickly straps himself into his seat and snuffs out his cigar. Out the small portal window, a white staff car is turning down a ramp. The jet engines begin to whine up. The small NO SMOKING/FASTEN SEATBELTS sign flashes on with an urgent chime.

The sergeant major leans over and allows to one of the two

retired colonels, "We don't wait around long when the commandant is on board."

Gray steps into the jet. The door is closed and locked behind him. Up ahead, in the cockpit, levers are pulled and safeties released. The C-20 rolls off its point.

As it picks up speed, Gray walks down the narrow aisle toward the men. He is wearing a set of impeccably pressed utilities. He is not a big man, but he is broad and blocky and hard as Monday morning: that peculiarly American "tough guy" look with the rolling, confident gait and a smile that could back up a ninja.

The two retired colonels rise in their suits and shake the commandant's hand as if he were a baseball hero or a movie star. Then they quickly sit back down and buckle up. The galley sergeant hands Gray a cup of coffee.

Gray walks directly to Barnham's seat and leans over him to speak. The commandant, who usually wakes at about five A.M. and runs his dogs and prepares for his day over breakfast, likes to hit the ground running, and shooting. Barnham pulls out his ever-present pad.

"You know those two young boys who live around the barracks?" asks Gray as he keeps his balance by holding on to the baggage rail. "The ones whose dad died? I want you to call them up and invite them to the parade drill." Barnham logs the order.

The C-20 now shudders for an instant and then it roars off down the runway. Up in the base control tower, the "CMC bird" is always number one for takeoff. It is a courtesy that, as today, generally catches Gray standing in the aisle without a seat.

"Gimme your seat," he calls out to the galley sergeant, who is just buckling himself into his backward-facing galley chair. The young man looks up, surprised. "You're younger than I am," says the CMC. "You go sit in the head."

The C-20, which is bound by no comfort-oriented commercial carrier flight procedures, leaps off the runway and bolts straight up for the sky. The two retired colonels pitch forward and bang their elbows on the collapsible table. Coffee cups slide and have to be caught. Gray smiles and shares a look with the sergeant major, who shakes his head in mild amusement, a pair of NCO types having a jest at the expense of the gentry.

As soon as the C-20 levels off, Gray is out of the galley chair and Barnham is at his side. Topic one is the day's itinerary.

First stop is Camp Lejeune, North Carolina, where they will be present at the retirement parade for 2nd Marines Sergeant Major Browne. Gray makes it a strong point to celebrate as many NCOs as he can manage.

The second stop will be at The Citadel, Charleston, South Carolina, where Colonel Smith, a Marine, is retiring from the faculty. "A cadet parade." Gray smiles. "They're great."

The Carolinas represent a major part of the Marine orbit. Although there are Marines stationed all around the world, serving in small units as naval security or standing guard at American embassies, it is the key posts in Virginia and the Carolinas, San Diego and Camp Pendleton (south of San Juan Capistrano), Okinawa and Hawaii where you will find most Marines who aren't floating somewhere on a "pump." Being commandant is something akin to being the emperor of a small kingdom, tightly held, but with small expeditionary forces bewilderingly far-flung. It taxes the mind.

Gray's next topic en route is the thorny issue of women Marine security guards. In the wake of the Moscow embassy sex scandal, the Marine Security Guard is pushing hard to include women Marines in their embassy mix and a Washington, D.C., women's group has seized upon the issue. Gray has been asked to address this group. He's peeved. Barnham nods and grunts noncommittally. His principal job as secretary is to listen. He is the CMC's sounding board.

"I don't know," Gray says about the idea of adding more women guards. "You know, we buried eighteen guards over the last four years: I mean outside Lebanon." He shakes his head. His mind is made up. "If these gals have any success in pressing this issue," Gray says of the women's group, "I think it's going to come down to a shoot-out at the O.K. Corral. I think I'll have to take one of them to lunch. Maybe I'll start some rumors." He winks at Barnham, who seems to think it's a good idea.

"Outside Lebanon" is what Gray said, and the very word *Lebanon* looms large and dark in the current Marine mythos. It was Gray who was in charge of the 2nd Marine Division in October of 1983 when those 240 men were killed in the Beirut barracks terrorist bombing. It was Gray who was in charge at the Marines' largest one-day casualty total since Iwo Jima.

If you ask Marine Corps old-timers for an indelible image out of the career of General Al Gray, this is one of the two they give you: General Gray speaking to the press in those first numbed hours after the bombing, dealing directly with the circling reporters, disdaining the ubiquitous spokesmen, calling the attack "a godless type thing, against a force that knows our God," and then, later, still taking the heat, leading the Camp Lejeune memorial service which was so publicly attended by President Ronald Reagan.

The other indelible image is of the fall of Saigon, where as commander of the 33rd MAU (during the Vietnam War the designation MEU, with that nasty word *expeditionary* stuck in the middle of its nom de guerre, was deemed too French for the delicate sensibilities of our friends in the Saigon government and was, therefore, changed to MAU, which stood for Marine *Amphibious* Unit, even though not a single serious amphibious operation was launched the entire war) Al Gray, himself leading the crack Battalion Landing Team, was the guy responsible for the final evacuation of the city.

It is a strange pair of memories between which to bookend the story of the commandant of the Marine Corps: two of the very sorriest disasters in recent American military history.

Still, few things give a warrior a taste for victory better than the acrid smell of defeat, and so his *presiding* over the debacle of Saigon must be seen as an essential ingredient in the readying of Alfred Gray for the job, and not a few senior Marines will tell you, though none for attribution, that his subsequent performance after the Lebanon bombing greatly endeared him to the president, which lent an added punch that scored heavily in the general's favor during the commandant-nominating brawl.

Barnham has been through most of this with Gray. Now, pad and pencil out, he's still by the commandant's side. Only the battlefields have changed. A new brawl is now gathering, five grueling days of weapons appropriations testimony in the Congress. Gray has been working overtime on his sales pitch. The problem for the next couple of days is to focus on the weapons hearing. As Barnham goes over the forty-eight-hour schedule, Gray blue-pencils it on the move. There are papers to read, meetings to attend, and hands to shake. "Action," he keeps reminding Barnham. "Gimme all nuts and bolts stuff," he barks like a bulldog.

For most of their history the Marines have been an off-the-shelf outfit, mainly off *other people's* shelves. Their planes are adapted from Air Force or Navy craft. Their tank and track vehicles are adapted from those made to the specs of other services and branches. Even their basic rifle, the M-16, has been modified for their own purposes.

According to Lance Corporal Hess, "When it comes to equipment, we're your basic hind-tit operation," and Gunnery Sergeant Chamberlain of Headquarters Company, Quantico, re-members that "when the troops got the word that we were good to go to Grenada, they all had the wrong packs, the heavy ones; so the PX's all over the place were jammed with grunts buying their own packware for the Caribbean."

A vanguard operation with a make-do armory, the branch that Americans seem to love the most is the one the military establishment funds the least. The years since Vietnam have found the Corps a stepchild in the house of war.

The Harrier "jump jet" program, for which the Congress authorized the acquisition, from Great Britain, of an entire weap-ons system for Marine use only, was a happy harbinger of better times coming. The new LAV (Light Armored Vehicle), a small, quick, amphibious "armored car," was derived from the Swiss MOWAG weapons system but reconceived specifically for the Corps. Gray is pushing the trend.

"You have that staff meeting tomorrow morning," says the colonel.

"Is it the one on weapons *theory?*" asks the general, curling his lip.

Yes, the colonel nods. The general says, "Cancel it." He'll use the time to study some papers on his own.

Barnham crosses out the meeting and tells Gray about a speech at the Alfalfa Club, a congregation of beltway movers and shakers. Gray nods. He'll take that one. These are good people to have on your side.

"Dress blues," says Barnham, sourly.

"By all accounts a fun evening." Gray smiles.

Two retirement ceremonies are then set, flowers are arranged for a widow, and a note is made to meet with some retired general about a new idea he has for gunnery ranging.

"Oh God," Gray says, finally settling into his seat, "the worst thing in the world—talking to an artillery man about artillery."

He turns to the two retired suits. They exchange the pleasantries of the morning and play a little game of service geography in which alternate players offer up the names of men who are then identified as "yes, I served with him here," or "sure, I commanded him over there." One of the suits, in fact, served under Colonel Smith of The Citadel, the other commanded Sergeant Major Browne. "Good men," all agree.

Then, although the old colonels haven't yet asked about the weapons hearings, Gray decides he wants to answer their questions anyway. Perhaps it's good practice.

No one doubts Gray's ability to send the right messages to his Marines. The doubts concern his ability to argue for them at the senatorial grab bag. The transition from the previous commandant, smooth, politically adept P. X. Kelley, to the gruff, blunt, bulldog Gray was widely, and perhaps correctly, seen as a rebuke to a number of Pentagon-wise Marine Corps commandants going several watches back. Yet, with the coming of these budget hearings, a lot of tongues that once cheered the end of the reign of the "political" commandants now bemoan the absence of such a one on the point.

Gray, however, is game. "The initial effort with the Senate hearings revolves around NATO and the INF treaty," he says, dismissively. "It has to do with the changing facts on the ground and the ramifications of losing the missiles.

"Now I'm portrayed as a guy who knows nothing about Washington or even where the Congress is located. I'm not concerned about that. The strength of the Marine Corps is honesty.

Be it with Congress or the Pentagon or the American people, the issue is credibility. Doing what you say you're going to do. Keep it on top of the table. No deals. I know how to do that. I may not know anything about Washington but I know a little bit about the art of getting things done. We'll see how we do.

"A man is what he is," the general reflects. "My own approach is common sense, common courtesy, stating the issues as clearly as you can. And it isn't like I've never been around," he smiles. "I was picked in 1979 to sell the Congress on how we were going to run amphibious operations in the future. And a couple of years ago I was the one who sold them on the Light Armored Vehicle [LAV]."

"That's right," says the sergeant major, "and that was one hell of a longshot."

"Look, I'm telling you the truth," says Gray. "With me, what you see is what you get. If the perception is that I don't know my way around, so be it. We'll just let that work for me."

But Gray is pushing a big stone up a steep hill. The U.S. defense establishment is on the run everywhere. Budget cutting is the mood of the moment. The Marines, always last at the trough in the best of times, have little fat to cut and many missions they hope to perform. These are bad times for "jarheads." They have, for instance, only recently carved out a niche in the NATO deployment, and now, with the Warsaw Pact turning toward democracy, it appears that the Marines have crashed the party just as it is ending.

One of the suited ex-colonels, undeterred as are most military men, was a tanker and wants to know whether, in spite of the current realities, the Marines are planning to upgrade their armor capabilities.

"We have some tough armor issues," Gray says, more than willing to play out the game. Not a lot of Gray's people are completely satisfied with the new main battle tank—the M-1 that fights so well in its television commercial. The Marine Corps, which must follow a doctrine of "light enough to get there and heavy enough to win," doubts that its firepower justifies its size.

"Frankly," says Gray, "I mean, really, should we even *have* the M-1?"

The two suits offer their opinions; both are against the new tank. Old soldiers tend to prefer old weapons. At the least, they knew how to make them work.

"Well, here's what I've done," says Gray. "I've invited guys in from the field. All our areas, all ranks. I want to let them in on it." He starts thinking out loud.

"You know, if you don't buy the new tank there's no free lunch because we still have to upgrade the M-60 at 1.3 [million] a mother. Gotta do that. I don't want Marines going out with National Guard tanks."

"No sir," say the suits.

"Or maybe we should go a little less," says Gray. "Take the M-1's but fewer of them. Problem is, it isn't so much their big bucks but their big size.

"Anyway. That's why I'm bringing in the ranks. The young guys of the future have to make these decisions. It's their Marine Corps, their tanks. The M-1 will outlast me by twenty years." Gray thinks about this a moment, decides he's right, nods. Besides, he likes the idea about involving the ranks in the decision-making process.

"The kids in the field know the difference between the way it is and the way it is supposed to be," says Gray, visibly warming up to his own idea. "We've got to get rid of the musers. What you see is what you get. We've got to start making real world decisions on real world inventory. I mean, if equipment can't respond [to training] in sixty to ninety days, what the hell is it doing in the armory? That's why, when you read that the Osprey has slipped a year in the budget, you have to read the fine print."

The Osprey is the experimental tilt-rotor attack plane that the Marines are developing for "vertical assault." It is bigger and faster and more heavily armored than any helicopter could be. As such, the Osprey represents an audacious sea change in vertical envelopment, with glitches and gremlins to suit. It is also under heavy attack from the budget cutters who want to declare a "peace dividend" in the wake of the collapsing Eastern bloc and the easing of the pressure of "the main threat."

In a matter of months the word will come down that the

Marines are to be cut back 25 percent, commensurate with the other armed forces. They will lose approximately fifty thousand men and a proportionate share of all weapons development and deployment. There will be, however—and it is something of a surprise—no serious call to disband the Corps or "fold it" into the Army. In fact several proposals will be raised that Marine assault ships, with their Harriers and the more conventional helos, might well prove a more cost-effective way of protecting American interests than the increasingly expensive Navy carrier groups.

In the meantime, Gray rides roughshod over the notion of a peace dividend. "The Osprey has slipped back a year in the budget," says Gray, putting a Marine face on it, "because we have also applied an additional two-hundred million dollars for research, at your commandant's request, because we will still get the airplane in the same time frame but it will be a better, more comprehensively tested airplane.

"I'm leaning on aviation. I'm getting tired of seeing aircraft introduced into the inventory and it takes us two years to be able to get up in them! I'm not smart enough to understand why we have to do that! When I put a weapon in the Marine Corps I want to shoot it the next day."

Rah-rah, rip-rip, go the suits. Gray rises and shakes their hands and moves out of the room up toward the front of the plane.

In a smaller, empty compartment, he takes one of the four seats and pulls a paper cup out of the dispenser on the wall. Then he rolls on his hip and pulls from the back pocket of his cami utilities an overpacked pouch of Red Man tobacco. He pops a plug in his mouth, studies the bottom of the paper cup, and says, "Okay, let's talk. You want to talk about me or the Marines? I don't much like talking about me."

Instead, a story is related. It comes by way of the former police chief of Point Pleasant, New Jersey, one Charles Bertolatus, who was a classmate of Gray's at Point Pleasant Beach High School.

According to Bertolatus, Gray wasn't called "Bulldog" then; he was called "Peanuts."

"True." Gray smiles and asks about his old friend.

Bertolatus remembered Gray as the smallest kid on the school football team, "but he had that grim determination and leadership." Gray smiles at that too.

They are still friends, the general and the chief. "You can be tough," said Bertolatus, "but it doesn't mean you're a tough person. Al has a tremendous amount of compassion and sensitivity . . . his men admire the way he lives; and we don't call him 'Peanuts' anymore."

Gray spits a brown wad into the paper cup and softens a little. He wonders why anybody would want to interview him for anything, then decides, "It's not me you want to talk about; it's the commandant. You know, they're not the same thing." He laughs.

Al Gray is by all accounts a warm and loving father, husband, granddad, dog owner, mower of lawns, repairer of bicycles, all that. Commandant Gray is another thing.

It is a paradoxical position, CMC. You rise to the very top of a demanding craft. You're at the pinnacle for four years; then you're out of work—not as in, back to being a general, as in unemployed.

"Well, yeah, but I just can't view this as a job," Gray says. "It's a profession. I've been at it a long time. I love the Marine Corps. I love the public service. I've really never spent any time at all, as an individual, worrying about what I'm going to do after."

In fact, just a few months ago he had expected to muster out, had sent in his letter of retirement. After thirty-five years of commissioned service, "protocol demanded I begin the process of separation," he says. "It's the law. At the time I wasn't under consideration for being made commandant; in truth I was supporting a couple of other people."

It was an advocacy that Gray took very seriously. "Your interests are always with the Corps and the country," he says, "but at the end of your career your interests go to the future of the Corps and what's best for the Corps. And you'd like to put personalities and friendships aside and make recommendations that really count for the Corps. And look, it had been kind of bumpy for several years for the Corps so that's the position I was taking.

"I had personal concerns that winter and spring, coming down the home stretch there. I mean Jan [Mrs. Gray] and I knew we had to get a house and live." That's not easy after having had housing provided for you most of your adult life. "No," he agrees, "and our other concern was taking care of my mom. We knew we had to put her in a home. And that was quite expensive so we knew I would have to go to work, get a job."

Just what kind of work does a Marine Corps general go looking for?

"Well, I don't know," he says. "I mean it never got that far. I had made a decision to continue to serve, one day at a time, right down to the end in June. There was this commandant selection business; a lot of harsh things had been said about it during the year. I was trying to work through that and I had some operational things I was trying to get complete." Implementing SOC, the special operations program, was one.

Time grew short for the general, and then shorter. In April he became what the Vietnam conscripts used to call a "two-digit midget," fewer than one hundred days to go. But Al Gray wasn't looking forward to leaving. As it turned out, "It wasn't until May that I was even called in and asked about my recommendations for commandant. So I told them about my thoughts about personnel and strategy and directions and whatnot, and then a couple of days later I found out I was the guy!" For Gray, the surprise was total.

"Well, we came in with none of the credentials that a commandant is supposed to have," Gray admits, "and we'll just have to wait and see what happens. I mean we tried to be a class act about it. You have to understand it had been a very tough year. The Moscow embassy scandal really hurt the team, and I'm a big believer in teamwork. But I'm also very fond of General Kelley, personally and professionally. And he did have a tough watch. I've taken to saying that we generals should have served him better."

This watch is going better. It's midwinter. There have been no more scandals, no more bombings. Training days are up. Morale is up. Relations with the Navy have never been better. In fact, Gray has just put through, despite many objections from former Marines, an order that will have "Anchors Aweigh" played before the "Marine Hymn" at all ceremonial functions.

There is an element of self-service in this order. In all the troubled times of the Marines, whenever their existence was seriously questioned, the bureaucratic remedy was generally to absorb the Corps into the Army. By more and more firmly positioning the Corps as the amphibious striking arm of the Navy, this kind of Pentagon shuffle becomes harder and harder to effect. Almost all new Marine doctrine after 1975 can be viewed in this context. Gray is not only its most recent proponent, he's its most vocal. Opportunities to promote it rarely elude him.

"Well, you know we have a whole lot of airlift in our military mix," Gray explains quickly (the unspoken "enemy" is always the Army Airborne, the most arguably redundant elite force), "but not enough sea transport as we need."

To be fair, this idea of involving the Marines more organically within the train of the seagoing Navy is not without some sound tactical foundation. Here, according to Gray, is the point.

"If we had a crisis today—you pick the place on the globe—and we decided to go there tonight, and we took all the airplanes we own, and the free world owns as we know it today, and loaded them up with soldiers and airmen and all the things of war, and flew to that place and fought for thirty days, what you'd have left at the end of that time wouldn't be much. But if you instead loaded three ships—out of Philadelphia or San Diego or Pensacola or whatever—and sailed them to that place, you'd be there well before thirty days, with far more men and materiel than was possible with all that airlift combined."

He spits a stream of brown juice into the paper cup and then looks up with a smile and prepares to clinch his argument.

"You see," he says, "the odds are that the point you had picked would be somewhere along the coastal area because most of the world lives there. Most of the economy is there. Most of our vital interests are there. So," he says, a little smugly, "if you want to go somewhere and stay long enough to gain a successful geopolitical decision on the other end—like winning—you better come from the sea and use your air as a support or you won't be there long enough to win."

Gray then addresses the bombing attack on Libya and Muammar Qaddafi (the U.S. reprisal for a terrorist bombing of a German café frequented by American soldiers) and the circuitous, perhaps fatal, route the strike planes took to get to North Africa. For Gray it points up a further benefit to sealift. "It gives us the freedom to maneuver," he says, "without basing rights, overflight rights, even without political arrangements with some of our allies who may be somewhat faint of heart or, in other words, afraid—yellow."

Having in a single blow laid low France (which had prohibited overflights in the Libya bombing), Gray smiles and targets his next objective, the broader subject of NATO. Marines man what is called the "northern flank" now. An odd image, Marines in white cami, on skis and sleds. The idea has come under attack from several strong points in the military establishment, but for Gray, any criticism of the NATO job is a camel's nose under the tent of the entire Marine battle role.

In fact, Gray has just returned from Norway, from a "very high level" NATO meeting. "I met Lord Carrington there," he says, almost boyishly. Gray believes in the NATO mission, or he says he does.

"Sea power!" he reiterates, "it should be the dominant player in *all* the vital interest areas, around the globe. Supported, of course, by Air Force and Army and in a number of cases our Coast Guard."

He spits in the cup again, returns to the pitch. "And this is where we fit in, with our amphibious capability," he says. "And now I'm going to get to the heart of why there is an *operational policy* that bonds your Navy with your Marine Corps, as opposed to [suggestions that the connection is] mere *politics* or *personalities*.

"You may not win the NATO war at sea," he leans forward and bellows, "but you certainly could lose it there. We must win the battle of the North Atlantic, just as we had to in World War Two and in World War One."

One of the retired colonels asks if he can come in and is invited to sit down.

"Now in recent years," Gray continues, "commencing in late 1975 and 1976 [which is, not uncoincidentally, the period of the Brookings report and the "malaise" that shook the Corps to its lance corporals], the then chief of naval operations began to think a little bit and talk a little bit about this kind of offensive navy versus defensive navy, and it was General Barrow, the twenty-seventh commandant of the Marine Corps, who gave the first public lecture on this new maritime strategy. Not the former secretary of the navy, John Lehman, or some of the others. It was a Marine."

The second of the retired colonels joins the first. A little court is developing around the commandant, as it often does, and, as is his custom, Gray plays to it, keeping eye contact with everyone in the tiny room.

"And since 1976," he says, "in playing war games, and in deploying forces throughout the Atlantic, particularly in the North Atlantic, and in conducting operations with our allies to reinforce the northern flank, we know that you must win the battle in the North Norwegian Sea. Or else you have to win it out in the wide Atlantic where you may *not* win it in time for it to be of any value."

The naval war planners always used to talk about winning the battle in the I-G-UK, the Iceland, Greenland, United Kingdom gap.

"No way," says Gray. "Not anymore. We realize now we have to win it *forward* in the straits of the Skagerrak and Kattegat and so forth, in order to keep the Soviet submarine fleet in their barracks. And so the striking fleet, with its operational manpower, is concentrated on going forward, into the North Norwegian Sea, and winning that battle. But how?"

There are expectant expressions all around the cabin. The sergeant major has heard this little talk, this skein of military logic, this Marine role rationale, a hundred times, like a long and favorite joke where the punchline always hits home. The colonels, however, lean forward so as not to miss anything. Playing the room, Gray leans subtly their way.

"To do this you need air power, the kind of air power that only comes from bases—Iceland, the Azores, and the like. And if you have bases you've got to protect them. That's one thing amphibious forces do! The other thing, more importantly, is that if you don't have bases, you have to make them, or seize them! That's what World War Two was all about.

"And what you need to understand today is that when people need help, what they understand is fighting men coming ashore. Jets zipping along at mach two, carrier groups sailing along over the horizon, that doesn't mean much to somebody who wants some help and a chance to be free. Men coming ashore. That, gentlemen, is what the Marines are all about."

Gray sits back in his chair. He looks over at Barnham and winks. The sergeant major smiles. Gray nods to him too. Then he returns to his point, softly.

"All of a sudden, amphibious warfare is a little more important, isn't it? The watery flanks of NATO are maritime in scope and *that's* why your Marines go to the northern reaches of NATO," he says. Then he explodes.

"Not to defend Norwegians or Danes! Not to be a second land army! Not, as was said in the middle seventies, about the Marines being a Corps in search of a mission! But because it is a maritime mission and I can guarantee you, as long as I have anything to say about it, whenever people talk about coming from the sea, sailors and Marines are going to have the dominant role!"

"Hooraw!" says the sergeant major, only a little in jest, and the colonels send up a couple of self-conscious bulldog barks. Gray laughs, and without even pausing to reload, switches to the Persian Gulf scenario.

"Why is the greatest nation in the world, the greatest navy in the world, having such a challenge protecting the shipping in the international waters of the Gulf?" Gray asks.

With Desert Storm many chess moves away, the United States was still "tilting" toward Iraq, so in the winding down of the Iran-Iraq war, in response to mainly Iranian predations arising from battle on the oil-route sea-lanes, America had "reflagged" a number of Kuwaiti oil tankers with Old Glory and undertaken the job of protecting them. The USS *Stark* was quickly missiled with much loss of face, not to mention lives, and the plan was soon drawing as much fire as the fleet.

"Because," Gray answers his question, "in order to control sea-lanes, you must have effective surveillance and reconnaissance, and that means controlling both sides of the land adjacent to those lanes, like in the Strait of Hormuz.

"Now obviously we can't go into Iran to do that, and as you know we have some difficulty, because of the political sensitivity and the downright commonsense problems of the Gulf Coast states. And by that I mean"—he pauses, as if weighing a thought, and then he leans forward and proceeds confidentially. "I mean if you were a Gulf Coast state, and you got a look at the U.S. track record lately in terms of staying power, you might be a little nervous. Better not open up your state to America because we just may pull out. After all, we left them in South Vietnam. We came back out of Lebanon, and we have done it elsewhere. Look at how we wavered in trying to give the freedom fighters an opportunity to take back Nicaragua."

That's another item troubling Gray, so he switches tracks to "the so-called low-intensity conflict." The invasion of Panama was a low-intensity conflict. "The term has become a buzzword in Washington," says Gray. "It has to be more clearly defined. It needs an improved definition. I'll give you mine," he says. "Low-intensity conflict is revolutionary warfare!

"Sometimes we need to either create a revolution, like we did in Nicaragua, or stop one like we are asked to do in many places around the globe. You only have to look at your naval history to see how, time after time, naval power was deployed in support of this kind of diplomacy. And so that thought is now being taken on board in U.S. Navy circles. It's been on board your United States Marine Corps as long as we've had a Corps!"

In a matter of months the problems in Nicaragua and the Persian Gulf will have become obsolete, moved off the front page of history by an Iraqi attack on Kuwait. Gray can't yet know or even guess at the Mother of All Battles which is to come. But he feels prepared for it anyway.

"The point is, it's always something," he says. "That's why we're making preparations with that same Navy that's needed to fight the NATO war. Flexibility. That's why we're teaching the basics of maneuver warfare and mountain warfare, and desert warfare, and revolutionary warfare, and a lot of these rules are the same—which are, one, don't ever do anything that's not right for the people in the country you're trying to help. Two, don't make any more enemies than you've already got. Maritime warfare and coalition warfare go down the trail together.

"And what does coalition warfare mean? It means to keep the shaky countries like Denmark and Norway and Turkey in the alliance. And keep the political alliance between Turkey and Greece. And figure out ways to bring over countries who are somewhat disenchanted, like Romania and Poland.

"We got to get them all going down the trail together. We don't do that very well. We have military men in different countries providing training and assistance. And in the same foreign countries we have our Senate Foreign Relations Committee denying them economic aid. It doesn't make sense. It's stupid. You ought to insist that people like me drive that point home in the Congress, instead of having these nice coffee klatches when we go over there to those hearings. We ought to get kind of tough over there about the real world and what's needed. Our own approach in the Marine Corps is quite simple. . . . "

He leans back and looks out the round window at the clouds passing below like sky pillows; heavenly sight, and seen so by the geese and the fighter pilots alike.

"Now you want to hear about the new training program we're putting in to implement all that?" Gray asks. "We call it warrior training."

He takes out his tobacco and pops in another wad and chews thoughtfully for a moment. The steward is a handsome young sergeant of Marines decked out in a snappy flight suit, whose job it is mainly to empty the ashtrays and serve the coffee on the big jet. He is cleaning up around us. The sudden realization is that Gray isn't ruminating; he's waiting for this un-warrior to leave. When the steward at last finishes up and slinks out, Gray leans forward.

"Everybody has to be a warrior if they're going to be a Marine. I don't care if he ends up driving a truck or cleaning up the ashtrays, pushing paper, fixing radios, or whatever. He's got to be a gunslinger and a fighter and a warrior first. That's why he came in our Corps and I'm going to make sure that happens.

"Okay, I think we have a pretty good Marine Corps," he says. "We have some units that are great. But we have some that aren't. Everybody's going to be great or they're going to go.

"That's why I've changed the training at Parris Island and San Diego. I've changed it once; I'm going to change it again, and we're going to change the whole program as to what happens after you get out of recruit training."

Gray glowers playfully. "I had to get rid of sixty hours of boot camp," he bellows, "that had to do with Navy Relief [a kind of in-service welfare], the Red Cross, and how to fill out a check!"

Everyone laughs. Gray lets a smile of his own bubble up too, and then holds up a hand for quiet. "But the course that really got me," he twinkles, "was something called 'the anatomy of a man and a woman,' whatever the hell that means!"

The place breaks up. Gray's shoulders, broad as the mythic blacksmith's, begin to shake with mirth. He may have the eyes of a man wanted for something terrible, but he has the timing of a stand-up comic.

"Our new guys are going to have to learn all about that stuff the way the Marines have always learned it. In town."

This time he rides roughshod over the titters. "I have replaced that stuff with an additional sixty hours of tough hand-to-hand combat, combat shooting, field craft, survival, land navigation, crew-served weapons mastery and etcetera, and *then*, then they're all going to go to infantry training school where they're going to get another four to five weeks.

"Before I get through, everybody, whether he's a corporal or a sergeant, will go through my version of squad leader school.

"And what about the Marine infantryman, the queen of battle, what's he going to look like? I can describe him in one word—commando. He's going to end up with twenty-six weeks of the toughest training I can devise.

"So this time next year, wherever you see a Marine, in O'Hare Airport or downtown Charleston, he may be loud or he may be quiet, but you better not screw with him."

The cabin explodes with laughter, some of it obsequious, some of it self-serving, but all of it hearty and most well meant.

"And so people ask me where are we going to find the money; training is expensive. We'll find it somewhere. We may have to do without something else but we're not going to go back on those standards. I don't care about the budget. We're going to take what they give us and we're going to make the kind of Marine Corps the nation demands.

"Now what I have in mind isn't going to cost a hell of a lot of money. The idea is very simple. I happen to think that our country loves our Marine Corps. The people support us. They pray for us. For some reason, and I'm not sure why, they make special demands on their Marine Corps. They demand that we be the best fighting force on this planet. They need to be secure in that knowledge. The best fighting force on earth.

"Now this afternoon, sitting here, I don't know if I can say that's true. But that's where we're going."

"Hooraw," growls one of the retired colonels, and there is a general harrumphing.

Gray spits into his cup. Discussion is his battlefield now and he's going to shoot at every target of opportunity.

In North Carolina, two Huey helicopters are awaiting the C-20 on the tarmac at the New River MCAS, their rotors turning. The commandant's jet dives on the station and hauls down to a stop between the helos.

One of the helos is flat green, the other is a bright sand-and-spinach cami job. A sizable red plaque with four gold stars is mounted at the nose of the cami one. Most of the entourage heads for the green helo. The commandant and his key people head for the other. The two helos lift off together and bank across the meadow and over the forest. It is late January, but this part of the Carolinas is gloriously evergreen.

It may only be an NCO's retirement ceremony to which he's going, but the commandant's helo is flying with its doors open, combat ready. The icy wind rips across the personnel compartment, making all but the commandant wish they were in the green helo with its heaters going and its doors sealed up tight.

Over their headsets Colonel Deforest explains to Gray how the new medals work.

"You don't pin them sideways now; you hang them like this, straight down."

Gray nods and tries out the new technique using the sergeant major as a model. The medal falls off. He tries again and bends the pin. He scowls.

"Why do they mess around with this stuff?"

Five white late-model Plymouths await the helos at the Camp Lejeune helopad. Gray makes it to his car first and moves off. The rest scramble to keep pace.

The vehicles turn down a back road and enter at a camp gate. The guards salute the motorcade with a special snap. So do the passersby. Heads turn.

A large red and gold sign says, "2nd Brigade, 'Follow Me,'" and behind it, out on the parade field, most of the brigade stands at parade rest in their company squares. Now they come to attention.

A sergeant opens the door of the commandant's Plymouth before it actually comes to a stop. The band strikes up the instant the commandant's foot hits the sod.

Ruffles and flourishes fill the winter air. Gray moves into one of the two grandstands. He shakes hands with several people and calls out "hiyas" to several more. In both grandstands people stand and crane their necks to see him. There are a lot of old-timers here, veterans of Tarawa and Inchon and Khe Sanh. Men like Herbert Newman know the commandant; others know of him or served with him and wish him to know of them.

The older these old-timers are, the more decked out they seem to be in their red 2nd Division windbreakers full of battle patches. Many are wearing those old, narrow semidress hats that were called campaign hats by everyone except the actual wearers, who named them rudely after a part of the female anatomy which they more or less resembled and which the wearers more or less missed.

Each old-timer comes with a small entourage of his own, usually composed of a woman his age, his wife; two or more much younger, his daughters and nieces; and a pimple-faced boy or two. These latter look a little proud, and awed, but also a little embarrassed, a little bored.

Gray exchanges his "hiyas" with as many old-timers as he can and kisses as many wives as he can and claps the shoulders of as many of the children and grandchildren as he can reach. The old men are all Gray's people. He wants their progeny to be Marines, especially the kind of Marines they were. Recruiting is always high on the priority list of any commandant outing.

The ceremony begins. The names of famous battles are called. With each battle named, a young Marine wearing a canteen and ammo belt and crisp utilities escorts one of the old-timers out of the grandstand and onto the parade field. Together they march, sometimes a trifle awkwardly, bearing a streamer representing that battle to hang on the division flag. After twenty minutes of this the division banner is festooned and there are tears in the grandstand. It's only a little military ritual, but a lot of the fallen lie behind it.

The young men in their ranks and files who stand out there at attention, looking back across the field at this ceremony, what must be in their minds?

Harry Truman's charge that they are the world's most propagandized outfit? The Corps accepts it, revels in it, maximizes it in every way it can.

The "pass in review" has begun. One by one, as orders are shouted across the wide field and echo back, the platoon leaders and company commanders report their units present and accounted for.

"Sir!" a Marine shouts across the field. "The parade is formed!"

The band begins to march around, filling the air with its tunes of glory. Bands once had a real role in battle; they set the pace of the march, the attack, the retreat, the regroupment, even the honorable surrender. They don't do much more than this now.

It seems a little silly to outsiders, sometimes. In fact, it sometimes seems a little silly to insiders, too: standing in the cold, back straight as a ramrod, a tinny band playing hoary songs and marching off to nowhere.

But in the grandstand the men in the windbreakers are at attention too, the music binding them to the men in the field. And that, of course, is what this is all about.

This is a club. Like an eating club at Yale it is all about having people to say "hiya" to forty years from now. Like a study club at Harvard it is all about the synergy of group effort.

It is a club with roughly two hundred thousand active members and another two million former members. How a group this large can feel itself as small as a chess club is a testament to Harry Truman's peevish jibe.

This is a fighting club. It needs to believe, really believe, that "the Marines always bring back their dead." This is why the Marines' share of Congressional Medals of Honor is top-heavy with stories of this peculiar type of heroism. It needs to believe in the unswerving help of the next guy. This is why training is based heavily on the tiny three-man "fire team" concept. The Corps needs to believe it can march better, look sharper, stand out in the wintry cold more snappily than anyone.

The belief that they can facilitates the fact that they do. The affiliation with their fellow believers, past and present, assures it.

It was Rudyard Kipling (who is as out of fashion as this parade ceremony) who left the timeless lesson in Akela's admonition to Mowgli: "The strength of the pack is the wolf. The strength of the wolf is the pack."

Sergeant Major Browne is now retired. "Anchors Aweigh" is played. Then the "Marine Hymn." There is a rustling of men in the grandstands. Of the men in the field whatever rustling there may be is buried inside chests. The men are as statues.

Celebrate the Corps and you celebrate the man; celebrate the man and he repays the Corps with gratitude.

The band has now taken up a station at the foot of the grandstands. The company squares march in review past it. Each company, at a precisely measured pace before the flag, turns eyes-right for the commander's salute. Perfect dedication to the mysteries of the order.

After the ceremony, Gray mingles on the field for a while. Then he joins the revelers at a party in the NCO club.

Like most bases, Camp Lejeune has an "O" club for the

officers, an enlisted man's club for the privates, and an NCO club for the sergeants. Typically, it is the NCO club which is the largest and most clubby. This club is such a one. Colorful unit crests adorn all the walls; an assortment of old weaponry gleams in glass casings.

Gray works the packed wood-paneled main room like the father of the bride. He pumps the hands of sergeants major and old-timers alike. He also chats up the few officers here, mostly field grade types, colonels and generals; the junior grade officers are not usually comfortable among this assemblage of older warriors.

Colonel Barnham stays close by. If someone asks a favor of the commandant, Barnham makes the note. If someone offers a good suggestion, Barnham makes the note. When Gray becomes surrounded by a knot of old-timers from the "2nd Marine Division Association," Colonel Barnham steps back and lets Gray have his way.

"Hell," Barnham says, eyeballing the patches on a couple of the windbreakers, "these guys were at Tarawa. We like to keep up at least the perception that we take care of the 'formers.' That's why they're always invited to these things. These are the guys that write their congressmen at funding time. And, besides, they take care of the current Marines, the actives. All these 'association' guys invite actives home for Thanksgiving dinner and Christmas and like that." It's all part of being in the club.

Sergeant Major Browne, the bride of the affair, moves around with a goofy grin, accepting handshakes and pats on the back and kisses on the cheek. His sidewalls are so "white" that the small tuft of hair on his head is almost a "mohawk." It is a haircut he would despise on a civilian. Here, it sends a different message.

Browne grabs the hand of a similarly coiffed sergeant major—one of those four-handed handshakes that go all the way up to the elbow. The two men bark at each other like bulldogs—Gray's bulldogs—then Browne moves on, leaving Sergeant Major Jose Martinez, of Lubbock, Texas, with his cup of punch and his ruminations.

Martinez is the top NCO in the 2nd Marine's very proud

Recon Battalion. "Good man," he says of Browne, but you get the feeling he doesn't really mean it.

"You know recon people." Martinez laughs. "We don't like anybody."

Anyway, he's not here to fete Browne. He's here to see the main bulldog. Gray, Martinez feels, is giving the Marines back personally to him. He doesn't need to shake Gray's hand or to talk to him or anything like that. He just wants to see him; that's enough.

"Big change," the Sergeant Major says. "Right track. Gray's treating us like Marines, not like prima donnas. Train for war, not to look pretty. You can feel it in the Corps now, from the lowest ranks up. That's what they came in for—to be warriors and to be known as warriors."

Martinez's eyes say, perhaps that was too strong. Like Lance Corporal Hess, like most Marines, the sergeant major has a small-town businessman's Chamber of Commerce way of talking about the Corps. Always positive, good to go, and Semper Fidelis. "Nobody likes war," he adds quickly and sips at the punch, "but a lot of people like to be warriors. If a guy is just going into the service to learn a trade, well, let him join the Army. We're going back to 'every man a rifleman'—the way it was when the commandant joined up."

A few steps away, Gray assures the men of the "2nd Marine Association" that their idea for a national "former Marine" association is a good one and pledges to give it all the support he can. Colonel Barnham makes a note. Then they move off.

One of the old-timers looks at the business card Gray has handed out. It is camouflaged! It's a combat-ready business card. It is good to go! The man flips the card over. The back is dead white. He frowns. Then he looks up at his fellows. "Think we ought to tell the commandant he might cami up the backs of these little suckers?" They all laugh. A couple of them bark.

"Every man a rifleman." Gray is saying it again to a WM who is covering the affair for the base newspaper. The CMC has been saying it over and over, at every opportunity, since his first week on the job. Now Marines are beginning to say it to each other. The reporter says she's already heard it "a hundred times" around the room. Gray grins. It is an impossible goal, of course. Training costs would be prohibitive. But, like the half-camouflaged business cards, the spirit here may be more important than the actual range performance.

A crewcut and somewhat gawky Lance Corporal Bless is introduced to Gray by Colonel Barnham. The Lance Corporal seems embarrassed by his own boldness and there's an awkward moment. Then, a little too loudly, he asks for an autograph. Gray smiles and backs, a little nonplussed.

"How you been? How you been?" he says, reflexively.

"Well, to tell you the truth," says Bless, "I'm having a little trouble reenlisting, sir." The commandant sizes up the kid and makes an instant decision.

"Keep at it," he says. He offers no help. A Marine with a sound record wouldn't be having any trouble reupping, and Gray really doesn't want to know any more about it. He gives the lance corporal the autograph.

"Truly an honor, sir," Bless says.

"Semper Fi," says Gray, and escapes.

On the way back to the helos Barnham is rethinking his decision of bringing Bless to Gray. Perhaps concerned about a dereliction of duty he says, of Gray, "He didn't look too pleased about that kid, did he? Not his kind of thing. Not his kind of Marine."

On board the cami helo, Gray has forgotten all about it. He straps on his helmet and hits the squawk button. "Good parade," he tells his men.

An hour later, en route aboard the C-20, Gray changes into his dress khakis for the Citadel ceremony. When he emerges from the private cabin he gets a smattering of applause from his people and Colonel Barnham pronounces him "sharp." Then Barnham asks the commandant what he will be saying in his address to the Citadel staff and senior classmen prior to the parade.

"What address?" asks Gray.

"You have to speak for sixty minutes," says Barnham. Gray does a vaudeville-style double take. There is laughter all around, but a minute or two later, when it is finally apparent that this is not a joke, Gray turns abruptly and walks back down the aisle to his cabin.

"Fine," he says over his shoulder, "we're holding to our M.O. Don't tell the general nothing till he's at the front."

The stark white turreted walls of The Citadel stand like an oversize crusader castle in the middle of Charleston, South Carolina, one of the prettiest cities in the nation. The school, one of America's several *other* military academies, is in fact a part of Charleston's charm. Some of its students may be rejects from West Point or Annapolis or Boulder, but the overwhelming majority are pure southern boys on their way to becoming pure Citadel men. The odd undershirt saying "West Point is the Citadel of the North" is not uncommon.

Generally, 16.5 percent of The Citadel graduates join the Marine Corps. Gray is seriously interested in raising that number. Another ceremony, another recruiting drive.

There are about 250 staffers and seniors packed into Jenkins Hall to hear the commandant's address. They wear the uniforms of all branches of the service and there is a sea of Citadel gray. Jokes are being told, some of them on the Marines. Stories are being swapped, most of them about the Marines.

"*Tenshun* on deck!" someone yells, and the auditorium leaps to its feet. Gray walks directly to the podium. He acknowledges the staff, particularly the Navy and Marine personnel. He looks out over the faces. He may have no speech, but he has a forum.

Forums like Al Gray and vice versa. He tells the cadets that since he has no speech prepared, "you're going to have to be stuck with sharing some time with me this afternoon while we ramble on about the 'big picture.' And particularly the young Marines here today, those that are from the Security Force Battalion and the others. It's not too often that you get a chance to find out a little bit about the big picture and you should do that from time to time and the reason for that is very simple. I believe that you have a right to know about what we are thinking about in Washington, what the policy making discussions are all about, and, most important of all, as long as you're in *my* Marine Corps you have a right to participate in the building of *your* Marine

Corps for the future, because it is you that will serve and you that will lead."

There are no lights here, no cameras, no Nagras, no reporters with notepads. This will be a military talk, direct from the commander to the commanded.

"Okay," Gray begins, "first we must understand that regardless of what some may say on television, in the media, in Congress, or *anywhere else,* we are a global power, and we will remain a global power, and the reason is that there are too many people on this earth we live on that are counting on us to help keep them free or to give them an opportunity to *be* free someday.

"The stakes are that high, not just today or the next decade or the decade after that, but as we spring off into the next century."

A silence falls over the room. Not merely a silence of attentiveness, but that special kind of silence, that total white sound, that kinetic emptiness you hear before, say, a grenade goes off.

Arrayed against this uncertainty, Gray says, is the United States of America with its millions yearning to breathe free, its motivated and dedicated armed forces, and, in the vanguard, the Corps. This is the way Gray launches his recruiting drive. The message, as ever, is: Are you good enough to join us?

"The stakes are going to go up," he says, not down. "So your Marine Corps is going to get leaner and going to get meaner. And if you mean to wear the Marine uniform, you need to remember that, too.

"I don't care if I have to drive the Marine Corps from two-hundred-thousand down to two-thousand. They're going to function at my high standards of excellence.

"We have a lot going for us. We're pretty well equipped right now. Better, relatively speaking, than any other military service in the world. And everything we have is ready to go tonight. We are the only fighting force on the globe that can go right now, with its entire force, and not have to mobilize one man. Think about that."

Gray scans the faces. They are curiously white, not just

racially, but translucently. You wonder how many of these pale young men are headed for the Corps, and how they're going to make it there. You wonder how many of them are thinking this.

"Our most precious resource is our people," Gray says, "the men and women who are privileged to wear this uniform. We have two-hundred-thousand Marines today and now almost ninety-eight percent are high school graduates. But that only tells you that they came from a family or from guardians or whatever that cared that they stayed and stuck it out in school. Doesn't tell you that they're smart enough to be my kind of Marines. We make them that, and we're going to continue to do that.

"I find the young people I'm privileged to serve with smart, tough, they want to be well led, they want to learn. And that's where all you as leaders and future leaders must dedicate yourself to a lifelong career of learning and teaching and providing that kind of leadership these people so richly deserve.

"No, let me say that another way. If there's anybody here who wants to wear this uniform, and isn't willing to dedicate himself to selfless service with a view towards taking care of the people you're privileged to lead, then don't apply for my Marine Corps. That adage, you take care of lower ranks and they'll take care of you, there's a living example. You're looking at him!"

Applause and dog yowls rain down from the students. The yowling quickly overtakes the clapping and Gray leaves to a dog pound chorus.

The afternoon arrives crisp around the edges and warm in the middle; the kind of day that makes living in South Carolina a very good idea. There is a sunset reception in the school president's spacious, Tudor-style home.

Local dignitaries pack the party rooms, balancing their wine and cheese on their laps or the antique furnishings. The piano has become a pickup point for spent plastic plates. A few children run underfoot.

Attractive young women, consciously or self-consciously southern, smile around the room in their hats and gloves and thin print dresses that billow in the breeze as they pass the open windows. Some are dignitaries' daughters. Some are from the local colleges. Some are looking for Citadel men.

Out in back, in the tended garden, the better part of the city's elite have escaped the packed rooms into the open air. Here are the car dealers, the television station owners, the newspaper publishers, the landowners, the well heeled or well bred, standing around in their knots of common interest, chatting, excluding, being.

Over by a shrub, General Al Gray has buttonholed a half dozen of the young Citadel cadet commanders. They are pimply and thin and unhandsome in their dress grays, but these are the school leaders, the top men, the good officer material. One has a girl on his arm. The rest are enthralled only by Gray, who is explaining, once again, why—if the Marines are amphibious forces—why are they also issued skis for mountain duty in Norway?

"But are you still going to be an amphibious force?" asks the cadet.

"Yes, we are the raiders from the sea," Gray assures. "And heck, that ought to be enough. You know, seventy-two percent of the world's population lives by the water somewhere. But we're also the ski troops of NATO and we're desert troops and we are the Marine Security Guards in your embassies, too. We are all that and more stuff because we are ready and we are able."

Marine General Victor H. Krulak, in his book *First to Fight* (unofficial required reading for the Corps' officer class), wrote, "Thus, we come to an unusual, and generally unheralded, aspect of the Marines' quality as fighters. Adaptability, initiative, and improvisation are the true fabric of obedience, the ultimate in soldierly conduct, going further than sheer heroism to make the Marines what they are." To which Gray likes to add, "You can't predict the future battlefield, you can only discipline yourself and your people to excel on it."

The cadets nod. "To cut through all the bullshit," the general tells them, "the key to battle, in fact the key to life, is to do something. Anything. Even if it's wrong. If you do it real well, who knows, it may turn out right."

Nobody barks. The six future generals stand stiff and attentive, waiting for more. Waiting, hoping, that General Al Gray, commandant of the Marine Corps, may, in the course of the banter, boil it all down for them, reduce it, squeeze it, crystallize their future into a bright-edged shard as clear as glass and hand it to them as a sword.

Instead, Gray tells them a joke.

"Train leaves London," he says, "and in one compartment are three old men in gentlemen's clothes. And they're all real quiet and real reserved.

"Ten miles out one breaks the silence." Gray clears his throat. " 'Smythe,' the general badly mimics a British gentleman, 'brigadier general, married, one child, physician.'

"Twenty miles out, a second gent can't take it anymore and decides to come out with *his* story." Gray clears his throat again. " 'Welles, brigadier general, married, *two* children, both *barristers.*'

"Thirty miles out the third man finally looks up. They look over at the guy. 'O'Boyle,' " Gray says out of the corner of his mouth, " 'sergeant major, *never* married, *three* children . . . all *brigadiers.*' "

The regimental commanders erupt in laughter. The point is made. Al Gray laughs with them. And the train, the United States Marines train, rolls on under Al Gray toward its destiny in the desert.

Sending in the Marines!

★

Back at Camp Lejeune, the "raid week" training of the 2/4 Marines continued apace. Twenty-four hours past SOC and two years from Kuwait, they were becoming warriors.

The Rigid Raiders' very successful seaborne assault on the "Carteret" rebel base at Camp Lejeune had not only yielded special operations qualification for Lance Corporal Hess and his battalion; it had, as the training swung into its third day, exposed the 24th Marine Expeditionary Unit to a newer, bigger "problem."

At a dawn briefing Lieutenant Colonel Sigurd "Big Sig" Jensen III, commanding officer of the 24th MEU's Battalion Landing Team, was told that information gleaned during the previous night's swamp raid indicated that the "rebels" were not isolated in the woods. They had the full support of the better part of the Carteret Air Force and were moving in force through several coastal areas.

Big Sig sat in a plastic chair several sizes too small for him, and rubbed the square jaw of his square face as Maj. Dan Conway, the MEU's intel officer, pointed to a map that showed where rebel forces now held twenty American hostages in a school building in a small built-up area not far from Hess's march. "Worse," said Conway, "they are in the process of consolidating a heavily fortified position in a larger town at these coordinates." He pointed on the map to Camp Lejeune's famous "Combat Town" facility.

It was decided to commit the full might of the 24th Marine Expeditionary Unit. A small force would take a platoon of LAVs, the light, armored, car-like fighting vehicles, and strike quickly at the school building to free the hostages. The main force, under Big Sig, would land in LVTs, the tracked landing vehicles, and proceed inland to cut off the reinforcement of Combat Town and prepare a full-scale attack on the town's defenses.

By midday several dozen LVTs were in the water, a mile out, line abreast, sunlight flaring off their wave-washed backs, churning earnestly toward shore.

These are sorry-looking vehicles, these LVTs, like shoe boxes with bird beaks. On land they run on tracks, like tanks. At sea they run on underwater jets. Like most amphibious creatures they are an ugly and ungainly compromise between disparate environments, not totally suited to either.

Inside the third LVT in the line twenty-four Marines, all strapped into their folding seats, stare straight ahead or at the floor. The yellow pallor of their faces is due in part to the lighting inside the belly of this beast and in part to the clammy, claustrophobic, death-trap atmosphere.

"These things can be floating coffins," Cpl. Roger Martin says and laughs over the din of the aqua jets that are laboring beneath us. Martin is the "pilot" of the vehicle, and he's got a healthy attitude about the job.

"They sunk one out here last year." He grins. "The guys all got out. It's just like a ship. It's gonna hold air, somewhere. Usually it'll be up around the cargo doors. It'll be, oh, about that much."

He holds up two fingers close together—too close for comfort, maybe a couple of inches apart. "If you don't panic you'll be okay. Of course, when you go under you lose your power and the lights go out and it gets real dark."

Martin got a lot of disaster training in LVT school. He went through two submerged escapes. "I'm cool in the shallow water," he says. "The deep water, well, this thing weighs twenty-six tons and it'll go down like a stone."

While the troops stare and sweat and try to keep the big green metal beast floating by the force of their will, Corporal Martin checks his revs and his speed.

"A lot of guys like to keep their tracks turning all the while they're in the water. You can do that. It helps keep the bow up. But it pulls power from the jets. I cut them off and then lock them back on as soon as I hit the surf. You have to get your tracks moving before you hit the beach. You hit that sand without your tracks moving and it'll slow you right down. You want to keep moving, keep the revs up. So you got to lock your tracks on when you get into the surf zone—whoa, and here we are!"

The LVT lurches into the surf with a sickening roll and at the same time the vibrations of the engaged track explode beneath your feet. Then, wham, you hit the beach. There are smiles everywhere inside the LVT.

Some twenty places down the line of attack, Big Sig's own LVT is up and running across the saw grass on the dunes. He hangs on to the rails and explains the situation.

"This is a strike force exercise," he says. "We've already concluded our individual and collective phase of training. We've gone through a series of basic skills training meaning individual, fire team, squad, platoon, and company tactics. We have evaluated our units and our individual Marines through an internal review of critique and analysis."

It was a night stage of that analysis that brought Lance Corporal Hess's Rigid Raider unit its hard-won SOC qualification, and the intel that underpins this exercise.

"Right now," says Big Sig, "we are undergoing a MCCRES, a Marine Corps Combat Readiness Evaluation System. For all intents and purposes it is a grade of A or F. It'll tell us all something about our ability to conduct our mission not as a series of small units but as a BLT.

"We are now fully composited, with all the attachments. I have a lot of Marines on the move. Five companies. Light armored vehicles, amphibious armored vehicles like this one, helos. This is our MAGTF, our task force. Excuse me." The colonel returns to the radio net on which he is coordinating the strike on the school where the hostages are being held.

By late afternoon the school is taken. By nightfall the hostages are being helicoptered back home. By midnight the LVT of the communications officer and Big Sig's own LVT are pulled back to back in the woods in a V-shaped field command post. Idle chatter is at a minimum. The radios are lit.

There are twenty people in the commo track, their wires and their radio transmissions crisscrossing. In Colonel Sigurd Jensen III's LVT there are another sixteen officers: fire control people, air control people, materiel people, operations people, all drawing their plans.

The main attack, the one against Combat Town, is now ready to be launched.

The commandant told the Citadel cadets that "the Marines are the only force that is ready to go, with all we have, right now." It may not be the *only* force capable of this, but it is most definitely one of the few.

Inside the command LVT, Big Sig stands by a map on an easel leaning against the steel wall of the track. His face is black with cami. His eyes are red with lack of sleep. He looks feral. But he sounds professorial, firm, clear, with an edge in his voice that says get this now because I'm only going to say it once.

"We are in the north end of the Camp Lejeune training area at the present time. We will be attacking basically to the south-southeast."

The orders Jensen received on deployment were of the type called "mission" orders. He was told to attack and seize Combat Town. The *how* and the *where* and the *when* were all largely up to him. With the commandant hammering away at every speech and ceremony about "maneuver combat," the field training has placed increasing emphasis on the role of the colonel in the field, the warrior colonel.

The map beside Jensen and the several acetate overlays representing artillery patterns and possible air strike avenues and such are the result of several hours of work on the part of the colonel and his staff.

His S2 (intelligence officer) has given him the best guesstimate of enemy strength and position. With his S4 (logistics officer) Jensen has worked out the kind and number of vehicles, ordnance, and other supplies for the order of battle. His S3 (operations) has suggested several plans of attack.

"We have evaluated all the courses of action with an eye toward feasibility and supportability. They've all come up with their recommendations. Based on what they all can support, based on what is feasible, we make our selection of what tactic we are going to employ."

Colonel Jensen has made a command decision. "I have picked out a double-axis attack pattern," he says, turning to the map. His gnarled finger falls on one of the two large arrows that mark the axes of this attack. It is, he says with a smile, "a very elegant plan."

Having folded back the acetate overlays Colonel Jensen traces first the attack marked by the large arrow labeled "Dani."

"Dani," he says, "will be our small force. They take the most accessible route to Combat Town, around the edge of this swamp here and through these wooded areas."

The plan is for Dani to engage Combat Town before dawn. There is no element of surprise here. Since they are using the most likely line of attack, they expect to be seen and encountered, and that too is part of the plan.

Jensen folds down one of the acetates so that its smaller arrows and symbols appear on the map.

"Once we've made our tactical decision, we write up an operations overlay on acetate, hand it out to the companies. The companies then take this order and return it with their own detailed order and how their individual companies are going to conduct their attack. We put that back on the situation map where we can see each company's plan."

The Dani attack can now be seen in both its larger and smaller components, the grand plan and its elements.

"Dani will engage the aggressors north of the town, right here, and then covered by the 'fog of war' [commanders always assume that 'the fog' will blind only their enemies] Dani will fight its way slowly away from the town down here to the east. We hope to pull their main counterattack here. Then we'll keep moving, playing a little game of 'catch me, screw me,' all the way to here."

The colonel smiles and points to a spot in a clearing. He waits for a visualization of the combat to sink in. Then he points to a second, larger arrow, east of Dani, which is labeled "Laurie."

"Laurie," Jensen says (the attack forces are named for the wives of the commanders in the field), "will remain buttoned up in their AAVs [amphibious assault vehicles] and LVTs, like a reserve force. But it's a trick, because then we'll do this enormous end run!"

The colonel's hand sweeps across the map and knocks some grease pencils to the floor. The Big Sig is six feet three and weighs 235 pounds, which was just about his playing weight when he was a linebacker at Colorado State University. When he gets excited, other men turn to look.

"Down this way," he bellows, his voice cutting through the commo chatter, "Laurie's AAVs will be rocking and rolling all the way down to the intracoastal waterway. It's way out of the way, but once we put in the water the AAVs can swim down the intracoastal at maximum speed all the way down to this point here."

At a point directly below the town, the AAV flotilla with the larger Laurie force in its belly will leave the intracoastal and ride overland for six or eight miles of good and probably undefended road.

"The men will deploy out of the AAVs at 'Area Dodo' here," says Jensen, "and attack Combat Town from the south. At the same time, a helo attack will reinforce Dani, taking the brunt of the northern assault."

When Maj. Dan Conway sees the plan in the MEU HQ he'll shake his head and mumble "too complex," and he'll smile that smile. "When you make something with a clockwork kind of precision, it better tick like a clock," he'll say. For Conway, "Jensen is always mapping out stuff like this. It looks great, but . . ."

At the map in the LVT, Jensen isn't even finished. "Here's the really elegant part," he says. "When the helos go in, that'll let Dani slide off here to the east, so that the force that was only a decoy force now becomes a fighting force cutting off the only route of escape."

Jensen cups his right hand and lays it against the map like

a mighty wall to the east of Combat Town. With his left hand he punches the town. "We take Combat Town," he says, and then, sweeping his left hand across the map's open plain, he smacks it against his right hand, "and then we turn all this expanse between Dani and Laurie into a killing field and start wiping all the bastards out."

It is, as advertised, an elegant plan, but it is also a curious one. The MCCRES doesn't test for "wiping all the bastards out." It is a "command and control" test. It seeks to know that all the head work being done down in this command post is being carried out in a timely and effective manner by commanders in the field who are beset with their own problems and connected to Big Sig only by his radio transmitter. Why go through so much extra trouble when the test calls only for taking the town?

"It's a paradox," says Maj. Glen Sochtleben, Jensen's operations officer and author of a good part of the dual-axis plan. "The idea of battle is to limit your casualties, but the fun is to create the enemy's maximum casualties."

Jensen claps Sochtleben on the shoulder. The major is almost as big as the colonel. Like Jensen, his eyes are red from lack of sleep. The third day's "problem" is scheduled to start in ten minutes. There'll be no rest tonight.

"Your watch," says Jensen, and he steps outside the LVT into the night.

The damp air is redolent of cypress bark and the pine needles underfoot. The call of an owl can be heard nearby.

"Watch out for the wire," Jensen says.

A narrow, serpentining column of razor wire winds its way from the outer defense perimeter to the back of the LVTs. It is invisible in the dark, but Jensen, who has walked the path a hundred times this day, negotiates it effortlessly on his way to the perimeter.

Big Sig points out the several vehicles of the command detachment which is scattered around in the woods, calling each of them by an arcane name or set of initials. None of their peculiar monikers is comprehensible and none of the vehicles can be seen, anyway.

"Oh, they're out there." The colonel laughs. "You can hear

one right over there. It's fired up right now because it has to keep its batteries charged so we can all communicate.

"The other vehicles that we have here are aligned, prepared to go, nose first, fully camouflaged, and pointed at a road down that way. The road's been reconned and cleared in case we have to have an emergency movement.

"If I had to move to a clear site, we would proceed in an orderly fashion, my vehicle in the lead, the command track, the backup commo track, and so on. We could blow out of here quicker than I could move my bowels."

At the end of the barbed wire serpentine is the opening of a double-wire perimeter fence. Here, a nineteen-year-old private pulling guard duty stiffens to a kind of attention. Jensen touches the young man's shoulder as a way of putting him at ease.

"Sir," the private mumbles in response, relaxing a bit.

Jensen nods. He takes a breath, stares off into the trees. Something is on his mind, something he'd like to talk about.

"Camp Lejeune is starting to get a little small for the forces that we have," he says. "Plus, we have a lot of ecologists running around here closing off areas because we have some species that are endangered—for instance the beloved wood beetle." The private laughs and then clams up.

Jensen smiles and his teeth—all Marines seem to take spit-shine care of their teeth—dazzle from behind his green face and red eyes; wonderful, terrifying.

"Equally loved," he smirks slyly, "is the crested wood-pecker, and of course, he makes his home in a completely different area. We've lost several tank trails and a darn good machine-gun range.

"And don't even talk about the blue whale. They're out there though, in their spawning area, screwing their brains out while we reroute the Rigid Raiders so as not to impose."

Jensen laughs. But the ecologists don't really bother the colonel. He is disturbed by something else, something that was said back in the LVT, something about "the killing zone," and also about "the creation of maximum casualties." He knows how that sounds. He'd like to explain it.

He lifts his hat and scratches both temples. Then he says,

"When I took command of this unit, it had just come back from a combined arms exercise. Immediately we were assigned as the opposition force for an entire division exercise; we were the aggressors. It was a force-on-force exercise," which means, roughly, that either side could conduct combat in whatever way it saw fit.

"We took on the entire division, this one battalion, and we did pretty darn good. That gives you an attitude, a good attitude about yourself, and your men."

He shrugs. He senses he hasn't made his point. So he tries again.

"You have to understand," he says, "I was always pretty athletic. I enjoyed competitive sports. I had a college football coach who played for the Cleveland Browns. And he always talked inspirationally about the challenge of sport. He had been a Navy medical corpsman and had served with the Marines. And he used to say, 'Men, if there's any service that teaches you about yourself, it's the Marine Corps.' That influenced me. Still does. So I guess, I guess there is really an element of sport about this endeavor."

Out there, ten or maybe twelve miles into the brush where the leather meets the mud, Hess and his Rigid Raider squad have taken up positions with Echo Company. They are forming along a quagmire road which is hard by the "line of departure," bursting to go as soon as the word to commence the "problem" is given.

Hess doesn't buy the sporting metaphor. "No," he says, "I don't feature the idea of taking somebody's life as a sport."

Hess, who's usually pretty unflappable, is in fact quite put off by the idea. "Preserving our way of life isn't sport." He bristles. "It's a challenge."

Then he turns thoughtful. "Commanders sometimes look at it like a sport because they are sitting there looking at a map, you know? But the good ones, the way they look at it is, the more of them that die means the less of us that die, you know?

"They look at it like, they hit an objective, that's good. They leave nobody left, that's better 'cause then who's gonna kill us? Nobody."

Hess likes Jensen, admires him. He feels that whatever the colonel says, or does, it is going to come out okay for everybody. Even if the metaphor is sport.

"He's got to think about us, our lives, the colonel," Hess says. "I mean, if he's a king on a chessboard, what good is he without his pawns and his knights and whatnot. That's the way he's looking at it, in my eyes."

At the command setup Jensen, actually the queen of this chess game, takes one last deep breath of the night air and with a bouncy kind of anticipation he turns on his heel and heads back to the LVT, leaving the private alone in the dark at his post.

The guard's name is Daniel Watson. He's from Wilburton, Oklahoma. The Marines have taken him far from home and he'll go a lot further before he's safely back. Watson is ready for whatever comes. He buys into the colonel's sporting metaphor. Watson is fresh in and buying just about everything the Marines have to sell.

"We're the best." He smiles shyly, explaining what he thinks his colonel meant. "We always wipe them out, it's always been said that we do. That's why terrorists always go after us so much, like in Beirut, the bombing. They all know we are the best and they all have something to prove. That's why we're the target of so much shit. We're the U.S. Marines. Like, there isn't even any argument."

Watson enlisted out of high school. His twin brother was an Airborne Ranger in the Army. Watson picked the Marines because he "wanted something a little better," he says.

"Now he calls me 'jarhead' and I call him 'grunt,' but it's all friendly like. I know he still loves me," Watson says, "but, well, there really is something extra special about me being a Marine."

For Watson it's not simply Jensen's correlative image of the all-conquering gridiron hero. It's weirder.

"My favorite thing to be, if I could live in any time I wanted to, I'd want to be a knight. And the Marines have always fought toward that tradition of knighthood, chivalry, being strong and the protector of the weak. The best part of the 'dress blues,' for me, is the sword. Problem for me is I haven't got to wear them yet. In fact, I don't own a set."

Then Watson tells what, for him, must be a very sad story indeed. "They had a clothing company go fraudulent on them," he says, "so they have a lack of them right now. So you have to have a job where you need them in order to buy them. But soon, soon. I'm looking forward to that. Very much so." He smiles at the thought, and then frowns.

"Well," he sighs, philosophically, getting back to the sporting metaphor, "maybe it's because I didn't play any team sports in high school." He seems truly disturbed not to be in total empathy with Big Sig's football notion of combat.

"I was into martial arts in high school," Watson says, almost defensively. "I mean, really, I did pretty good. I was a second degree green belt. I even did pretty good in my state tournament. I don't like to talk about it much." He leans in close. "You talk about that around here and everybody wants to take you on," he whispers.

"I'll take you on," comes a voice from the bush. You can barely make out the green face.

"This is Private Ferguson," Watson says, introducing the voice, "he's also from Oklahoma." Ferguson has been standing there throughout the entire conversation!

He too is on guard duty, in the middle of the night, out in front of the command HQ. He had been killing time by having a whispered argument with his friend Watson, an argument that was interrupted by the arrival of the colonel.

Now, as men come and go in the dark and are waved into the barbed wire serpentine with a password and a proper countersign, Ferguson, whose regular Corps job is in supply, continues his thesis that the U.S. Marines are once again preparing to fight the next war with the tactics of the last one. His target is the Corps' commitment to what it calls the "over the horizon" attack. The commandant spoke of it at The Citadel. Hess ran one the other night. Ferguson doesn't buy it.

In Tarawa, he argues, the ability to hide over the horizon would have been a spectacular advantage. But new electronic techniques now render you visible to the enemy *wherever* you are. "They got Exocets, man, that come and get you in the bathtub!"

"Ferg," says the younger Watson in a nevertheless avuncular fashion, "it's what you learn after you know it all that counts."

Watson is uncomfortable as he puts down his friend's argument. There is an element of truth in it, of course, but Ferguson is a wise guy whereas Watson is one of those kids who wants to believe.

"Halt," he stops a figure in the dark.

"Hiya, Watson."

"Kind of password is that?" says Watson.

"It's me, Cavanaugh."

"You got that green shit all over your face. How the hell do I know it's you?" says Watson. "You could be damn Gorbachev talking like you."

"Fuck Gorbachev," the voice says, "and fuck you too." It's been a long night for Lance Corporal Cavanaugh, too. "Hey, that you Ferguson?" he says, turning in the dark to the other man at the barbed wire opening. "What the hell's the password?"

"Plastic," Ferguson says. "Whyn't you write down these things on your cuff?"

"I can't see my fucking cuff!" says Cavanaugh. "Okay, plastic, Watson, plastic."

"Automobile," says Watson for the hundredth time that night, and he waves Cavanaugh inside the barbed wire.

"Pogie bait; whattaya bucking for, jack?" Cavanaugh mumbles as he passes Watson.

"Get the fuck outa town," Ferguson calls back into the enveloping darkness. But Watson just smiles. *Pogie* refers to candy. *Pogie bait* refers to kids. *Jack* refers to a sergeant's stripes. *Bucking* means trying hard to get them. Watson is all of the above.

"What the goddamn hell do they think they're doing!" a voice bellows out of the command LVT and silences the entire detachment.

Inside the command track, Colonel Jensen is sitting on an edgewise ammo case staring at his map and rocking back and forth. All around him, the junior grade officers are either caught between conversations with their headset people in the field and listening to the happenings inside the track, or else they've rung off their field people altogether and are staring at the little drama by the map.

The operations officer, Major Sochtleben, is doing the talking now. "Training headquarters," he repeats, "has directed us not to cross our line of departure any earlier than oh-one-hundred."

All of the BLT's "assets," all its men and materiel, are coordinated in place, time-synchronized, and ready to roll; but they've been held by an administrative order. In what few cracks and crevices the major's green facial cami has failed to cover, a smart reddening of the skin burns through.

"Essentially sir, to be honest with you, it's so they can have the aggressor force in place."

Jensen smiles. He knows what's happened. He's seen it before. His operations officer continues.

"I've explained to the MEU that if we do not cross prior to oh-one-hundred we're gonna end up landing our helicopters in Combat Town in daylight. They say 'sorry.' It's probably because we've already pushed the aggressors to a point where they would not be ready for a predawn attack down in Combat Town."

The MEU and the evaluators have decided that for the benefit of the problem, they would hold up the attackers to let the defenders get a better position.

"That's unrealistic," says Major Sochtleben. "We're ready to go, real world. They should let us go."

Colonel Jensen patiently explains that it's not real world, that it's not force on force, and that the MEU doesn't see it as a game to be won or lost, or an event at which to excel; all it is, is a MCCRES, command-and-control exercise. The major doesn't buy it. Truth is, the colonel doesn't either.

"Obviously the aggressors thought we were going to go some other way"—the Colonel smirks—"and they're just not prepared to take us on. They thought we were going to come down this way on axis Dani. Now they see what we're doing and they're trying to skedaddle down this way. We caught them with their trousers down." What does the BLT get for this masterstroke?

"Basically, we're stuck," says the major.

"Oh, get me on the horn," says Big Sig. He'll give it one last go. He'll try to haggle it out with the higher HQ.

As the artillery people return to their headsets to try to replot their fire patterns and hurried calls are put in to the different Marine air units to retime sorties, Jensen raises the MEU commander on a field phone and tries to plead his case. They lose contact almost immediately. It is 1240 and counting. Now every second is a minute lost.

An intelligence officer comes in to report that the recon units have seen six tanks move into Area Dodo and not come out. The aggressors are on the move.

"This is Samurai," says Jensen into his field phone, "repeat, Samurai. I am reading you again, over."

Jensen listens to the commander's transmission, nodding his head, pursing his lips. Then he says, "Yes sir, but I understand that you don't want us crossing the line of departure until zero, one."

The commander transmits another message that only the colonel can hear, but that doesn't stop several of the other officers from leaning his way anyway.

Colonel Jensen transmits back, "Roger, then we will be crossing at zero one hundred and consequently the attack on Combat Town will be post-BMNT. Samurai out."

Part of playing the game is following the chain of command, unhesitatingly. Jensen plays the game.

Major Sochtleben suddenly leaps to his feet and begins marking the map. "Can I show you something, sir?" he says.

Jensen approaches the map. Sochtleben points a green cami finger at a red line drawn on the acetate.

"The line of departure starts way up here, but the finish of it curves way around here down by this tower."

Jensen eyeballs the map. The line of departure follows a ravine that runs mostly east-west, but at the very edge of the training area, the ravine makes a sharp turn south toward Combat Town. The red line follows it, carving out a narrow salient pointing like a dagger at the heart of the town.

"Technically, we could move Golf Company all the way down here," says Major Sochtleben. "We'll pick up all that headway, and not really actually cross over the line of departure till oh-one-hundred."

Jensen is already on the horn. "Hello, Golf," he says, "this is Samurai!"

The new plans are laid. A half hour later, at exactly zero-one, Big Sig's task force hits the line of departure on a dead run and moves out on the assault. They immediately roll up a surprised and unconsolidated aggressor flank as they go. The game is finally afoot.

In the command track where the dual attack is being co-ordinated, Jensen and Sochtleben sit at the map as reports come in from the field. The reports are brief, sometimes only one word. As each unit passes by a checkpoint or completes a task, it radios to command a single code word on prearranged lists that are taped to the inside wall of the track.

"Cadillac."

"Mashed potatoes."

"Chicago."

"Dental floss."

"Elvis Presley."

"Big lips."

They all mean a milestone made, a bridge taken or destroyed, a known enemy stronghold engaged. There is a thick babel of chatter inside the LVT, but it is all about artillery strikes and air raids and recon reports. It is not about the march of battle. That unfolds in clear, quick code words, no mistake about who's where and why. There are no misunderstandings. No excuses or rationales or postmortems. Just the odd "pantyhose," or some such, which means a company has achieved some objective. Command and control is the strong yellow beacon in the fog of war.

A report of an anti-armor unit along a secondary road is brought to Jensen. He checks the location on the map and sees the possible danger. "Okay, let's let Echo eyeball that; put their nods right on it," he says, and the word is sent to a company in the field.

Weather reports are brought to Jensen by Sochtleben. These are critical for the coordination of the predawn helicopter lift.

Showers are reported "in and out" and high winds near dawn. The winds are the problem. Night ops with helos are always dangerous and wind shear compounds the problem. It was a side-winding Marine helo, caught in a wind shear, that bumped its neighbor and left all that steel and wet stuff in the desert on that abortive Iranian hostage raid, Desert One. Helicopter accidents are among the most common cause of death in night training.

Sochtleben is to fly in the lead helo on the assault, but it is not the danger that worries the major and Big Sig. They are more concerned that the people running the problem will prohibit them from using the helos.

"We need to give the S4 [supply] a heads-up on this and get him up here to talk about possible alternatives," says the colonel. Unlike his earlier pique at the "line of departure" problem, Colonel Jensen now betrays no emotion whatever. His speech is slow and deliberate, carefully measured. The right words are chosen and delivered without flourish or embellishment or any hint of connotation.

The samurai once spoke like this, plainly, briefly and effectively. A samurai was as praised for his ability to press a point with concision as for his sword work. We get the modern haiku from that. Not for nothing has Jensen chosen "Samurai" as his personal radio code.

The S4 arrives and plans are laid to substitute trucks against the advent of a decision to cancel the helos for the raid.

Dani and Laurie advance according to plan. The latter's long line of AAVs, behind a small screen of riflemen acting as a decoy force, are running full tilt beyond the trees for the intra-coastal. The vanguard of the Dani force, backed by LAVs (light armored vehicles), is bearing down on the most forward defenses of Combat Town.

As hoped, the aggressors take the bait. Dani's potent spearhead engages them a mile before their FEBA (forward edge of the battle area) and maneuvers to begin the preplanned slide to the east. The code word "hamster" is passed to the command track. There are smiles all around.

"Where is Golf?" asks the colonel.

"We lost commo with them, sir," says a communications

officer calling over from his cramped console.

"We want to support them with eighty-ones [mortars] but we lost commo with him," says an artillery officer, or arty, at the next console.

"Right now I just want to know where he is," says Big Sig. Golf Company is the key player in Dani. He has not called in his code word. Has he failed to take an objective? Has he bogged down? Has he stalled? Or is it just a problem with the radio?

"We're trying to get everybody to come up with radio checks, sir," says the communications officer.

Golf calls in. The company's veered off course just a bit but is making headway again. The colonel checks the map and pinpoints Golf Company.

"We need a new series of targets," he tells the arty, "all the way down from the base magazine area to [Area] Hawk."

"We have two preplot targets in there already, sir," the arty man calls out above the general din.

"Yeah, we need to initiate a *series*," says the colonel. "Can you do that?"

"We're plotting one now, sir; it'll cover the movement north and then their run down the hardball [paved road]."

"Well, eyeball the intersection of Marines Road and the road north out of Combat Town," says the colonel.

"That's part of the series, sir," says the arty man.

"How about from the garbage dump to the stream south towards Hawk?"

"We have one at the dump."

"Add the stream," says the colonel.

"We have three recon teams along that stream, sir," says the artillery.

"What do we need recon teams in there for!" says the colonel. "Never mind; they're no further north than Hawk, are they?"

"Oh yes, sir," says an intel officer. "We've got them all the way along there, all the way up north."

"Can they adjust fire?" the colonel asks.

"Well, they're recon units, sir, they're not artillery people," says the artillery officer. Big Sig stares at the arty man for a heartbeat or two. "Well, yeah, I guess so," says the arty officer.

"Good," says the colonel, "'cause I want Golf's route sanitized all the way into Combat Town."

The attack is back on track. The chatter becomes a low hum. Colonel Jensen seems pleased. The code words are rolling in again. "We're making it happen," says Big Sig, and he smiles.

The colonel hails from New Rochelle, New York. Like Lance Corporal Hess, he is a boating enthusiast. "Learned how to sail when I was eight years old, out on Long Island Sound." Also like Hess, the boating background had nothing to do with his becoming a Marine; and as with Private Watson, it wasn't a family tradition either.

"My father was a pilot in the Air Force," he says, "we served in Vietnam together. He was the base commander of Da Nang AFB."

Jensen was in the Air Force reserve, discharging his military duty during college in the hopes of having an uninterrupted career in professional sports, when "things began to happen." This was the time of the Cuban missile crisis; the time of the death of President John F. Kennedy.

"The people of our generation responded very uniquely to those particular traumas," Jensen thinks. "What Kennedy said, 'Ask not what your country can do for you; ask what you can do for your country,' was almost an ethic that drove many of our generation to extraordinarily magnanimous contributions. You wanted to do your duty.

"After my reserve obligation was over in 1969, about the time of the Tet offensive in Vietnam, in which a college friend of mine, a Marine, was killed, I enlisted for active duty. I didn't have a career in mind. I guess I had my old football coach in mind, my old friend in mind. And I wanted to be a Marine."

Jensen stands up and puts his hands on his hips and looks around at his men. "Look around you," says the Big Sig, and with a sweep of his hand takes in all the men crowded into the LVT. They are an undeniably impressive lot as they work away on their headsets and receivers, and crisscross the tiny access way of the vehicle as they add and subtract missions to the map. Only one of them is what you might call short. None is what you might call fat. The rest are uniformly tall, muscled, hand-some, and bright-eyed.

"These are your high school quarterbacks," says the colo-nel, "your college wrestlers, your big men on campus, your lady killers. They're all heroes. That's why they joined the Marines."

Jensen arrived on active duty in Vietnam during the waning months of the American involvement. "It was a time of transi-tion, a lot of the American facilities had closed down. The Marine Division had already moved back to Okinawa and our job was to take out a security patrol from time to time. I saw the U.S. Marines shooting the last American artillery salvo and then com-ing down off their guns and turning them over to the Vietnamese who were taking over their own defense.

"I met an ARVN general named Lam. He was a very gre-garious, strong, large commander in the Second ARVN Division in Quang Ni. I visited his HQ. I was there with a senior Marine officer. General Lam gave me the impression at that time that with the right logistical support, with the assets that the United States had promised, his men would be able to keep the North Vietnamese army at bay. But he said that his people were very tired. And he didn't know if the national will was as strong as his men. His prophecy proved to be correct."

Jensen returned from the mud to Washington, D.C., and the "8th and I," the ultimate Marine spit-and-polish outfit.

"Marine Drill Team, Color Guard, Special Ceremonies, it was three very wonderful years." The unit is also tasked with providing security for the president in Washington, D.C., and at Camp David, but it was the ceremonial function that caught Big Sig's fancy.

"It was a wonderful social whirl and," just in case anyone is inclined to sneer at such duty, he adds, "it was a wonderful kind of opportunity.

"You see, during the seventies, people were searching for majesty in the backwash of confusion over Vietnam. We sort of personified and gave people a good feeling about the military. The commandant at that time, General Cushman, used 8th and I to present the Marine Corps in its best light post-Vietnam. We had sunset parades, evening parades. We had demonstrations at the Iwo Jima Memorial, Arlington National Cemetery. The people that came were looking for answers, looking for support, looking for someone who still believed in himself. We did. And we shared that belief with them."

After the spit and polish it was back to the mud of an infantry unit. "You serve where you're assigned," says Big Sig. He has confidence in the career monitors who review officers' records and move them around. "I don't ask for assignments. I don't politick," he says. "After the infantry I did four years of recruiting. I sure as hell didn't ask for that!" Then he found himself director of the Drill Instructor School. Of all this, his mind always goes back to the close order drill of the 8th and I.

"We traveled sometimes and everywhere we went, despite everything that had happened, there was this tremendous outpouring of patriotism. It was a precious time. In 1973, we were marching down the streets of San Antonio, Texas, to open their Spring Festival, and every time the 'Marine Hymn' struck up you could hear the response from the crowd. It was like we were telling them that we were all still on our feet and they were cheering us for it."

Two officers call out the colonel's name simultaneously as each has monitored a transmission on his radio.

"Sir, you've got a broken track . . . "

"Sir, you've got a fire . . . "

Apparently, there's a fire raging in one of the axis Laurie AAVs and everything has come to a stop while they check for casualties.

Like the snakes in the swamp and the alligators on the banks, like the munitions that go off unexpectedly and the helos that go down in faraway hills, real life has a way of intruding on the war game.

Reports are sketchy and transmissions broken but the sense of urgency in the command track is now palpable. These are their Marines out there in the dark, fighting the fire with small extinguishers, pulling friends out of harm's way.

Then another report comes in. A jeep has flipped and one of the Marines inside it has broken an arm. There are no casualties confirmed at the AAV fire but the Marine in the jeep has a compound fracture and has to be airlifted out.

The Laurie attack is grinding to a halt. The fog of war which first afflicted the defender, who sat in the dark and didn't know which enemy was moving where, now descends upon the attacking force which knows where it wants to go but can't get there. This, as Lance Corporal Hess would say, is real.

Colonel Jensen and Major Sochtleben are up at the map with their grease pencils scribbling and erasing a half dozen contingency plans. None will allow them to be in position for a predawn attack on Combat Town. But one will allow them to maximize their forces for a second surprise, a split-up of axis Laurie. Jensen likes it.

"Fire the preplanned artillery," he tells arty, hoping it will serve as a decoy, "and then what we're gonna do is this. We're gonna zip on down here by the Golf-five impact area; then we'll go through Zeus, go to Gander, and then to checkpoint eleven, and then they'll work their way into access right here." The map is marked.

At the different consoles different officers begin putting out the word. No problem, can do, Semper Fi.

"Sir!" a voice rings out. "Enemy tanks operating south of Golf-five, sir!"

"Shit! I thought Echo was supposed to sanitize that area!" says the colonel.

Someone says he has anti-armor assets nearby, but when they are contacted they report back that they are presently pinned down.

"This is like giving birth to a porcupine," says Big Sig. Another option comes in immediately from air. A heads-up is sent to Golf about the air strike.

Move and countermove, the "problem" moves on through the wee hours. Every hour puts the attackers a half hour behind as the snags build one upon the other.

As a foggy first light begins to throw an indigo band around the blackness of the eastern horizon, Big Sig the samurai sits down at the open door of his command LVT and ponders what went wrong on his stumbling advance toward Combat Town.

"The one thing we try to do, and we keep pushing it on all levels of combat," he says, "is maintain your momentum, maintain your momentum, maintain your momentum. Do not allow yourself to be pulled off. Do not allow yourself to be bogged down by a squirreling attack. Continue momentum because once you've committed yourself you have to use speed and maneuver and close down the enemy quickly.

"Now what happened was, as Echo Company moved down the route, they ran into that tank force and pulling over to the side one of the jeeps flipped upside down and that Marine got himself winged and another guy in the jeep got a concussion. The commander on the scene said we got to take care of this right now.

"That was the delay that backed everything up. And we didn't know about it for about twenty minutes. That really bottled us up. We were moving very quickly and then bingo, we were way, way behind on our checklist."

A lieutenant hands Jensen his first good news in the past couple of hours. Despite the fog, the BLT has been given the go-ahead to launch its helo-borne attack. Almost at the same time, the wacka-wacka-wacka of a Huey can be heard in the clearing behind the command post.

Major Sochtleben is already aboard that helo. He declines a pair of the night vision goggles that the pilot and copilot are wearing. He knows there'll be nothing for him to see until dawn.

The plan is for Major "Sock" to lift off in the command helo, rendezvous with the troop helos, and tethered to Big Sig by his radio, lead them in the attack on Combat Town.

With a lurch and a rush of cold, wet wind, the Huey rises up into the foggy dark. Strange feeling, floating in the dark. You can't see anything. The two guys up front, insectlike in their night vision goggles, are faring quite a bit better. Like most innovations, the night vision gear was resisted at first by the helicopter people, who, like most pilots, value the "seat of the pants" point of view. There are no doubters now. The night belongs to the helo driver with the goggles.

As the fog lifts, first light washes over the dome of sky above the helo. The elements of attack begin to come together. The Laurie force that swam the intracoastal is now out of the water and moving north on the town. The part that broke off is moving in from the east.

Dani has fought its way down to a position also on the east

flank of the town. The helo troops that were to attack from the south now will come from that direction with Dani.

Below the helo you can now make out U.S. 17. There is some early morning traffic, trailer trucks with their running lights on, automobiles with their headlights on—some of the drivers now flipping them off. It's another day in Carteret County. Where are these trucks headed today? Who are these guys in their automobiles, on their early morning trips? Salesmen? Shop-keepers? Eager beavers from the department stores and barber-shops and factories needing to get a fast start on another day?

But you're way up here, poking holes in the sky with this Huey. Semper Fi, mac.

The Fine Young Lieutenant

———————————— ★ ————————————

By eight A.M. the Phillips 76 gas station on the road leading into Camp Lejeune—"Pawn 'n Gas—We Buy Dress Blues"— was crowded at all the pumps. Park 'n Pawn, across the street from the Tarawa Terrace housing area, was empty. The Marine training facility was in full swing.

The morning fog had burned off and below it, on the dew-wet terrain of the "TNG Area," Colonel Jensen's mock battle against the aggressors was moving into its final phase.

Bloodless, except for the accident that had bogged down the attack, it was the most perfect of engagements. No arms or legs or heads littered the field. No entrails stuck to the boot. There were no gold teeth for the interested grunt to pry out with his bayonet. This was all a game of fire and maneuver and supply and dash. Real war has maggots.

Several of the older commanders and NCOs knew that and kept the knowledge a very special part of the memory, a good way deeper and darker than the part reserved for sums and multiplication tables.

Sometimes, during the course of the exercise, you could see this memory being tapped in a man. It is almost always followed by a brief period of quiet, or else a shout or a grunt, ill timed and noticeably out of place, having more to do with the man than with the man's operation.

For the rest it was as Private Watson would have wished: a game of knight errantry. Slap a bug, challenge a man in the dark, move forward. Take a road, blow a tank, radio your progress. Find the stronghold, call a strike, overrun.

Though the assault had bogged down—and in the MEU HQ the heads of several senior officers which had nodded in approval at the presentation of the elegant two-pronged attack now were scratched by idle hands as the discussion turned to overcomplexity—still, command and control had been excellent.

Each disaster had been met and quickly remedied. No large units were lost or out of the combat. They had not done all the things they had set out to do, but they were *doing,* and that, as the commandant said at the party, was the key to combat, to life.

In the days to come, in the officers' mess and at the club, the offhand assessments of this exercise would divide the colonel's peers into two groups. The pedants would rip him for his grandiose plan. The pragmatists would applaud him for his flexible pursuit of it. But this would be just so much shoptalk. Like ballplayers who discuss the art of hitting ad infinitum, or wives who discuss their husbands in the same way, there is nothing decided, nothing taught or learned, only positions taken and selves expressed. Anyway, neither the battalion's plan nor its pursuit was being tested by this exercise.

The point of the maneuver was to determine how well the different parts of the BLT could communicate with each other and with their commander. Could they move, far-flung and in the dark, in an efficient manner? Could they fire and move? Could they move and support? Could they spot opportunities and turn them into gains? They had done all of that. They had passed all their tests.

All that was left was the taking of the objective. It is one of the oddities of the training regimen that this is the least important aspect of the game. To a soldier at war, or a child at play, it is just about everything. But in truth, all a good commander can do is position his men well for the attack. The rest depends on courage, and that cannot be tested when the guns are firing M-82 blanks.

There is thought given, every so often, to removing this attack phase altogether. But it is not easy to tell a battalion that's slogged through real mud and stepped on real snakes and missed another real night's sleep that the game is over, they've won, and it's time to go home. It's not good for morale. So, as ever, Combat Town will be taken.

It won't be easy. Charley Company, First Battalion, Second Marines has been given the job of holding it against the MEU, and like most aggressors they're taking it all very seriously.

"They've taken sixty-percent casualties!" shouts Lt. Frank Mahler, twenty-four, from Syracuse, New York, as he circles the top floor of the main house. He is tall, slender, and just a tad hyper. He has his men set at every window. He has his platoons in every building. He has fifteen minutes to get his people up for the biggest battle of his brief military career. He is not being tested. He is not even being monitored. He has nothing at stake in this exercise. But he has that gleam in his eye.

"We can hold them!" he shouts. He's made up the news about the casualties. He'd happened to overhear something one of the red-tagged exercise monitors said about the attack being bogged down and he simply turned it into a figure that his men could understand and rally around. As for holding the town, it never happens. The monitors won't allow it. This is an attack exercise. The town is always taken.

"Check this out," Mahler says. He takes the stairs two at a time, past a platoon of his men who are on their way up.

On the ground floor of the house there are more men than there are upstairs. Here they are two and three to a window. Mahler pushes his way past a knot of them and puts his hand out and twangs a piece of barbed wire that's strung across the open window.

"They don't have real windows in the town, just these open casements. So we scored some barbed wire last night and strung up all the windows with it. The two/four thinks that they're gonna come running through here?" *Twang!* "No way."

The wire gleams deadly in the sunlight. Real razor wire, the death of a thousand cuts.

"Too bad they bogged down." The young lieutenant laughs quietly. "Their intent was to attack us before first light. I'd pay to see those gents hit these windows in the dark."

A monitor wearing a major's oak leaf walks past and overhears. He smirks, puts a hand to his mouth, and walks away. It's hard not to like this young hero.

Mahler yells over to the next building, making sure they are all wired up, too. He twangs a third strand and walks off, talking into his walkie-talkie.

He's telling someone, "Lookit, tell your men I don't want it breaking out into fist fights but we're holding this position, whatever it takes."

The key here for Mahler is to make his people want to hold the town, really need it. He's not being graded on this. But guys like Mahler are what the Marines are all about. They're always grading themselves.

"They're walking into our trap!" he says, and leaves the house to his troops.

"Actually, we're dog meat," he says when he gets out into the sun. He is outnumbered five to one and the BLT has armor and helos. "But, what the hell," he says, "we'll give it our best shot."

All the buildings of Combat Town are constructed of thick timbers and are built to last. The style of house suggests a tiny farming village in Central Europe. The expiring Soviet Union, despite much to indicate the contrary, nevertheless continues to be referred to as the "main threat." The layout of the buildings, however, is something like a Southeast Asian hamlet. Military training always tends toward refighting the last war, or the one before that. Combat Town is a little bit of both. If Al Gray had a crystal ball he would set up Combat Town like a defense of armed sand berms in the desert. But he doesn't have a crystal ball; all he has is a plan to ready his men for whatever it is that future battle may bring. The town will do just fine.

"I really do wish they'd have come at night," Mahler says. "We've been digging in since yesterday afternoon." He points out all the booby traps. The place is ringed with trip wires and mines. Then, with palpable pride, he shows off his machine-gun placements. For Mahler they are the centerpiece, not just for this battle, for the Marines.

"Backbone of the Corps," he says. "Sure, we've got high tech, like all the services, but we're light infantry and so it's the good old machine gun, developed in the First World War and improved since then right up to this baby, which is the big hitter for the defense of a Marine unit."

Mahler has been able to deploy five. "Their tripods are locked for a grazing fire through two wide triangles, basically the most likely routes of approach, which we helped delineate by setting up the concertina wire."

After deploying the placements in the dark, Mahler had his gunners mark off with a length of twine all the strong points and choke points of both areas. "Up to four hundred yards in any direction," he says, "we'll be zeroed in on everything that moves."

He walks to the center of one of the killing grounds and looks back at his setup. "I love this; I really do," he says. "I'm a platoon commander and this is my first chance to command a company. I mean this kind of thing happens historically all the time in combat, but it's a clear opportunity for me to play the game, to maneuver this large an element." Quickly, he mentally checks his positions yet again.

His men are dug in but not very well concealed. With the coming of dawn they began working on the latter and are still at it. "It's not that big a deal," says Lieutenant Mahler. "When the shooting starts, they'll know where to find us." For him, the important thing is, "We can throw up a wall of continuous fire— the human body cannot penetrate that wall of steel." Then he shrugs embarrassedly. "If we were using real bullets."

He walks back past some of the very sharply barbed concertina wire. "We were setting this stuff out all night," he says. "No moonlight, no *illume* of any kind." He checks the wire. Solid.

"We're in good shape. I expected Jensen to hit us when we were most tired, say, two in the morning. We had one hundred percent alerts three different times during the night. That really helped motivate the men, too." Mahler's first night of company command had not passed smoothly.

"Well, we were a little tired after marching up here, and so, about three hours after we started digging in, I took a look around and things were just not progressing as we wanted; so I got all the platoon leaders in for a little old-fashioned ass-chewing." Mahler encountered no problem in finding the right words.

"I've worked with these people for over a year now. I know that they're good leaders. I know what they're capable of. I told them that. And when I looked at their lines and inspected our defenses at about five-thirty in the morning, about an hour and a half later, they'd done more in the hour and a half than they'd done in the three hours before.

"And take a look at them this morning. They're up for this now. Their motivation is high. Nights like that are good for the soul. They let you see what your men are made of. They let your men see what you're made of."

A loud explosion rocks the ground and then a second one. Men begin shouting. Mahler puts a hand on top of his unstrapped steel pot and runs back to the big house. All the way he is talking on his walkie and the incoming shells are booming.

"Is that them?" he shouts into the walkie.

"Yes sir," he hears, "we're taking a lot on incoming on the north, either side of the road."

"Disregard, repeat, disregard. That's bait. They're gonna be coming in from the east."

Mahler bursts into the house and flies up the steps. A few of his men flip him thumbs-up signs and ask if this is it. He winks back and takes care of business.

He radios a forward post. They now have visual contact with the forward elements of Jensen's BLT, a half dozen LAVs supported by infantry.

"This is it!" Mahler yells to his men. "Make your rounds count. Don't waste them!"

He goes out a window and swings up onto the roof for a better view. His men throw each other the thumbs-up sign.

All the roofs are full of platoon leaders straining for a better view. You're reminded of how expendable such men are, made so not merely by orders from above, but by their own willingness to sacrifice for victory.

U.S. MARINE CORPS PHOTO

The Tracked Landing Vehicle is the culmination of a weapons system development that goes all the way back to the 1920s.

U.S. MARINE CORPS PHOTO

Marine Corps Commandant Al Gray tests communications during Operation Desert Shield.

U.S. MARINE CORPS PHOTO

Marine riflemen of the 3rd Marine Division supported by a tank during Operation Kentucky in the northernmost area of South Vietnam in May 1968

PHOTOGRAPH BY CORPORAL M. T. MINK

A recruit from M Company, 3rd Battalion, tackles the combat assault course in the rain at Parris Island, South Carolina.

PAINTING BY SERGEANT TOM LOVELL, USMCR

2nd Division Marines at Belleau Wood, World War I, 1918

PHOTOGRAPH BY CORPORAL D. M. KEEGAN

Gunnery Sergeant ("Gunny") Michael Bacon (shown here at right as a staff sergeant) is serving his second tour as a drill instructor on Parris Island, South Carolina.

PHOTOGRAPH BY CORPORAL D. M. KEEGAN

Gunnery Sergeant David O. Pozorski looks on during a commander's inspection at the second recruit-training battalion.

PAINTING BY SERGEANT JOHN CLYMER, USMCR

Marines of the USS *Wasp* in action against the HMS *Reindeer*

DEFENSE DEPARTMENT PHOTO

An artillery piece is being offloaded from an early version of a landing craft in Culebra, Puerto Rico, 1923.

DEFENSE DEPARTMENT PHOTO

Company G of the 24th Marines waits for the tanks to blast the pillboxes of Iwo Jima, February 23, 1945. The company has already sustained 40 percent casualties.

U.S. MARINE CORPS PHOTO

The fallen are visited by their Leatherneck buddies in the Roi-Namur Cemetery on Kwajalein Atoll in the Marshall Islands, 1944.

DEFENSE DEPARTMENT PHOTO

The Marines storm ashore at Inchon, South Korea, September 15, 1950, in one of the swiftest and most successful amphibious landings in history.

U.S. MARINE CORPS PHOTO

Marines prepare to fire an M-60 machine gun mounted on an M-998 High-Mobility Multipurpose Wheeled Vehicle (HMMWV) known affection-ately as a "humvee."

PHOTOGRAPH BY MASTER SERGEANT G. W. HENSON

The official photograph of General Al Gray, Commandant of the Marine Corps, 1987–1991

U.S. MARINE CORPS PHOTO

Marines being towed ashore during amphibious landing on Santo Domingo, May 1916

PAINTING BY H. C. McBARRON, JR.

The uniforms of the Marines in 1779 consisted of a green coat with red facing, white woolen jacket, light-colored cloth breeches, and a round hat with a white binding.

U.S. MARINE CORPS PHOTO

Marines set up a machine-gun nest against the Germans during World War I in the Meuse-Argonne, France, 1918.

U.S. MARINE CORPS PHOTO

Leathernecks fight to save a Marine fighter plane, a Grumman "Wildcat," hit during the battle of Guadalcanal, December 1942.

U.S. NAVY PHOTO

The amphibious assault ship USS *Guam* departs for the Persian Gulf in support of Operations Desert Shield and Desert Storm, August 1990.

PHOTOGRAPH BY SERGEANT D. E. RENNER

A Marine from the 1st Tank Battalion fires an M-16A2 rifle equipped with an M-203 grenade launcher, Operation Desert Shield, September 1990.

PHOTOGRAPH BY CORPORAL D. HAYNES

The versatile LAV (Light Armored Vehicle) shown here in its "L" (Logistics) form, speeds across the Saudi desert in Operation Desert Shield, October 1990.

U.S. MARINE CORPS PHOTO

An AAV (Amphibious Assault Vehicle) convoy chugs toward their ships during Operation Team Spirit, South Korea, 1990.

U.S. MARINE CORPS PHOTO

A female recruit fires her M-16A2 rifle from concealment on Parris Island, South Carolina.

U.S. MARINE CORPS PHOTO

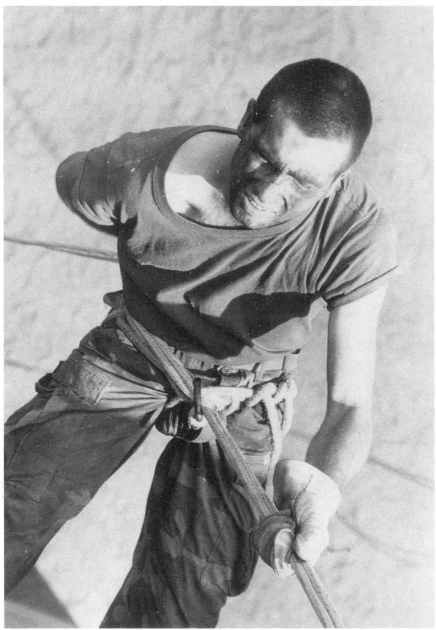

Trainees rappel from a forty-five-foot tower as one of their last tasks before completing basic warrior training, Parris Island, South Carolina, 1990.

Female recruits practice various defensive maneuvers. Here they defend a disabled vehicle, Parris Island, South Carolina, 1989.

U.S. MARINE CORPS PHOTO

Morning runs are a regular part of the rigorous physical fitness program beginning with basic training and continuing throughout Marine life, Parris Island, South Carolina, 1990.

The radio chatter is high. The force to the north is small; perhaps Mahler is right. Perhaps they are coming in force from the east. But then everything stops.

Jensen has decided that with surprise gone, with dark turned to light, a rapier attack will fail. He has paused to regroup. He will use the sledgehammer instead. And it can come from anywhere. A waiting game begins.

Mahler is now down from the roof. He is deployed and confident of his position. He has nothing to do now but sit and stew and keep his men on the boil. He goes from grunt to grunt slapping butts and patting backs. Then, in that hollow before the howling, he has a moment to himself.

He slumps down by an upstairs wall and cracks a can of apple juice. "Sweet," he says, but it's only the heightened level of his senses.

Private Watson said he loved the Corps because he was a patriot. Colonel Jensen said he loved it for the sport. If you ask Frank Mahler why he loves being a Marine, he'll agree with both, but he is hard put to choose between the two.

"All Marines love America," he says, "and I'm right in there. I mean, I'm a Democrat and have been since I've been voting. I'm not your dyed-in-the-wool, right-wing Republican who believes that might makes right. But I do see that what I do has a purpose."

It goes with what Mahler calls "the philosophy of the contemporary America. I think America has a role in the world to play. I think the Marine Corps has a function within that role. So I guess I do this because I am a patriot. I want to serve my country and this fulfills me."

Mahler thinks that "most of the guys are like this. We like going home and wearing the dress blues. I've worn them about five times. Each time it's meant a lot to me. The red stripe on the trousers. That's for the dead shed in the war with Mexico, Chapultepec. We've been around as long as the country. We're damn proud to be Marines generally."

He takes a long pull of the apple juice and pockets the container. Don't want the enemy picking up any information.

"Don't get me wrong. I'm not naïve. I know we have our five percent that joined for all the wrong reasons and are on their way out from the day they got there; but the majority of my Marines will tell you they joined for the country."

There is, Mahler says, rising and peeking out a window, "a flip side to all this." He peers out into the sunlight trying to see troops behind trees, LAVs behind hills, Big Sig Jensen drawing his plans against the town.

"There is a thrill of the hunt attached to all this and we all feel like we're the type of person who's attracted to a life-style like that. The big challenge. The grand sport. Red flag material." He smiles.

"It's a sobering reality to come to terms with that. To realize that you want something, or need something like that. But what comes with that is you get to see what men are made of, and what you're made of. That's the ultimate challenge to me.

"I always remember that quote from Rudyard Kipling, the 'If' poem. 'If you can keep your head about you while others are losing theirs.' That's what it's all about for me. That's my goal."

Mahler leaps up and huddles with one of his sergeants. Then he returns to his window. He has sent a recon team out to scout around. He's had enough waiting.

"I've not been in combat," he says. "I would be lying if I said I didn't want that experience. Not that I'm bloodthirsty," he assures. "I'm certain that the first minute after the bullets start flying I'll decide war is hell and I don't want to be here anymore, but it all gets back to being part of the challenge. It's why you join. It's why you want to be a Marine."

A squad of men pounds up the steps to take the place of the men who went out on patrol. Mahler quietly eyeballs the leader and points to an empty window and then another.

"Yes sir," the man says, "motivated and dedicated," and he divides his men between the two shooting points.

"We thought we were going to be committed last year in the Persian Gulf," Mahler says. The United States had begun reflagging Kuwaiti oil tanks with the American flag, but Iran had not stopped shooting. "At night, in the ship, I would lie awake thinking I will do everything in preparation for this combat that I am trained to do, especially so that my men do not become stressful, they do not see fear, my fear. I'd be a liar if I said I wouldn't be fearful. I was a day away from having a lot of people shooting at me. But to control that fear and accomplish my mission and do my duty, that'd be my goal. Business as usual."

Mahler is described by one of his platoon leaders as "one of those guys who numbers the wonders and lets the chickenshit slide."

Mahler admits, "I'm upbeat." He will, for instance, tell you that his night on the float, awake and wondering about the fields of fire to come, "was my third greatest moment as a Marine."

Mahler can name all the moments. Induction, first day of basic school, graduation, commission, "wetting down the bar," assignment to Europe.

That's where he had his second favorite Marine moment. It came as he was winning a ski race staged by the British Royal Marines. The British and American Marines have a training exchange program and Mahler spent three months "over there" last winter.

Mahler's eyes flash as he recounts the race that pitted him against a battalion of men he says were, even by Marine standards, "extraordinarily physically fit!"

They "go at these ski races all the time," he reminds, "and train long and hard in the frigid climate of Norway, in the subzero weather."

Across 1,500 meters of Nordic terrain Frank Mahler raced for the glory of his uniform, "the only set of Marine green utilities among a hundred of the Brits," he says with a wink, "and you know, they're very proud of that little beret they wear. Just to do well against them would have been enough. Beating them—that was a very proud day."

Mahler was charmed by the Royal Marines, perhaps a bit expanded. "For one thing, they laughed at all the patriotic stuff," he remembers. "Maybe that's what fourteen hundred years of history does to you. You kind of take that stuff for granted. They love their country just like we do but—"

Mahler lets the thought trail off. "They're a great bunch of men, extremely professional. They're a corps of only nine thousand and that smallness and the quality of training makes them, well, I'm not going to say more elite because no U.S. Marine will ever admit another force is better than us; but they are real Marines, great ones, amphibious little green monsters like ourselves."

The source of Mahler's envy, if that's what it is, now becomes unfortunately clear. "I think Britain," he says, "despite all the independence movements in Africa and all the immigrants that have come to Britain since the fifties, they're still primarily more homogeneous than the United States is and their Corps is primarily—" He screws up his face against something and then decides to let it all out. "White, Anglo-Saxon, Protestant," he says.

"I don't think that's necessarily an advantage," he continues quickly, as if to cover. "But they do have all those traditions and they're a very tight-knit group of men with a proud history."

He excuses himself, the negative thought gnawing away at a spot inside him, a spot he thought he protected. He goes around his men again. Many of them are black. "The strength of the wolf is the pack, and the strength of the pack is the wolf."

As Mahler makes the rounds he curries each of his pack of wolves, reminding them, reminding himself.

When he reenters the main building he is smiling again, flashing those laser eyes around, ready for hell. He asks, "You want to know my favorite moment as a Marine? It's happening right now!"

"Fire!" yells a man at a window.

There is automatic weapons fire to the north.

Mahler hears that his forward people are engaged. For a moment it is not known whether the fire is being directed at his observation post or at the patrol that is out there, somewhere, reconnoitering.

"Lieutenant!" shouts a pfc. at the window. "I make six troops, at the tree line, two o'clock."

Mahler looks out at the tree line.

"Two fingers right of the big pine," the pfc. says. The lieutenant holds up two fingers and aligns them to the right of a big pine tree. He makes the men.

"They're not walking too tactical," he says.

In fact, they're strolling.

"Sir," shouts a man with a radio. "The fire is O.P. Number Three." That's the one to the north.

"Shit! Those men are ours!" Mahler shouts. "Hold your fire! They're friendlies." He turns to the radio man. "We want fire to suppress, fire to suppress all along the left. That's our recon guys coming in and I don't want them hit."

The radio man sends out the order and fire erupts from all the observation posts to the left of the battle area and one of the machine-gun nests lights up.

"Come on you devil dogs!" Mahler shouts at the recon team, which, hearing the fire, has broken into a trot. The lieutenant has only a short company of men to hold the town and he doesn't need to lose any more.

"Get your asses in here! Move it! Move it!"

In the excitement a short, blocky, freckle-faced private at the window near Mahler opens up with his M-16. Tat-tat-tat.

"Hold your fire, hero!" Mahler says. "What are you shooting at?"

"Sir?" says the radio man, interrupting, "they just got word we have to move O.P. Five. They're in the woodpeckers, sir."

Mahler rolls his eyes. He has set a position in one of the protected wildlife areas. "Leave them there," he says. "The 'peckers are just going to have to deal with it."

"Can't sir," says the radio man. "There's a team from the EPA out there, sir, and they say we have to move."

Life has intruded on Mahler's wonderful moment. He's got bureaucrats on his battlefield.

O.P. Five commands the east, the direction from which Mahler thinks Jensen will come.

"Move them," he says, unfolding a map. "But let's do it quickly, and make sure it's not too far to the north."

As the recon team runs past below and makes it into the building, the anxious private at the next window opens up again. Tat-tat-tat. As in, take that! You rats!

Mahler throws him a baleful glance. Six spent shells now litter the bare wood floor in the corner by the window. One rolls toward Lieutenant Mahler. He nudges it with his toe and it rolls back toward the young private, who shrugs, caught in the act.

Mahler smiles back at him like a mildly reproving older brother, then he turns to the map and gives orders to the radio man which reposition O.P. Five.

The recon team runs upstairs and reports. They saw five of the big AAVs, hull down, just off the road to the north. Mahler screws up his face and thinks about this. Where the hell *is* Jensen?

The answer comes in a storm of gunfire. "North!" someone shouts.

"Hold your fire!" Lieutenant Mahler shouts. He grabs the radio and alerts all his people to the east.

They radio back that they are taking no fire; they see nothing. "Just giving you a heads-up," says Mahler, "wait for it."

Now men can be seen, Jensen's men, moving over a rise to the north.

"I make five AAVs," someone shouts. These are the vehicles that the recon unit saw. They're moving forward firing their big machine guns.

Mahler works with the radio, contacting as many of his people as he can. Excitement rises in the faces of the men at the windows. A private takes an extra ammo clip out of his pocket and holds it in his mouth. Another sights and sights again.

Then the building to the right rocks with gunfire. It sears out of every window, tiny tongues of flame, the deadly lick of the M-16.

"They're coming from the east," someone shouts.

Mahler smiles; got it in one. "Okay! They're not getting in here!" he shouts. "They're not getting in! Open up! Open up!"

The men begin to fire from the windows, raking the field to the north where Jensen's small force is on the move. From time to time they glance over to the next building, wondering what's behind it that they can't see. What, who, and how many?

Mahler is getting the report now. Two companies are attacking the eastern face. Two O.P.'s are already overrun. The forward edge of the attack is within a hundred yards of the first building.

Down on the ground the monitors in their red-taped caps watch the action, assessing the movements of the battalion landing team. Every once in a while one of the monitors will wave a man or a group of men off the field. They've been shot. Sometimes they complain.

"I didn't see anyone shooting at me!"

But the monitors' job isn't to determine personal, man-to-man combat. This isn't some weekend "paint ball" game. This is the cutting edge of America's foreign policy arsenal readying itself for the real thing. The battalion is being tested and every so often the monitors have to deplete it, randomly if necessary, to simulate the attrition of real war. "Death" by "death" the men draw closer and closer to Khafji, a town they've never heard of, in a sheikdom they never in their wildest dreams thought they'd get to visit. Kuwait is one morning closer. Gray's warriors are one day better trained.

Inside Mahler's building the now familiar confusion of "play game" for "war game" is taking place. As the north attack axis comes within lethal range the sharpshooters stop area shooting and start drawing beads on individual attackers. It's off-putting to drill a man quite neatly through the face and have him keep coming at you.

"Hey! I got you, you moffer fuffer!" the private with the ammo in his teeth yells from a window. Then he turns to his friend next to him. "Hey, man, hey! That son of a bitch down over there is dead, man!"

His friend just keeps firing away. A monitor standing nearby waves the two of them away. They've been "killed."

The private whirls and spits his ammo clip out into his hand. "What you say!?"

The house on the eastern face falls. Mahler is up on his roof now, running back and forth. He waves the brave survivors over to his house.

Men of both forces now race through the area between the buildings, shooting at each other, getting waved off by the monitors.

A group of about twenty men make it through the BLTs and the monitors to Mahler's building.

Mahler swings in through the window. "How'd that wire work?" he asks.

"Cut the fuckers up," a man giggles. Then Mahler gets down to more serious assessments.

The house has filled with acrid smoke. The gunfire, at first sporadic and then explosive, now seems a dull wall of noise. Deadly Muzak.

Mahler has the radio pressed to his ear now. Suddenly he pulls his head back and roars, "Alright!"

He starts moving around his men shouting, "They're pulling back! Pass the word! The first attack failed! We threw them back!"

Like a dying engine the gunfire sputters out. You can hear the shouts of men calling after the retreating BLT. A cheer erupts spontaneously in several of the buildings of Combat Town. Mahler leaps up onto the roof again to confer with his platoon leaders and assess damage and casualties.

The company is severely depleted but no thought is given to abandoning the town. The eastern face is quickly reinforced.

A platoon going into the building that was briefly taken encounters two sappers who were left behind. They are taken prisoner and waved off by the monitors.

Mahler leaps back in through the window. He is as high as a windy kite. The radio man says the EPA wants to use a truck for passage through the battle area. Mahler gives it his okay but warns, "Take them down the south end, don't let them see all those long-needle pines we cut down for fire lanes."

This is for the troops, and they all laugh. No pines have been cut down. Only Jensen's BLT.

Mahler has no way of knowing if the exercise is over but the monitors haven't left so he assumes that there will be a second attack. He consolidates his men. The house on the eastern edge of town gets a machine gun and twice as much rifle support as it had before. The first-floor window holes are rewired.

Then Mahler returns to the main house. He checks to see that everyone has plenty of ammunition. Then he sits down to endure again that most detested thing of men at war, the wait. "They're dog meat!" he yells to no one Marine in particular, and is answered by dog yowls from all.

Mahler loves these men he commands. He compares them favorably with the Marine unit he served with in Europe.

"Just as fine," he says, "and we were crack over there, really top-notch."

After the training with the British and the scare in the Persian Gulf, "We had to do an operation in Turkey and we were the only company available so we had to play the role of a whole battalion, four companies. And we beat everybody we went up against."

"Granted we were going up against the Italians. Not to be condescending but they're not at the level that the U.S. Marines are. And we beat them soundly in every phase of every operation we did. I was very proud to be a Marine then."

He looks around at his men at their windows. "This company's like that company. They're guys you wouldn't hesitate to go to battle with. I'm proud to be with them."

He laughs suddenly at himself. "I guess I'm proud to be a Marine all the damn time, aren't I?"

He gets a message that the BLT is moving in the east. The guns begin to blaze before the message is complete.

The second attack has begun. Mahler is everywhere again. He's on the roof with his binoculars. Then he's downstairs with a platoon leader. Then he's back upstairs yapping at his men, "They're attacking where we want them! Open up! Open up! Selective engagement! Make it count!"

The fighting in the easternmost building is fierce. The machine gun scythes down a wide swath in the advancing line and the monitors sweep the men away with waves of their arms.

Mahler goes to join the fight in the house. The BLT is at the gates and at the windows. The fighting is hand to hand. Fistfights break out.

Mahler stands at a wired window firing his sidearm. He is shouting for the BLT to come and get it. But they keep coming and Mahler is forced to pull back and retreat with this decimated platoon to the main house.

Now the guns boom in the north. Mahler goes to a window and sees a hundred or more Marines advancing in a line backed by AAVs and flanked by LAVs.

"Damn!" Mahler says.

It is another of Big Sig Jensen's elegant attacks, this one a double feint to the east and a main attack from the most obvious point.

The BLT is walking straight into Mahler's most heavily

booby-trapped area. But Mahler's guns have been thinned by battle and maneuver and Jensen's AAVs are riding down the barbed wire.

Mahler's people open up with everything they have, which now, concentrated in the main part of town, is considerable.

Jensen takes hellacious losses, but his force is too great. It bears down inexorably on the town. As it nears the "plaza" between the first buildings in its path it is caught in the cross fire of two machine-gun positions, and it stalls.

But AAVs pound up the gun emplacements and the BLT drives onward. A BLT platoon, moving too quickly, reaches the main house. They make the windows on the main floor. Mahler's people fight furiously to repel the invaders, who, unsupported by the main attack, are killed to the last man.

Mahler moves to reconsolidate. "Pull them out!" yells one of the monitors, a major.

"What?" says Mahler. "Are you kidding!"

"You've received orders to fall back, Lieutenant!" the major says stonily. "Now pull back!"

The two men lock eyes for an instant. Then Lieutenant Mahler whirls and shouts, "Fire to suppress! We're pulling out!"

He runs from man to man screaming. "Nobody stays! Nobody leaves gear! Keep up your fire!"

The Marines of the BLT are at their throats. Only a narrow corridor is left through which to retreat toward the south end of town. Even now LAVs are racing to cut that off and turn the town into a Big Sig killing ground.

"Okay!" shouts Mahler. "Let's high-diddle-diddle the hell out of here!"

The men of Mahler's company leave the house firing. They have to fight their way through to the rear but they make it before the LAVs. For a moment it looks like the BLT might pursue them, try to overrun them before they can reach the full cover of the woodpecker area. But the battalion has taken heavy losses and their turning back reflects Jensen's desire to pause, consolidate, and lick his own wounds before trying to inflict any more.

When Mahler met later that day in the woods with his platoon leaders, safe at last from the blank rounds of the BLT, there was much back patting and hand slapping. They had done well.

"I didn't want to give it up," said Mahler. "That was my battalion executive officer, second in command of the battalion, who waved us out of there. So I guess it's all okay.

"There's more politics involved in this maneuver stuff than anything else, but really, that was more 'free play' than we usually have."

The "politics" of war gaming is the approximation of real world battle scenarios. "We're supposed to be working on what we might do in Panama or the Persian Gulf. We all like the 'free play' aspect but the rules of engagement are very limiting.

"The fact of the matter is that the MAU, the Marine Amphibious Unit of which the BLT we were facing is the spearhead, they are important for the national security of this country. They will go out and do battle wherever they have to do it and the commandant says that when they do they will be special operations capable. That's why they go through this work-up.

"And this is a real outstanding unit. We gave them a run for their money but these guys are good. Colonel Jensen and his operations officer had a real fine plan and we did what we could with it." Mahler breaks a twig and throws the pips away. "We did as well as we did," he smiles, "probably because we were so young and hungry."

The platoon leaders agreed enthusiastically. "I got carried away a little bit with my cursing and whatnot, but these Marines here, if this were real, they wouldn't have given away that town. The BLT wouldn't have taken it. I was very excited about our performance. If there were real bullets in those guns, they would not have taken the town. We would not have given it up."

Lieutenant Mahler was one of those bright young men you meet from time to time who have their feet on the ground and their heads up in the sky and their eyes on tomorrow. You got the feeling Mahler was going places, which is good. But you also got the feeling that the places he was going to were a ways off and that for now he was just passing through.

"I don't have a Marine tradition in my family," he said, almost apologetically, as if he were caught in a social gaffe. "My father was a minister, one of the more *liberal* types during the sixties. Initially he had some anxiety about me joining up. But not anymore. He's very proud. Very happy. He's a patriot and the Marine Corps is an extension of that, and he can separate that from the whole moral question of death and killing and the stuff I may be called upon to do."

It was not a happy thought so Mahler changed the subject. "I'm getting married next Saturday," he said. "She's graduating Georgetown University." Mahler knew her in high school, dated her in college. "She's got a cum laude," he said proudly.

The week after that he was scheduled to receive his promotion to first lieutenant. "I guess I'll go from a honeymoon to a 'wetting down' just like that." He smiled.

Generally, when a group of Marines is promoted they throw a bash with their collective increases in pay. These parties have been known to get out of hand. You got the feeling Mahler's wouldn't.

"No, I don't think I'm going to make a career out of this," he said. "I have my plans. I want to run for Congress by the time I'm thirty. I'm twenty-four so I have six years to come up with some money, maybe win a medal. I'd love to have that, but so far it hasn't happened.

"Look, I've always wanted to serve my country. I'm doing it now; I want to do it the rest of my life. Not for money, for— you know."

Yeah, we know. You could feel the young lieutenant's discomfort. But he knew what he wanted and he was going for it.

"I'll have the home field advantage," he said. "My family has deep roots in my home district. And I think the people in my district, I think all the American people have the faith and courage to sign off on someone who's new but who wants to do what's right. I am a man of conscience. I'll be middle of the road. I know that I can do it," he said. His road was clearly mapped.

"My plans are to stay the tour, maybe make captain, try to get a recruiting assignment up there in Syracuse, get my face seen all over in dress blues." The Marines try to send recruiters to their hometowns in order to take advantage of their knowledge of the terrain. For Mahler it will work both ways. And then he's going to call in all the family debts and go for his dream.

Mahler shrugs. "Running for Congress is something I've wanted to do for a long time and come hell or high water, I'm going to do it."

Score one small but important loss for the U.S. Marine Corps. Well, that's what Marine recruiters are for. They bring in those fresh new Mahlers every day, or at least they try. The recruiting job Frank Mahler is trying to land in Syracuse is not as easy as it seems.

A Few Good Men

------------------ ★ ------------------

Clouds are moving in from the west and the upstate New York town of Poughkeepsie, unpretty at its best, is waking up in a gray mood.

Rush hour hasn't begun yet. The men chatting away in the coffee shop by the railroad station are night shifters, getting off at last. They grouse about the reflagging of the Kuwaiti tankers in the Persian Gulf. They hate Iran and the Ayatollah. They are happy the U.S. is "tilting" toward Iraq, sending Saddam Hussein the weapons for his war of attrition against the slowly withering Iran. Of course, they don't care much for Iraq either. They mumble their discontent and move on to baseball.

The streets are empty of pedestrians. Only an occasional milk truck or farm produce van rolls by the traffic light, which otherwise blinks red and then green for no one.

At the joint armed forces recruiting center, on the main floor of a modern building in the town center, both the Army and Air Force are still closed. Young Sergeant Page, a survivor of the Lebanon barracks bombing, is sipping coffee in the darkness of an unopened Marine Corps office.

Across the hall, two sailors in white play cards. They are open, but nothing is happening.

"Nothing much ever happens up here, anymore," says

Bos'n Mate Mike Daniels, one of the card-playing Navy recruiters.

Up here, when a kid walks in off the street, which is rare,
he either goes to the Army for training or to the Air Force for
what the locals call "the life," or to the Marines for reasons that
Bos'n Mike doesn't understand.

"I don't know how they do it," he says of the Marine
recruiters across the hall, "but ninety-eight percent of the time
they just kick our ass."

Lately, that's been 98 percent of a very small number. The
business of getting people into the services went bad in this area
a couple of years ago and it's been getting even worse. About
eight months ago, says the bos'n, the Marine Corps sent Gunnery
Sergeant David Chelstowski up here to run things for their office.

"Gunny Ski" was something of a "top gun." The big, bar-
rel-chested, thirty-five-year-old campaigner had won several
"Recruiter of the Year" type awards, and for a little while, the
Marine Corps' little corner of the Poughkeepsie station generated
some real action.

"In fact, I think he won one of those recruiting awards up
here," the bos'n says, and shakes his head in something like
amazement. But then the numbers "took a hit" again.

"He's a nervous person now," the Navy recruiter says.
"This job tends to get you that way. You got a quota to meet
every month. But I'll tell you what. Even with all the bad news,
Gunny Ski is good to his people. He's into reality. When a kid
reneges on him, or else on one of his recruiters, he doesn't get
all emotional. He just gets on with it. He knows that shit happens."

Gunny Ski arrives with a big smile that fills the room across
the hall. "That's him," says Bos'n Mike, indicating with a nod
of his head, but it's not necessary. You'd know Gunny Ski, the
Marine recruiter, anywhere. He's big without flexing and loud
without actually having to speak. He's all creased, starched,
brassed, and spit-shined. The gunny just commands attention.

Ski snaps on the lights, pats Sergeant Page on the back,
and dives into the morning reports. Like Ski, the office is bright,
a morale builder just to be around.

There are twenty-two "Eagle, Globe, and Anchors" in plain sight. They're on flags and posters and coffee cups and loose-leaf covers. There is even one on the clock in case you're the kind who's bent on watching that.

Across the room there is a big red felt board with a bulldog in the middle, and, radiating out, the Polaroids of the station's recruits in their dress blues. There are 120 men on the board and two women.

Next to that board are the charts for the six different sub-stations under this office's command. Pins are stuck in maps. Calendars are marked.

There's a clipping from *The New York Times* pinned to one board. The headline: "ARMY TUITION AID DRYING UP UNDER BUDGET CUTS." Anything for a little lift.

Below that is a glossy 8×10 photo of the porno film star Vanessa Del Rio, personally autographed to "Gunny Ski."

"She's a body builder now," Ski hastily explains, and you notice the pair of guns that hang down from the short sleeves of his own khakis. "She doesn't do those skin flicks anymore."

"Unfortunately," says someone under his breath.

Ski laughs like an innocent man. Why not? This is a good morning. "We're putting a WM in." He smiles. "She wanted avionics and the school was closed so I talked her into the reserves. She's going in today."

Ski gets on the phone as he goes over the reports. He tells HQ about Terry Morgan, the woman Marine who is going in today. They are pleased. In return, they give the gunny a problem.

It seems one of the men he put in a month ago has had a run-in at Parris Island. He has filed a complaint against a D.I. The recruit says he was punched. The young man's parents have called twice.

Gloom spreads over Ski's face but dissipates almost as quickly as it begins. "Let's get some information on that," he tells his captain. "Let's get something I can take back to the street."

He pulls a single cigarette from a breast pocket, and with a polished move meant to impress no one but himself, snaps open his Zippo with a one-hand twist. He fires up the smoke and in the glow you see that the silvery lighter, too, bears the eagle, globe, and anchor.

With his captain on the other end of the line, Ski goes over the rest of the impending day. They go over the list of "working applicants" and Ski gives a status report on each. Some are awaiting interviews, some are awaiting tests or the scores of tests they've taken, some have arranged to have one of the recruiters visit their homes. "Good to go," Ski says over and over again.

When he finishes the phone call he whirls around in his swivel chair and informs his men about the kid who got hit by the D.I. Page shakes his head. Sergeant Waltham, who's just come in, says, "typical," even though it isn't. Lance Corporal Mihocko says, "He's probably full of shit."

Mihocko has just graduated the avionics school that was closed to Terry Morgan. He is spending two months in his hometown as part of a Marine recruiting program that sends recent school grads back home for thirty days as temporary recruiters. It's good duty, almost a vacation, and it lets the happy grad loose among his old friends, one or more of whom just may be impressed enough to join up.

Ski has Mihocko working with his Delayed Entry Program people. The DEPs, who are also called "poolies," are recruits who've signed up for future entry. They too mingle at the mall and the community center with all those prospective clients of Gunny Ski's Marine Corps recruiting shop. "I'll get'm any way I can," smiles the canny Ski.

Today is going to be a tough day for Gunny Ski. He is going to make the rounds of three recruiters in his outlying towns who aren't going to meet their month's quota, again.

"Windshield time," he says. "It's about eighty percent of my day. Mostly it's visiting schools and customers and whatnot. Today it's, well, kicking butt."

Before he leaves he goes around to each man in his own office, one by one, as he does every morning, and dispenses a little morale-raising chitchat. It's not a pep talk or anything like that. Just a query about the family or the girlfriend or whatever he can think of at the moment. It's just to let the men know he's with them.

Waltham seems nervous, needs calming. Ski says, "You got a guy in Albany, he's good to go, right?"

Waltham reminds him that "we've lost six guys up there, all in the last two months, all at the last minute."

Ski says, "Take a car. Pick the kid up. Drive him all the way down. Make him feel obligated. Just see that he raises his hand and says, 'I do.'"

Waltham perks up. He and Ski exchange can-do winks and a thumbs-up. Then the gunny picks up his cover and he's out the door.

Sergeant Page suddenly remembers that he's got a friend who's a D.I. at Parris Island. He calls out to Chelstowski that maybe he can find out something about the recruit who got punched.

"Call him!" Ski shoots back.

Later, as his big late-model Chevy rolls down Route 9, Gunny Chelstowski's smile fades slowly into worry. He's concerned about his station's numbers. He's worried about his men. But most of all he's in a quiet snit over this punched-out trainee.

"He's got a friend who's also a working applicant," he explains. "And apparently he wrote the friend a letter. So this friend is going to come to me. I know that. He's going to want to know what happened to his buddy who went in. This kind of stuff can spread around a community like wildfire. You join the Corps; you get hit by a D.I. I need to know the what and the why. This will hurt you if you don't have a story to come back with."

There are three kinds of recruiters. Some are on a temporary duty assignment like Mihocko. Some are on a two-year "unaccompanied tour," the proper discharge of which is a key to advancement through the ranks. Some, like Gunny Ski, are career men. Recruiting is their specialty.

Ski has been at it for twelve years. The last field work he performed was as a mechanic on an F-4 Phantom jet. The last time he qualified with a rifle was back in 1977. This is still, however, only a job. If it gets screwed up, says Ski, "I'm back in the fleet."

Last year's awards don't mean much to a recruiter. In fact, last month's don't mean much either. Each month's new quota must be met, or else Gunny Ski will find himself back in overalls. Would he like escaping the starch and shine pressure cooker of his current job for a "pump" with the rest of the grunts? "It'd be—interesting," he says grimly.

Ski pulls into a tiny, disused mall. Next to a boarded-up car wash, behind a Chinese restaurant, is a small row of attached offices. One displays the patriotic poster, "We're looking for a few good men."

Inside, Sergeant Hamel rises at his desk to greet the Gunny. Hamel is in his twenties, married, pimply around the chin. He's distressed. He knows this is no social call.

"How're you doing?" Ski says, grabbing Hamel's hand and pumping it. "Tough times?"

"It's okay," Hamel says.

"Can I see your books?" Ski asks.

Hamel hands him his detailed recruiter's diary. When the services lost the draft, recruiters across the board found that their shoot-from-the-hip approach to their job was not getting it done. One by one, the services went to what Ski calls "a sales oriented" approach. The Marines were among the first to tap major business for this kind of sales training. Gunny Ski was trained by IBM. "The first major change," he says, "was the detailed diary." Through that a salesman can detect patterns, see where and how his pitch is failing.

As Ski goes over Hamel's diary a call comes in from Sergeant Page. He has some information on the recruit who got hit. "Fifteen stitches," says Page. Ski winces. "And he's making a lot of noise. Went right up the chain with it."

"Stick with it," says Ski, and he turns his attention back to Hamel. Ski kicks butt softly. He begins by telling Hamel what he's doing right.

Hamel is closing a fair amount of his contracts—which means that when he signs a guy up, he usually puts him in. His percentage is low but acceptable. Where he is lagging is the initial contact stage. He's not "opening" enough people.

Ski is familiar with the syndrome. "When you feel it's going bad, that telephone becomes a mortal enemy. It's how you get most of your rejections. So you stop using it."

Hamel nods and grins, happy to be understood. Gunny Ski

continues to manipulate. He says he wants Hamel to get out more. He tells him to go visit the local schools and community centers.

Hamel has a reasonable excuse for avoiding each. One school has a liberal staff and an administration that frowns on recruiters. Another is "good turf," but, Hamel says, "the student body is all blacks and Hispanics" and he is afraid they won't pass the entrance tests.

"Yeah, typical, shame," Ski says, not really believing it but trying to herd Hamel along any way he can.

"No way we get an NROTC out of there," says Hamel. Ski frowns and looks for something else he can use to get his man moving. He sends Hamel out for coffee and uses the time to peruse the office.

He looks at the faded photographs on the desk and the dog-eared posters on the wall. A softball sits in a loving cup on a shelf, covered with the thin layer of dust that clings to everything else in the tiny space.

"He's putting on a little weight," Ski says. "This is a lonely job. It's hard to keep up the *esprit de corps* when you don't have other Marines around you all the time reminding you who you are. Especially for him. He and his wife live off the base, so they don't even have the support of the wives and the guys. He's drifting away."

Hamel returns with the coffees. Gunny Ski puts on his biggest smile. "Smiles and dials!" he says, and claps the young sergeant on the shoulder. It's Ski's prescription. Just get on that phone and smile and dial.

Hamel agrees with a smile. "I made one phone call yesterday and got two guys for interviews—twins!"

"That the McDonalds?" asks Ski. HQ knows everything about everyone in this district.

Hamel answers in the affirmative and Ski launches into a story about a set of twins he once put in and how they had to be separated.

"Couldn't tell 'em apart?" asks Hamel.

"Couldn't *keep* 'em apart!" Ski laughs.

Ski launches into a review of phone procedures. Call at dinner time to make sure your prospect is home. Cut off prospects after four calls; but call the prospect's mother before you cut him off.

Hamel notes it all in a book. How many times has he played this out with his boss? Hamel's definitely got that "tough job" look. "Got a beautiful spot here for a radio operator on a C-130, six-month reserve, but I can't even fill that," he almost whines. "I get a guy who wants it but it turns out he has an irregular heartbeat."

Hamel spits out the last two words like they are an indictment against himself.

"You send the guy to his doctor?" Ski asks.

"Yeah. He'll be okay. He's trying to talk his brother into coming in for it."

"Attaway," Ski says, and someone walks in right off the street. Ski and Hamel share a look. No one ever walks into this shop off the street.

The young man is twenty-four with unkempt hair and unclean clothes and a jailhouse tattoo fading across his knuckles. To Sergeant Hamel he is the second coming of Chesty Puller.

"I wanna be a cook," the man says.

Hamel pulls out the paper. "School?" he asks. But it turns out the kid never graduated high school.

"You gotta get that diploma, son," says Ski.

"I can get an equivalency," the man says, but the Corps does not except that. "Also, I got a record."

Ski listens to the rap sheet and frowns. "We can work around some of that stuff," he says, "but you have to have that sheepskin."

"Hey, man, I'm a little old to go back to high school!" the man says, growing testy.

Ski really doesn't want to pursue this, but the paper chase that drives the recruiter in him forces the words from his lips. "If you have some college credits the high school dip can be waived."

The man says he has six credits of cooking school. Ski asks if that was all he needed to graduate. The man says he is still twelve credits short.

"Thrown out?" says Ski.

"Yeah," the man mumbles.

Ski scribbles a note and hands it to the man. "I want you to talk to this guy. He's up in Poughkeepsie."

"He can get me into the Marines?"

"He can get you into the Navy, if you're lucky."

The young man rises, smirks, turns on his heel. "Hey, thanks a lot, man." And he's gone.

"Fifteen years ago we'd have taken him in," Ski says. "But that's when the Corps led all the services in AWOLs and disciplinary actions. Now everything is changed around. We can't make deals with judges. It's actually written into our orders that we can't do that. It's for the best, I guess. We got a really solid Corps now. But in the bad old days we were competing with the jails then and now I'm competing with the colleges." General Al Gray's "warrior training" is not for the poorly motivated, and the new Marine schools are not for the hard of learning.

Ski remembers a story from the bad old days, back before he was a recruiter, when he was just one of the grunts.

"Back in infantry training," he says with a little swagger, "Combat Town, Camp Lejeune, there were these six guys who no matter what were always sticking together. We could attack or defend or whatever and these guys would stick together.

"One day the C.O. comes by and asks, 'Anyone here know how to play a musical instrument?'

"All six of these guys raise their hands. The C.O. says, 'Where'd you guys learn how to play?'

"'Prison,' the guys say."

Ski laughs at his own story and then turns to Hamel. "Call that kid's brother. The one with the bad heart. In fact, call his mother, ask how the one brother is doing and invite the other one down for a talk. Hell, man, you gotta do what you gotta do."

"You gotta," Hamel agrees.

"You gotta," says Ski, and then, to Sergeant Hamel's great relief, it is time to go and bust someone else's butt.

Back in the car Ski sympathizes with Hamel's plight. "Doing well in independent duty is very important, and that just adds to his pressure. You screw up an independent duty and you can hang it up for promotion, or even reenlistment. Hamel's gotta make his two a month."

Ski stops for take-out burgers on his way to pick up Terry

Morgan's high school papers. "Personally I don't know why women do it. I don't get it. But a WM counts the same as a man so I don't knock it either."

Ski talks and drives and eats with enviable dexterity. "You get so good at this," he laughs, "I can drive through downtown, eat a pizza, and not get anything on my tie. Hey, I can one-hand a Big Mac."

At Terry Morgan's high school Ski picks up the woman's papers. They are all in order, and they are excellent. Ski is pleased. He ducks into a phone booth and calls in to his office to report the latest and get his messages.

There is further word on the recruit who got hit. It seems the recruit in question hit his drill instructor first, then got himself decked. This means that, in addition to the fifteen stitches, Ski's young man can also look forward to some form of military justice. This darkens Ski's mood.

"We're supposed to follow them through training," he says, sitting forlornly in the phone booth, his hand on the telephone hook. "We're required to write two times, to talk to the family and to get together after graduation. We get a training failure like this—it goes on our record."

He puts in a call to his wife and then he closes the phone booth door.

On the half-hour ride over to Sergeant Kane's station he admits, "When things go badly that's usually the first thing I do. Call the wife. Maybe I should have told Hamel to do that."

Sergeant Kane's office is part of a nice little suite off the main road in the lake town of Mahopac. It is larger and cleaner and better appointed than Hamel's but it is no busier.

The slight and slender, redheaded Sergeant Kane greets Ski with a smile and a loud hand clasp. As far as Kane's concerned, he's good to go. So he opens the meeting with an old "war" story.

"Best interview I ever had," he says, strutting up and back like a bantam cock, "was in a high school right around here. This was the best kid in school—quarterback, class prez—but it was Halloween, see, and I had an appointment with this guy right before some big party. So he's dressing and his mom tells me, 'Don't be surprised.' Okay, the guy comes downstairs wearing a cheerleader's outfit and makeup and the whole nine yards. And he was cute! I interviewed him as a cheerleader and signed him up right there."

Ski laughs dutifully and asks for Kane's books. "Right here," Kane says, and leaps to the task. But the spidery lines of worry begin to creep about his eyes.

As Ski eyeballs the numbers, Kane expounds on his trade with a swagger that belies his situation. He says, "I don't do shoppers. Shoppers go to the Army or the Air Force. The dreamers go to the Navy. They walk right by me here and leave me alone. I don't deal with shoppers. I deal with the high school athlete who comes right into this office and says, 'I always wanted to be a Marine.'"

Ski looks up. "You had three hundred and thirty-four phone calls last month."

"That's right," Kane snaps.

"And only one interview?" Ski asks.

"That's right," Kane says and sags.

The phone rings. It's for Ski. The office calling. You remember Terry Morgan, the WM who wanted avionics but got closed out and talked into the reserves? Well, there was a mistake. Avionics has a slot. Ski's boss wants him to talk the girl out of the reserves and back into the full burst.

"Right," Ski says, dry-washing his face with his free hand. He calls Terry Morgan and they talk about the avionics class and the reserves and the relative merits of each. She agrees to meet Ski at his office at 5:30, which is when she gets off her job at an ice cream store.

Meanwhile Kane has changed his tune. "I gotta tell you, man, this is killing me," he says. "Last month I had twelve signees and all but two skipped on me. I had to get treatment for a rash on my neck. Nerves, that's all. Just nerves."

Ski wheels around in his chair and delivers a verbal smack in the face. "Get it together," he says, quietly. "We need all the help we can get. Gotta max everything. Gotta max your area canvass. Go to the supermarket, go the the ice cream store. Go where they are hanging out. Why don't you buddy up with Hamel and go down to the lake. It's always easier with two guys. Wear your PT gear, look good, have some fun. And when you find these guys you got to max them. Gotta get interviews in people's homes. Not in the office. You invite guys into the office because it's easier for them to say yes that way, but it's also easier for them not to show up. Gotta max those home talks. Gotta max Mom. You can pull it out. I know you can do that. We're sitting on a donut. Zero."

Kane opens his mouth but for a second nothing comes out of it. Then, "Ski, I signed twelve guys last month but—"

"I know, only two went in."

It is not widely known in the big cities, but signing up to go into the service in no way obligates you actually to do so. The Corps, like the rest of the services, likes to keep up the fiction that it's an ironclad contract, that if you sign you go, but it is just not so, and in the smaller communities like this where the word goes around real fast, it's doubly hard on the recruiters.

"You can have everything right," says Kane. "You can have a good guy with a good test score and a good school for him and even an enlistment bonus, and that guy could talk to a friend and the friend could say 'you're crazy,' and that guy will want out. And if he wants out, you'll lose that guy." There's no law that compels them to go in.

"Yeah, we try not to let them know that," Ski admits. "But they all get a little scared as the time approaches and if they have a friend who makes them wise, well. . . . "

"That's why you need the mom," he says. "She'll cry some, but she'll make him go. Moms believe in contracts."

Sergeant Kane suddenly snaps out of his funk and obeys an inner command planted long ago in Parris Island. He gets up and straightens himself. Then he goes to his desk and quickly straightens that, too.

"It's tough on you guys on your independent tours," Ski says. "I know what it is; whatever unit you came from you had the respect. You were all Marine sergeants and when you said jump, good men got right up off the ground. Then you come out here and you're all alone and most of the people you meet treat you like you're a jerk in a monkey suit. It's gotta be hard."

Kane smiles. "Dealing with it," he says. "I know I'm a little down right now. Hell, I can see that. And I got a couple of family problems too. Car's laid up, can't afford brakes till Friday. Wife's stuck in the house going a little crazy. It'll all work out."

Ski laughs lightly. "Know it will, but in the meantime I'm gonna dump a little more shit on your pile. I want you leading the parade colors at the high school picnic this weekend. Means you're gonna have to work Saturday."

Kane stands ramrod straight. "We'll make that happen, Sergeant," he says.

The two men shake hands and Ski climbs back heavily into his car. "You know what my favorite movie was," he says, as he cranks the old beast up one more time. "John Wayne in *Sands of Iwo Jima*. That's where the Duke takes the battle and then watches them put up the flag on Mount Suribachi and then he lights up a cigarette"—Ski reenacts the moment by one-handing a cigarette of his own—"and then he gets shot in the back by a sniper."

He pulls out into the street and heads for home. He says: "Whatever keeps you going, you know?"

He's logged over three hundred miles this day. He's tired. But he is still crisp. And when he parks his car and gets out, he puts his cover on his head where it belongs.

"Out here, nobody'd know if I just carried it in my hand. But I'd know."

The HQ is winding down a hectic day. The parents of the troubled recruit have been made aware of the pending disciplinary action against their son. Messages expressing their support of the Corps are waiting on Gunny Ski's desk.

He calls the parents and thanks them. He jots down the names of a couple of key kids from the delayed entry program with whom he will go over the case tomorrow. He will need these DEPs to counteract whatever "bad vibes" the recruit has "leaked out into the community."

In the corner of the office, Sergeant Page, still creased and trim, is going over a list of June graduates with another DEP. This is a problematical-looking kid in Jams and a torn T-shirt, gold chains around his neck and unlaced Nikes on sockless feet. His assessment of Page's list is equally suspect.

"He's an asshole. This guy joined the Army. This guy is going to college but stay on his case because he's gonna flunk his ass out in no time."

Page scribbles little notes next to each name, quickly. The DEP is on a roll.

"This guy's okay, maybe. This guy is tough as a boot but he's the biggest douchebag in school," he sneers.

"How do you spell that," Page asks wryly.

"Just write shithead," the DEP says.

"Put him in the Corps," Ski yells over, "betcha we'll straighten him out."

Page puts two stars next to the douchebag's name. All of a sudden he's fire team leader material.

"These two guys are okay," says the DEP, "but they were arrested for vandalizing the gym. This guy's a pussy. This guy's great but I think he's already gone across the hall. He's a Navy DEP, but he wanted to be a Marine, man. I think he's sorry."

Page remembers talking to the young man. "He wanted one of the engineering schools and it wasn't open."

The DEP shakes his head. "He'd come back, man, just talk to him."

Page won't. "It's an unwritten rule that we don't raid other service DEPs," Ski explains. "Even though they can get out of their contracts and switch, it's too hairy. It's like a service-wide recruiters' agreement. It'd be too cutthroat without that."

The place falls silent for a moment and the DEP, more to make conversation than anything, asks Page about Lebanon and the bombing.

"He doesn't like to talk about it," Ski calls over, but Page turns to the DEP and smiles thinly as if he'd maybe like to give it a try this time.

"The company I was in lost nineteen people," says twenty-five-year-old Michael Page, Mansfield, Ohio. The other recruiters turn to listen. Page has never told them his story before.

"Well, actually I was sleeping . . . it was Sunday morning and I don't remember too much . . . all I remember is I woke up and I thought I was dreaming . . . I could hear everybody yelling and stuff like that."

He stops and clears his throat. Ski clears his throat, too. Then the DEP.

"That's when I realized I wasn't dreaming. I thought we must've got hit by an artillery round or a rocket or something."

Actually, it was a suicide bomber in a dynamite-laden truck who had simply driven through the lightly guarded front gate and deposited death at Valhalla's door.

"I was on the third floor . . . but I guess it wasn't the third floor anymore . . . I couldn't move . . . I was covered with debris."

He clears his throat again. "My injuries weren't really . . . I had a broken jaw . . . my cheekbone . . . my hand. I was scared. I started to join in the yelling because I figured that was the way to get rescued. I did that for forty-five minutes to an hour. Then somebody said, 'There's someone over here.' Then one of my friends from Lejeune dug me out.

"I really don't remember this but they tell me that I just got up and walked out and stood outside looking back at the building. They finally put me on a bulldozer that was clearing a path. That's how I got a lift to a makeshift hospital facility. I felt like somebody had hit me in the head with a hammer. They put me on a stretcher and tied me up for head injuries and neck injuries and flew me out to a hospital. I didn't find out about the deaths until four days later. Lot of friends. A lot." That's all he can say. And there is nothing to say in response. Everyone goes back to work. The DEP goes to the head, perhaps to think about things.

Terry Morgan calls in. "Good news, young lady." Ski launches into his pitch, but she cuts him off. She's decided to go to college. Ski goes into his GI Bill spiel. How she can pay for her credits and get great training and see the world and be a WM, and even get avionics. But she's gone.

Ski leans back and pops his Zippo and fires up the last cigarette in his pack. "Okay, let's call it a day!"

Mihocko, the peach-fuzzed guy, right out of training, claps a hand over the receiver of his phone and shouts out, "I got a guy here who says he wants to be a devil dog."

Everyone laughs. "I'll take it," says Gunny Ski. He scans his school's availability sheet, takes a breath and then: "So, young hero, you say you wanna be a Marine."

D.I. Bacon:
The Green Marine

———————————★———————————

"**H**up, four, do-it, do-it!" the drill instructor barks as he marches his platoon up the road to "Combat Square." Overhead, the ancient oaks of Parris Island are hung with Spanish moss and the scrubby palmettos are rich with bugs and Kuwait is a summer away.

Staff Sergeant Michael Bacon, twenty-eight, crisp in the August heat in his sharply creased khaki shirt and olive slacks, watches the platoon go by. Parris Island is a wonderful, terrible place. "A lot of guys come back here on a duty assignment or for vacation or whatever and they look at the lush greenery and the red brick buildings and the pretty lakes and they say, 'Wow, this place has changed.' But it hasn't changed. They're just getting a chance to look at it without some D.I. like me shouting into their sorry face."

Another platoon marches by. "Yup, yer leff, yer leff." Each D.I. has his own distinctive cadence call. Like the platoon that just passed, this one is part of training sequence 1088, and Staff Sergeant Bacon is the senior drill instructor for this series, responsible for everything.

"You!" he bellows. "What kind of friggin' way is that to

march? Get into your Cadillac; where are my Cadillacs!?"

Several young men with shaved heads throw back their chests and put a little strut in their march. The platoon starts looking a bit sharper.

Bacon nods and turns and walks off after his men in his own, very highly polished "Cadillac." He is a big man with chiseled facial features and he sports the V-shaped torso and equine legs of a man who holds black belts in several of the martial arts. Like the other two D.I.'s, he is black.

"I always tell them that their legs are their wheels but their chests are their Cadillacs," Bacon says. "Anyone can walk far if he's forced to; marching is more attitude."

It's amazing that among all these smart-stepping, seemingly identical, cami-clad men, a D.I. can actually spot the one "'cruit" with the flagging attitude. Bacon turns and laughs quietly. "I didn't see anyone, really. You just yell it out and they all straighten up a little."

Combat Square is where Marines learn hand-to-hand. It is, depending on your point of view, one of the most fun-filled, or fear-filled, stations in the training cycle.

Today, the well-muscled hand-to-hand instructors are laying out the pugil sticks for a battle on "the bridge." Pugil sticks, staffs with soft-padded ends, are a training device as old as armies. The Marines are instituting new ones this month. They are shorter than the ones they've been using, the better to mimic the length and feel of a Marine M-16 rifle with bayonet. They weigh about the same and are balanced about the same. The new padding is smooth and light and hard to the touch. The Marines like these new fighting sticks a lot.

It was a terrifying incident in the old style of pugil-stick fighting that led to what Bacon calls "the current philosophy" of training in both the Parris Island and San Diego recruit depots.

In the last month of 1975, back in the bad old days, a so-called problem recruit who had been rejected by both the Army and the Air Force was subjected to a series of bouts against the best men in a platoon. Beyond fatigued, and increasingly helpless against his endless string of opponents, he was finally beaten into unconsciousness and died in a hospital three months later.

The New York Times, referring back to a previous training

disaster—the infamous Ribbon Creek "death march" of 1955, in which eight Marines on a disciplinary night march drowned in a swamp—commented, "once the elite of the United States armed forces... not all Marines have yet learned to draw the line between toughness and sadism.... A few training officers seem to have difficulty in distinguishing between the tough but human disciplines that build men and the perverted sadism that degrades and destroys them."

Part of the ongoing comeback of the Corps has been the evolution of a training regimen that emphasizes toughness without sadism.

In today's Corps, pugil-stick fighting is something of a sport. Three other training series will compete today with Bacon's 1088 for a trophy. The D.I. of each series will send its men out, one at a time, onto a narrow platform, raised three feet off the ground. Each pair of combatants will fight it out, the winner gaining a point for his series.

A small crowd has gathered for the festivities. Two junior grade officers from another company have stopped their car to watch. Three young girls on bicycles, post brats, have come by to giggle and ogle. A couple of whole families are here, relatives not of the combatants but of the training personnel.

"Okay, listen up," shouts an Asian sergeant who leaps onto the bridge with a white pugil stick in his hand. Like the rest of the hand-to-hand staff he wears severely tailored cami trousers and a black T-shirt with a red skull device. He swings the stick in a graceful arc.

"You will kill your opponent by stabbing, slashing, butting, or throwing him off the bridge; pretty simple, huh?"

The four series, seated in formation at each corner of the bridge, bark in unison.

"You will not, repeat not, get credit for a slash to the chest because that's where your enemy is wearing his body armor. You will get credit for a slash to the face or to the neck; pretty simple, huh?"

Bark! Bark!

"You will not, repeat not, get credit for a stab to the chest unless you stop your opponent's forward momentum. And you will not, repeat not, get credit for an underhand butt smash to the lower abdomen or to the testicles unless it's hard enough to bug the guy's eyes out." He flashes a smile. "Pretty simple, huh?"

Bark! Bark! Bark!

The battle begins. Staff Sergeant Bacon takes on the role of the corner man. As each of his 'cruits is handed a stick Bacon checks the man's helmet, his protective cup, and his headgear. Then he grabs the face mask and shouts something inspirational into the man's face.

"Go in straight; hit him hard; don't back up!"

Meanwhile the 1088 sits in formation and roots for the home team. They break into little cheering routines. "Eighty-eight, better than great," is kind of basic. Halfway through the matches they shift to something a little more flowery.

"Ready to fight. Ready to kill. Ready to die but never will! Ready to fight. Ready to kill," and so on.

One by one they run up onto the bridge. They scream as they advance. They batter one another with the sticks. Some bouts are over in the first charge. Some take a minute or more with arm-weary blows falling this way and that. The smack of leather on forearm is painfully clear. The bark of stick against helm rings out again and again from the bridge.

Bacon's men are taking a beating. They are down eight or ten points. Bacon refuses to get ruffled. He continues to check each man and shout into each face. "Don't give it up!"

The other three series are cheering too, and chanting and barking.

One of the 88s misses on a wild charge and throws down his pugil stick in disgust. His opponent walks up behind the man, and with a wide gratuitous whomp in the back of his head, knocks the hapless troop off the bridge. A huge war whoop goes up. The instructor signals the kill. Bacon leaps to the fallen man's side. He grabs the young man by the face mask and lifts him half off the ground, or close enough to bend into him nose to nose.

"Don't you friggin' ever drop your rifle again!" He throws the man back down in the dirt and turns his back on him and walks away.

Back with the men he launches into a loud harangue. "I

don't want you friggin' quitting on me now. I wanna see your goldarn courage. It ain't how you friggin' start; it's how the heck you finish."

His quaint little wordy-dirties belie his fury and make him sound a little like an out-of-control choir boy. But that isn't Bacon talking. Staff Sergeant Bacon is a regular guy who can curse a blue streak with any jarhead who ever split an obscene infinitive. But another important aspect of "the new philosophy" is that the D.I.'s are not allowed to curse at the recruits.

Despite a magnificent comeback, 1088 loses by a point or two. In a ragged, postmatch assembly, Bacon, who has come in second, must present the pugil-stick plaque to his friend Staff Sergeant Moore, whose series has come in first. Moore's men get to cheer. Bacon's get to stew. He lets them stand there until all the other series have marched away. Then he turns to them and says, "Goldarn great comeback. You sons of B's really friggin' showed me some heart."

Some muted barks rise wearily from the tired and battered ranks of the platoon.

"Shut up!" Bacon bellows. "Lay-eff face! Forward, march! And yo leff! Yo leff!"

The recruits are picked up by another D.I. and marched off for their third-week haircuts. This gives Bacon a half hour to dash back to his barracks before midday chow. He needs the time because he has to change uniforms.

"We change usually two, three, maybe even four times a day," he says as he pulls an identical set of khakis out of his locker and throws them on a battered ironing board; it's the only way to stay crisp in the summer. "Gotta keep that snap and pomp," he says, as he tests the small iron and goes to work on the creases of the olive slacks.

Bacon's "house," as it's called, is a small room in the corner of a barnlike brick and cinderblock building kept at a pleasant 67 degrees.

The men of 1088 sleep in the big room, double bunks, two yards apart, open shelving in between, covers on helmets, toilet articles arranged as for a parade.

Bacon lives off-post, but with his workday averaging sixteen hours and often running to twenty, he sometimes finds himself too tired to drive home at night and ends up sleeping on the "rack" in his "house."

"Do a lot of laundry, too." He grins. "You get pretty good at this. In fact, you get to be a goddamn expert. Snap and pomp. Half the time you gotta do the laundry that comes back from the laundry!"

Staff Sergeant Moore comes down from his squad bay on the second floor of the two-story barracks and pours a cup of coffee from Bacon's pot. "You ain't squat at the pugil sticks," he ribs, "but you're a hell of a homemaker."

Moore grabs a can of Scotchgard from an open shelf and sprays his khaki shirt with it. "It doesn't keep you from sweating, but it keeps you from showing it."

Moore and Bacon chat about their charges: who's looking good and who's not; who's a candidate for being dropped. A D.I. is judged on how his recruits do. A drop is a bad mark for everyone, but a guy who can't cut it hurts the whole series.

"You gotta turn them around," says Bacon as he deftly edges a pleat. "You can't just drop a guy. You gotta turn him around. That's your job."

"Yeah, right," says Moore, wincing at the first taste of the boiled-out coffee.

"You gotta go up against the guy and challenge him," says Bacon. "A lot of these guys come in for the fantasy, and when it gets hard they forget all about that blue pants kind of crap. You gotta go up against them and ask them why they wanted to become Marines in the first place. Everybody has something in there somewhere, they just forget it and you gotta bring it back out. Or else you gotta carry them a little."

"I'd pop a hern carrying some of my sorry individuals," says Moore.

"I got a thirty-year-old guy," says Bacon. "He used to be in the Army. He wants to come back in as a Marine. This guy's a real ragged situation, man. He's flatass last in everything but he's busting it to get by. I want to carry a guy like that, see if he can make it through at the end. I won't drop a guy who's busting it that hard."

They are joined by Staff Sergeant Dingle, their senior. Dingle, who is also concerned about drops, wants to know which of the recruits need to be held back from a physical training test scheduled for the next day. "I wanna produce some good numbers," he says.

Dingle also brings another problem; there is a new first sergeant coming in.

"The man's walking around with a ruler and he's measuring everything that don't move," says Dingle. "That eighteen inches?" he asks Bacon, indicating the amount of white sheet showing on the D.I.'s incredibly tight-made bed. "It looks a couple of inches short."

They measure. It is exactly sixteen inches. "Let's fix this shit up," says Dingle, "I ain't fucking around."

The recruits think the D.I.'s are supreme beings, way above it all. They're supposed to think that. The D.I.'s know better. "Shit rolls downhill," Dingle explains.

Dingle's second problem has to do with the roving bands of depot inspectors who ride around in white pickup trucks and make sure training is being conducted according to "the new philosophy."

Dingle thinks orders must have come down from higher. "They are all over the place!"

"The new colonel?" Moore suggests. One of the reasons Bacon has his iron out is that he "burned" two fresh khakis drilling for the change-of-command ceremony which was held the previous morning.

"The new colonel," Bacon agrees. He whips on his shirt and pulls a pair of long black elastic suspenders from his locker. He attaches one end to the tails of the shirt and then bends at the waist and attaches the other end to the tops of his black socks. When he stands up the tails of his khaki blouse pull down sharp and tight. He pulls up his pants and turns his back to Moore, who holds flat the two large kidney darts as Bacon buckles up smartly and correctly.

The three D.I.'s fall to discussing the state of the current training methodology. The discussion, as it often does, takes the form of an argument over which movie most correctly depicts

Marine basic training, Stanley Kubrick's *Full Metal Jacket*, a product of the post-Vietnam 1980s, or Jack Webb's *The D.I.*, a product of the post–Korean War 1950s.

Moore favors Kubrick because "*The D.I.* was ancient history. We can't make guys go out and bury sand fleas in six-foot holes anymore."

Dingle, nevertheless, favors Jack Webb. "You still have to tear their bodies down and make them speak with a new voice," he says. "We don't do as much physical stress now as they did then but the procedures are still there and we just produce the stress in different ways, mental ways. We still stay on them the way Jack Webb did. We still make them shout louder, louder, and make them do everything fast-fast-fast. We still scream at them."

"Can't hit them no more," says Moore.

"No," Dingle says. "Funny, 'cause they do it in the fleet, you know. Can't hit them here, no. But hey, look how the world has changed. Back in the fifties your goddamn gymnasium teacher could hit you. Now your parents can't even hit you. But we can get on them. You yell in their eye? I yell in their eye. You get right up close and yell right into their eyeball, and spit a little, and don't they blink, and don't they flinch back?"

"Yeah, I do that." Moore snickers.

Much of the yelling and screaming is an act. It is put on to instill in the recruits a sense of military bearing. The most important thing a Marine must demonstrate, more important than pull-ups and sit-ups, more important than pugil sticks and barking, is the ability to stay unrattled under pressure. It is why they shout back and forth and why they are given only ten seconds to polish a belt buckle. Of course, a little later on in the training cycle, when the series starts to fall behind a bit and the D.I.'s begin looking over their shoulders at their own superiors, then the yelling gets serious as a heart attack.

"You got that right." The three D.I.'s laugh and Dingle returns to his point. "We press them," he says, "and we can bully them when we want to. We don't march them through Ribbon Creek no more," the senior Dingle says, "hell no, but we can take them down to the sand pit."

Every group of D.I.'s finds its own special way to come

down hard when they feel they have to. For 1088 it is a pit of
coarse sand out behind the barracks. When things get a bit
bumpy, physical training is moved from the grassy field to the
sand pit.

"You work out in there for a couple of hours," Dingle says
with a grin, "and they get that sand in their boots and down
their neck and in their balls. They get mighty uncomfortable
with the deal.

"Hey, look, we can't do with these people the shit that
Jack Webb did with them. People aren't as disciplined today as
they were back in the fifties. You can't just all of a sudden dump
it all on them. They won't take it. And they are smarter now.
Smarter than we were, that's for damn sure."

They all laugh. "Yeah, I gotta explain to them why we do
every fucking thing," Moore says. "They all wanna know everything. 'Why do we do this?' 'Why do we do that?'"

"We're supposed to explain everything to them," Bacon
says. "That's the whole idea."

The question is, does it work? Dingle and Moore are en-
thusiastic about the recruits they are turning out. Bacon remains
silent a moment and then shrugs and lets it out. "The Marines
we graduate out of Parris Island today are weaker than the ones
we graduated with. They're weaker mentally and physically."

"No," the other two say, almost in unison.

"It's okay," Bacon says. "The warrior training picks up the
slack. They all go on to the school of infantry, so it's okay. But
we don't do the job here we used to do. You can't. Society has
changed. You're starting off with folks who are weaker and you
got to follow training rules that are softer. It's still the greatest
fighting outfit in the damn world but, hey, you know. . . ." He
lets the idea trail off and hang, like stale smoke, in the room.
They have this discussion a thousand times each training cycle
and it never turns out any other way.

"Okay, sure, we have our ten percent," says Dingle, ever
the cheerleader for the team. "We've always had our ten percent
but it ain't nothing like it was when I came in."

Like Gunny Ski, Dingle remembers that in the seventies
the Marines led all the services in AWOL rates, desertion rates,
drug abuse rates, racial incident rates; just about every negative

statistic you might care to ring up came down hard on the Corps.

"We had a lot of Vietnam-era hangovers," Dingle theorizes. "They had put the manpower levels too high in order to fight the war and we were getting in all kinds of guys who shouldn't have been here."

"A year in jail or four in the Marines," says Moore, echoing the lament of Gunny Ski.

"Damn right," says Dingle. "And we had to make them perform as Marines. I came smack into it, first tour as a D.I., and it was bad. We had race problems. We had drug problems. We had riots. We had fragging. But we dealt with it. Some of those guys are good Marines now. Most of them are just plain gone."

In 1975, the year the recruit died from injuries received in pugil-stick fighting, Commandant Louis H. Wilson, citing "a manpower quality problem," ordered something be done to turn things around.

Four thousand "unsuitable" Marines (the snarled epithet "unsuit" is still used by drill instructors to terrorize the lagging recruits) were dropped from the rolls and a standard quota of 75 percent high school graduates was set for Corps recruiters. That figure is now close to 100 percent, but back in 1973, the post-Vietnam bad days, it was an astonishing 46 percent.

The new quotas had the effect of sharply decreasing the percentage of black enlistments from 19 to 15. Commandant Wilson said, "I think this is about right, 15 percent black, because they constitute about 12 percent of the population. I think this would be a good mix."

What was ignored by Wilson, and continues to be ignored by men like Bacon, Moore, and Dingle, all three of whom are black, is that the majority of the four thousand unsuitable Marines who got discharged were black, and that the Marines have historically viewed a "good mix" as being the whitest mix the defense posture will allow.

According to Marine Corps lore, at least three black men served in the ranks of the Continental Marines during the Revolutionary War. The first, according to pay records, was John Martin, or "Keto," a slave of William Marshall of Delaware. Keto was recruited, without the slave owner's knowledge, by

Marine Captain Miles Pennington for service aboard the Continental brig *Reprisal,* which in 1977 dashed itself to bits against the Newfoundland Banks, where Keto perished with the rest of the crew.

And things didn't get much better for blacks in the Corps for quite some time. Even the service's official history of blacks, *Blacks in the Marine Corps,* admits, "those few black men who have been identified as Marines from surviving Revolutionary War records were pioneers who were not to be followed by others of their race until 1 June 1942."

The Continental Marines went out of existence shortly after the British went home. In July of 1798, when Congress reestablished a separate Marine Corps in order, among other jobs, to provide security aboard the the frigate *Constitution,* the new commandant, Major William Ward Burrows, instructed his recruiting officers to "make use of Blacks and Mulattoes while you recruit, but you cannot enlist them."

Though thousands of blacks began serving proudly in the Army and the Navy, distinguishing themselves particularly in the Civil War and the Indian wars, there is no known record of black Marines serving in any of the various wars of the nineteenth century.

Peking was defended without the benefit of black Marines. Belleau Wood was fought without blacks. Whenever America cried, "Send in the Marines," only white Marines answered the call.

On the eve of World War II, President Franklin Delano Roosevelt signed Executive Order No. 8802 establishing the Fair Employment Practices Commission. "All departments of the government," it said, "including the Armed Forces, shall lead the way in erasing discrimination over color or race."

The Marines remained silent on the issue. Then, just a few days after the attack on Pearl Harbor, Marine Commandant Holcomb finally responded. It wasn't what blacks wanted to hear. "The negro race," he said, "has every opportunity now to satisfy its aspirations for combat in the Army—a very much larger organization than the Navy or the Marine Corps—and their desire to enter the naval service is largely, I think, to break into a club that doesn't want them."

Nevertheless, the secretary of the navy ordered that the Marines begin taking in a thousand black recruits a month.

An all-black boot camp was activated at Montford Point near Camp Lejeune. Two months later the first black unit was activated, the 51st Composite Defense Battalion. All its officers were white.

Though blacks were becoming Marines they still faced an iron wall of segregation, and, just as infuriating, a policy of assignment that was keeping them off the front lines.

Black units were almost exclusively used as labor units and stevedore battalions, freeing other, white Marines for combat.

Though some units eventually got to the front (the 3rd Ammunition Company received a Presidential Unit Citation at Saipan, and Pfc. Luther Woodward won a Silver Star in the invasion of Guam) the tale of black Marines in World War II is told in the casualty reports. Though ambition was high and bravery was abundant, the 19,168 black Marines suffered a total of only 9 dead and 78 injured—not much action at all.

Still the record showed that black men could serve the eagle, globe, and anchor. Commandant Alexander A. Vandegrift said, "The negro Marines are no longer on trial. They are Marines, period."

But when President Harry S Truman signed Executive Order No. 9981 ending segregation in the armed forces, the Marines again were the last to get in line. Commandant Clifton D. Cates agreed in "principle" but maintained that "the problem of segregation is not the responsibility of the Armed Forces."

Of course the rest of the armed forces had already gone ahead with desegregation, and in the end, the Marines were dragged along.

The first Marine units to be integrated were the Corps athletic teams. Then the black boot camp at Montford was closed and black recruits began going through training at Parris Island and San Diego along with white recruits.

In Korea black fought alongside white and both fired their weapons from the front lines. Two blacks won the Navy Cross and Major General Oliver P. Smith, who commanded thousands of black Marines, said, "They did everything because they were integrated and they were with good people."

But the Marines' "good mix" was still lean. The war in Vietnam is widely perceived to have been disproportionately fought by black Americans. The numbers bear this out when viewed across the broad spectrum of the armed forces. But of all the Marines who served in Vietnam, only 41,000, fewer than 10 percent, were black.

In 1973, when the war was over for America, the Marines could boast of only 282 black officers out of an officer corps of 20,000 men. That was when the racial problems were at their peak. Lejeune registered 160 cases of racially motivated assaults in one year, including homicide, and more racial violence was flaring in Hawaii and Okinawa.

"That's where I came in," says Dingle, and the others nod quietly. "But see, society was racially violent then, with all the black power stuff and the riots and whatnot. The Corps can only reflect what's going on in the society."

The drug abuse rates have been brought into line with the other services by a vigorous and successful program of testing, treatment, and punishment. Dingle thinks a lot of "civilian society" ought to "look into the program."

The racial incidents are down, too. This is true in part because, in the society at large, the eighties were not as racially contentious as the seventies. But a large part of the credit has to go to an antibias program as rigorous as the one for drugs. "You want a bad rating, go get yourself hit with a bias thing," says Dingle.

"Quickest way out of the Corps," says Moore, who finishes his coffee, rinses his cup, and taps his cami watch as a signal to Dingle that it's time to leave. Bacon says he'll catch up.

He puts away the ironing board and takes down his "smokey" hat from a wooden device that keeps the wide brim rigid with snap and pomp. Then he confronts his blackness.

"I'm a green Marine," he says. "That's a saying we have. There are no black Marines and no white Marines. There are only green Marines."

But are there lighter and darker shades of green? Bacon "would hope not." He tucks his things carefully away and continues to struggle with the question.

"I'm not your stereotypical ghetto black," says the big D.I., who hails from East Orange, New Jersey, a black but socio-economically mixed suburb of New York City. "I come from a family with a mommy and a daddy living there, two sisters. Never had any problem in the streets. High school grad. Went straight into the Marine Corps because I had a desire to be a Marine.

"Not all my people are like that. I have black kids from broken homes, hard lives, knocked around a bit, joined up because they didn't know what else to do. I deal with them. But I deal with the white guys, too."

General Frank Petersen, jet ace, senior black officer in Vietnam, ended his career recently as commanding general at Quantico. In his closing comments to the press he said that "there is as much racism on the black side as on the white side" and because of that he never let his decisions "be predicated by race." There was the inevitable grumbling that Petersen never reached out to a black man.

Bacon nods. "I don't blame him. He's the true green Marine. I agree with that. I'm not here to make black Marines. I'm here to make green Marines. I enjoy all that black history and stuff. I study it on my own. But I don't dwell on it with the troops. It wouldn't be fair.

"I treat my recruits fair, across the board, no matter what race they are or where they come from. I treat them as they are. If they're good Marines I treat them as good Marines. If they're bad Marines I treat them in a way to make them good Marines.

"Of course I may understand my blacks a little better. They may have come from an environment or have an experience that I can relate to a little better. Yeah, I can totally relate to black recruits. I went to an all-black high school. I know what it's all about. I can especially help out the ones on the edge. I got guys from the inner city in Baltimore, Detroit. They're not used to certain things, to certain discipline things. I tend to help them out. I enjoy that. I do them a favor, yeah. I make them work hard. They earn what they get.

"Sometimes, I think, maybe I'm a little too hard on these people. Come down on them too hard. Specially if the fuckup has something to do with their, you know, sociology. I don't want to embarrass the race, you know?"

Bacon laughs. He's a little embarrassed already. "Anybody

looking for a juicy race story isn't going to find it in the Marines. That's history. Sure I hang with Moore and Dingle and like that. People all have a tendency to hang with their own. But I party down with the white sergeants too; we all tear up the clubs when we've a mind. We do it all together."

He puts the "smokey" cover on his head, where it perches with a menacing tilt below the eyes. "Dingle's right about the racial stuff in the Corps mirrors the stuff in society. It's been quiet. It's getting noisy again. Our people read the papers. They know that this stuff is happening again. It could all explode again here. The Corps is a lot smarter now, more educated. But a lot of educated people still do a lot of uneducated things. It could happen here. I hope it won't. But it could."

Bacon walks out the door to a blast of August heat. The fetid aroma of the tidal "fluff mud" fills the air. But the sky is clear and the humidity is down and the stinging sand fleas won't be rising for another month or two.

"Yo, 'cruit!" Bacon yells to a lone trainee ambling along in the shade. "Get in your Cadillac!"

Bacon doesn't know what is in store for the men of 1088. Pumps, floats, deployments to small insurrectionary republics? Or the sands of the Middle East? So they're getting ready for it all. When Bacon is through with them they'll get a weekend pass and then it's on to grass week. That is where they'll stop being boots, and start becoming riflemen.

The Rifleman

━━━━━━━★━━━━━━━

During the Vietnam War the Army switched over from the aging M-14 rifle to the M-16. The M-16 was lighter and more compact, and was able to fire many more rounds in lightning, deadly bursts. If the weapon's range was somewhat shorter than that of the M-14, that was all right with the Army. If the shot was slightly less accurate than the M-14, that was all right, too. In fact, the M-16 didn't even have a hand-adjustable gunsight.

The rationale behind this rapid-fire, short-range, marginally accurate weapon was an Army Infantry Board study which concluded in the mid–1950s that modern infantry combat was increasingly being fought at ranges of three hundred yards and less, by soldiers who were becoming increasingly less expert at aiming their weapons, firing at enemies whom they could not even see. The M-16, the new rifle of choice, was therefore designed as a close-combat spray gun. The Marines hated it.

Never mind that since the trench warfare of World War I the trend on the killing field was tending less and less to rifle-inflicted death and more and more to artillery and other munitions. Never mind that the rifleman now scored only a tiny fraction of the kill while accounting for almost the whole of its casualties. Never mind that despite the development of "smart" bombs and guided munitions of virtual pinpoint accuracy, virtually every modern armed force in the world has moved from the riflery concept of "aimed fire" to the massed concept of "area fire." The United States Marines still believed in the "one shot, one kill" combat philosophy, which had been born in the rigging of the ships of the Revolutionary War.

Few Marines believed more strongly in this manly art of riflery than Maj. D. J. Willis, who in the middle sixties set about the legend-making task of redesigning and refitting the scatter-shot M-16 to suit the battlefield needs of that good old "Marine marksmanship."

Now a full colonel, the cueball-domed, hawk-faced Willis honchos the Marines' Weapons Training Battalion, which is charged with oversight of the entire marksmanship package, from "snapping in" the recruits to grass week to competition shooting teams that compete worldwide, even to research and development.

He jogs every day to keep that lean Marine silhouette, and he shoots almost as often. Smiling at his interviewer, Colonel Willis squeezes off the last rounds in his M-16 A2, the U.S. Marine version of the weapon; then he steps off the firing line and pulls the foam stoppers from his ears.

"I didn't invent it," he warns, "this isn't a story about how I got up one day and smacked my head and said, 'Wow, this is the way we can fix up the M-16!' "

It is, according to Willis, a story about a lot of men, frontline men and competition men, rear echelon men and businessmen, all getting together to solve a few little problems with a weapons system. Willis wants you to know that. Like all legends, modesty comes easy to him. Which means it will be a long way to the story of the M-16 A2.

His strides are long and graceful as Colonel Willis glides across the grassy slopes to the low building that houses his office. His clear eyes stare straight ahead. He seems just a little bit hard of hearing, that certain sign of age which wears particularly well on an old warrior. He puts a hand to his ear. "Nine-millimeters," he says.

Indeed the Marine Security Guards are out shooting today, changing over from the old .38 to the new 9-mm. Willis nods. He is on top of that weapon, too.

"The guards are able to carry loaded weapons now. That comes, in part, from Weapons Battalion here. See, anytime you arm a man with a loaded weapon you have to be sure what you're doing is totally correct. These guards didn't even used to carry loaded weapons.

"When the nine-millimeter pistol came into existence—although it wasn't a Corps push to get the pistol we are part of the Department of Defense arena and when they said 'take it' I took it—I could see from looking at the safety features on the weapon that we could put a round in the chamber and put the safety on and make our people as safe or safer on post than they were with a forty-five and their rounds in a pocket or a desk drawer.

"I mean, to ask an individual, based on an MSG school philosophy of safety, that he's gonna walk a post and he's gonna carry his pistol here on his hip but his rounds are gonna be a ways over there, and then expect him under pressure, or a matter of life and death, to make a decision on a use of deadly counterforce and then to pull his pistol and open it up and go get his ammunition and load it and *then* first bring it to bear—that's just wrong. If you don't trust your man to arm him with a round in the chamber and the hammer back and the safety on, then you might as well send him out with a billy club and a whistle.

"Now, for the first time in history we have, on a regular basis, not just in nuclear facilities, Marines who are walking their guard posts with a round in the chamber and their safety on. And though that don't seem like much to a lot of people it's been a big boost in morale. Just ask a Marine Security Guard."

The pop-pop-pops of the 9-mm's fade away as we gobble up the hillside in the sixty-inch pace. Everything about Col. D. J. Willis says Marine.

"Came in back in 'fifty-three," he says. "Didn't think about a career. 'Lifers' were weird and to be avoided. They were the ones who assigned you to the latrine detail."

Willis went to sea school and spent a couple of years on a heavy cruiser, then another two years and three months—"I counted every day"—as a guard on a missile test site.

He put in for officer and was turned down; no college. So he left the service.

"My wife was pregnant. I had no money. I was really pissed. They didn't pay for the baby, of course. He's now a helo driver, by the way."

With nothing to his name but his little family, a part-time job, and a beat-up old Ford, Willis enrolled at Long Beach State, and got his degree in three years. Then he turned around and went right back into the Marines.

"It's not that I missed the reveille or the harassment or anything like that. But I missed the camaraderie. And the kind of people I trusted. All the time I was out I had the feeling no one was in charge. And they wouldn't let me be in charge. And that didn't make any sense to me."

He made OCS in 1960. He was assigned to Hawaii and there he fell in love—with shooting.

"We had a platoon on Molokai and I was the shooting officer and we got called to take part in the division matches. I remember talking to this colonel who had red hair and a deep voice and I remember the palm trees swaying and I was saying to him, I didn't want to get stuck in shooting competitions because it'd suck me up."

It did. Willis joined the Hawaiian Marine Rifle and Pistol Team.

"Now, once you get into this family of competition shooters, you bump into them everywhere. No group is as tight in the Corps as your competition shooters."

It is one of the best testaments to the Corps' ability to propagandize itself that just about every group in the branch thinks this of its own. But Willis's old buddies in the competition program would come to play a key role in the redesign of the M-16.

We reach the office of the colonel and are let in by an aide. "He's one," Willis says of the man at the door. "He can shoot the eyes out of a gnat at a hundred and fifty yards. Always has the coffee hot, too." A steaming mug is sitting at Colonel Willis's desk.

He sits down and quickly looks over all the paperwork that has been left there during his brief absence. "You can look around if you like," he says.

It is a huge office, four times the size of Gunny Ski's room, but it too is filled with the accumulated trophies of a life. Here and there, everywhere really, are plaques and statuettes and silver plates attesting to the marksmanship of Willis and his men.

On a long conference table that runs along one wall, a pile of reports and recommendations on weapons or weapons training sits in disarray. There are books and charts lying everywhere. "You all can look through it if you like; see if there's anything interesting. I find stuff in here all the time. Surprises the heck out of me sometimes," says the old colonel.

But the most surprising thing about the room is its John Wayne stuff. The likeness of the Duke is no stranger to the Halls of Montezuma. Your basic jarhead may not know that the actor George C. Scott (who played Patton in the film of the same name) is a former Marine. He may not know that Gene Hackman is one too, as are George Peppard and Robert Wagner. Most of them, however, do know that John Wayne was *not* one. But it does not seem to make a bit of difference. They love the Duke most of all.

Willis's office is a testament. There are photos of Wayne everywhere, eight by ten stills from motion pictures, small figures of him and replicas of one kind or another. There are film posters from *Sands of Iwo Jima*, Gunny Ski's favorite movie, and *Rooster Cogburn*, and a dozen more.

There is a John Wayne doll standing straight and two feet tall on a side table. It's dressed in the cavalry uniform of *She Wore a Yellow Ribbon*. There are the painted plates you buy on mail order and the bourbon decanters long since emptied, and there's a woodcut of the man, and a pound jar of "Big Duke" chewing tobacco. It's a kind of shrine, this room.

"I like him best in *The Green Berets*," Willis says as he sits down, takes a sip of his coffee, and in a dozen tiny fussy ways prepares himself to be interviewed. "My own experience in Vietnam," he warns me, "is somewhat different than the Duke's."

Willis went to Vietnam attached to an air wing. It wasn't exactly duty for a sharpshooter, but by the time the hostilities became "really interesting," the colonel had ranged pretty far from the rifle business anyway. "Far, far from it," he says with a sharp, rasping, razor laugh. "In fact, I was running O-clubs in Okinawa."

It didn't work for Willis. "I didn't understand what was going on," he says. "And I couldn't figure out how to steal any of the money."

Willis really wanted 'Nam, wanted it like the Duke. He didn't think it was going to last very long, so he decided to volunteer for everything that came down the pike.

"I finally got into it as a top secret commo officer out of Da Nang. That was no good. I had to keep track of all that crypto-message stuff with a war going on all around me and people grabbing at the stuff all the time. Everybody in Da Nang was worried about the damn Viet Cong except me. I was worried about an inventory!"

Again and again Willis tried to "get into the grunts." He was one of the best shooters in-country so the requests made sense. But that didn't make it happen.

"I wound up getting out of commo and into processing," he says. And that's where he encountered the M-16.

"The M-16 when it came in was called the AR-15. It had been originally thought up by General Curtis LeMay, who wanted something small and powerful for his Air Force, but the Army, which is the action service on small arms, got into the act, too."

It was a good marriage, says Willis. The Air Force's need for something small that didn't need a lot of "real good, eyeball marksmanship" dovetailed nicely with the Army's assessment of the modern enemy being only three hundred yards away and out of sight to boot.

"But there was a philosophical difference of opinion when it came to the Marines," who would also have to use the new rifle.

"Every weapon we had, going back to the M-1, we had used a big bullet in a big gun." Remember, historically, the Marines were snipers in the rigging, and later it was their marksmanship, born of long hours of shooting practice, that had carried the day at Belleau Wood, that had in fact given birth to the reputation the Marines enjoy today. It wasn't just some theory of ballistics that was being challenged by the advent of the M-16. It was the very stuff of the United States Marines.

"Bigger is better," Willis thought then and says now. "This was the first time since the late 1800s that we were being asked to shoot a smaller, lighter bullet."

The M-16 caused controversy almost immediately. "The secretary of defense, [Robert] McNamara, loved the gun. He was always for uniform weapons systems and this did that for him, or at least he thought so. Meanwhile, the president, who was John F. Kennedy, he hated the weapon. He came to like it later, when he had no choice, but at the beginning he despised the M-16, but for all the wrong reasons."

Kennedy, like everyone else in the military enterprise, was getting reports that the gun jammed in combat, that it couldn't be taken through the mud. Vietnam was made out of mud.

"That wasn't the weapon's problem," Willis says. "It was okay. Colt had made a pretty good piece as far as that goes. It took a little more care and feeding than your average GI was willing to give it, but if you took care of your M-16, it'd take care of you, mud and all."

The Marines, for instance, had far fewer problems with the jamming complaint. "Training," Willis suggests. The Marines put in a few more hours on weapons cleaning, and a lot more hours on equipment discipline. In the end, it didn't matter who liked the M-16 and who didn't. The war was in full cry. Industry was geared up. The papers were all stamped and signed. The M-16 was good to go, ready or not.

"By 1967 it was brought over in massive numbers and fed into the system. We solved the problems with clean and feed and so did the Army, and to tell you the truth it became a fine weapon, for the purposes it was developed for."

But it just didn't make sense to the Marines. "All through the 1800s and the 1900s our credo was 'one well-aimed round.' Okay," Willis admits, "artillery was making people keep their heads down on the battlefield so a lot fewer people were actually being rung up by one well-aimed round, but in the end of the fight, when you had to get up and take the position, you know, mount the rubble and send the bad guys home, it still had to be, from our point of view, one well-aimed round.

"I mean what's firepower, anyway!?" Willis raises his voice. A muscle plays high in his cheek. "More rounds got off? Or more rounds on target! Bean counters will tell you that it's the rounds you got off, or the total poundage of lead or whatever. Well, that's because that's all they can do—count!"

Marines, according to Willis, work on a different set of criteria. "Like the longbowmen of Agincourt, we reckon on hitting people on purpose."

At Agincourt in France, in the fifteenth century, Henry V defeated a vastly superior force of French armored knights by the skillful marksmanship of his men and the cutting power of their longbows, whose long, feather-tipped shafts could pierce a knight's armor and actually pin him to his saddle.

Nearly a century earlier at the battle of Crécy, this light "infantry" weapon replaced the unwieldy crossbow and marked the beginning of the end of the age of mounted men in armor. At Agincourt, faced by phalanxes of archers with longbows, the knights had made their last, bloody stand.

Willis stops himself and takes a breath to cool the blood. "The M-16 was an automatic weapon, and not a bad one. It could have been a special weapon for a special job. It fit okay into the jungle-type environment. Vietnam, Grenada, Panama, you can't aim at what you can't see. But even those places aren't all jungle. And back in the 'Nam, when the Cong were all around and the NVA was coming down and we were beginning to flood all our units with the piece, I don't think that even General William C. Westmoreland ever thought that the M-16 would become the 'service' rifle. And it did."

When you ask Colonel D. J. Willis straight out how he'd compare the 'Nam-era M-16 with its predecessor, the M-14, he says that "the M-14 was better," and then, after a pause, "and so was the World War Two M-1 Garand."

What Willis means is—for the Marines. When you are taught to engage at five hundred yards rather than three hundred, and when you, like an archer of Agincourt, are shooting one well-aimed round, the M-16, for all of its hi-tech, rapid-fire ability, has far too many shortcomings.

"You lose the ability to read the wind, to gauge the effect of ambient temperature on a bullet, you lose that pride of a group of men who are proud of their ability to put a bullet on a man."

What had developed in 1967 around the M-14 and M-16 was a classic apples and oranges argument. The question of which gun was inherently better than the other had to do mostly with your theories of fire and which gun fit the profile of the theory of choice.

"You talk to ten generals about tactics and you will get ten theories," says Willis. "Right now, if you talk about suppressive fire, part of our philosophy is if you can pin them down, if you can suppress them, then you can move and maneuver and infiltrate and all that stuff.

"The first principle is you can back the hell off and pound them with artillery and let air take over. Or at the least bring your machine guns in.

"But still, you're suppressing to get in a position to overrun. And eventually artillery pulls back and you have to physically take the ground. That calls for precision fire. That's a Pfc. with a rifle. He has to pinpoint your remaining targets. He had better know what he's doing, and have a good weapon to do it with.

"Hell," says Willis, "even the U.S. Army stayed with the M-14 when it came to using it as a sniper's rifle."

The M-16 was unquestionably lighter than any of its predecessors, no small benefit to a man carrying a sixty-pound pack, and it could fire a cloud of rounds in a heartbeat, but it wasn't a marksman's gun and that rankled Willis. It rankled all the Marines.

"We will accept no weapon, no standard service weapon, that won't let us acquire targets at five hundred yards. I know what the Army says. The Army says—what's the number—eighty-five? The Army says that eighty-five percent of all rifle battles are fought inside three hundred yards. I say bull. And I say so what if they're right anyway? What about the fifteen percent that are fought outside three hundred yards? You gonna sit there with your head down and your thumb where the moon don't shine?"

It's been more than twenty years since D. J. Willis took in his first M-16. Conversations like this still make him mad. That muscle in his cheek is working overtime now. He starts shifting papers back and forth around the table with no apparent reason other than to have something to do with his hands.

"They didn't want to spend the money on a second gun is what the problem was!" he roars. "They were saving on the money. They had what you could call a specialty jungle weapon here and Westmoreland goes out and he orders 150,000 of them!"

It is nearly impossible to look into Colonel Willis's fast reddening face and not want to play the devil's advocate, if only to watch him explode. So you ask him if the advent of smart bombs and laser-guided munitions hasn't reduced the sharp-shooting rifleman to little more than a romantic relic of a bygone era, hasn't reduced his battlefield role to that of offering himself up to be slain as human target material for artillery and air strikes, to be a counter, a body count number by which to judge the ebb and flow of the next great hostile action.

Willis counts to ten. He is the old guard, standing at the gates against the rising tide of techno-barbarians.

"Listen," he says low, "one well-aimed round will be the most important element of the next great European war, or, if there isn't going to be one of those for a while, of the next great war wherever it is going to be. And don't tell me about smart weapons." He takes a long sip of the steaming coffee.

"You know what a rifle is?" he asks, and then answers his question. "It's a gun tube that has a spiral groove cut into it so that the shot that comes out of the business end has a spin on it. That way the bullet isn't shot-putted, like out of a musket. It's rifled out, like when a good quarterback makes a pinpoint spiral. A rifle is a 'smart' weapon. It's a smart musket." He nods to himself. "No matter how you bomb and shell and strafe and fire, you're gonna have to take and hold the terrain, piece by piece. And to do that, you're gonna have to have people. And these people better be real smart riflemen who can hit a target, on purpose!

"Don't you guys ever get it? In Vietnam we had air supe-riority. Total air superiority. We could truck in ammo and fly in ammo and load the ammo off the ships. It's no wonder we got into the habit of just throwing the stuff at the enemy. You may not have that in the next war. You may have to keep your head down. You may have to shoot what you got and pray to God for sunrise. You ain't gonna be jerking off no thousand rounds into the bushes then, are you? You are gonna be damn sure that when the howling bastards are right up in your position and they're this close to making your wife a widow, you're gonna want to put one lead ball on one man, again and again, and just hope to God that you got more balls than they have. That's what a real rifleman does."

Willis stands up and walks around the room. He looks up at one of the John Wayne posters, makes as if he is about to say something, and then he doesn't.

"You want to know how we changed the M-16 into a rifle fit for real riflemen to shoot?" he says. You nod. He sits back down. He hands his spent coffee cup to an aide and says, "Get Jack Cuddy in here, will you?"

Lt. Col. Jack Cuddy, a smiling, open-faced man, comes in with two coffees, for himself and Willis. The two men worked together on the M-16 A2 and have been a team, more or less, ever since. In fact, Colonel Cuddy's new assignment, to Okinawa, is in the process of being "finessed" by Colonel Willis at the highest level.

"Back in 1967 I was on a wound team," says Cuddy. "We were studying wounds. The M-16 was an impressive wounder. The entrance wounds were very small, almost like a .22, but you look inside and it was all sinew and bone in a kind of pudding. You could dip it out."

Cuddy too had heard all the complaints about the M-16's inability to make it through the muck, but it wasn't until he ran into Willis that he began hearing the complaints on its inability to target a single round.

"We were getting the aiming complaints from Marines in the fleet," says Cuddy.

"And if it's coming from the fleet," says Willis, "you have to give it your best support. The Marines are a very small outfit and the generals are very close to the men in the foxholes. Everything we have we use to support the rifleman. That's what we're about. All this stuff that the commandant is bringing in, 'every man a rifleman,' well that's what we've been about for a very long time. He's just reminding us that we've been slipping away."

"In other words," said Cuddy, "when the question was raised by the fleet Marines about the M-16's effectiveness at long range, the Corps listened."

And in addition to the problems in the fleet, Weapons Battalion was also hearing a lot of negative feedback from its competition shooters. The Marines are justifiably proud of the worldwide record of their competition shooting teams, and problems in this area are also taken up with the utmost seriousness. Both Cuddy and Willis had been competition shooters and many of the complaints they were hearing about the M-16 were coming in not from their fellow Marines in the fleet, but from old friends at the shooting matches.

"In fact," says Willis, "we first attacked the barrel-length problem through these competition matches. We have access through these matches to three or four hundred men who are crack shots and who are firing over a range or a course of fire endeavoring to win a medal. You listen to them. You watch them. A guy will tell you the stock is too short, it doesn't lay right against your cheek. Or he'll tell you that his bullet sailed, or that he couldn't see straight through the sight.

"You come back from all these matches or you take in the reports and you begin to think about what your best shooters are saying and you begin to realize that they are saying the same things the guys in the fleet are saying and you remember that this is what you yourself thought when you first fired this thing in 'Nam. You got to do something."

From these reports by sharpshooters and fleet Marines, Willis and Cuddy were able to secure permission for an official Marine board to study the matter. Willis was a major by this time and had recently taken command of the Weapons Training Battalion. He had some say.

"We got around a big table like this one," Willis remembers, "in fact it was right here at Weapons Battalion, and we had a bunch of colonels and majors and a warrant officer who was a sniper, and we said there has got to be a better way than this; how do we make this gun better?" They talked back and forth for a week and came up with four key ideas for remaking the M-16 in the Marine image.

They wanted a longer barrel with a tighter "rifle," or groove.

This would send out the bullet in a tighter spiral and help it "ride the wind" better than it did out of the short barrel of the M-16.

They wanted a hand-operated gunsight that could be adjusted for distance and windage. The M-16, which was never really meant to be aimed, had a relatively fixed gunsight that was adjustable only with a tool. It was supposed to be a set-and-forget sight, meant only to "zero" the weapon, to align the barrel with the soldier's line of sight. It was never meant to be used to draw a slow bead Marines were trained to draw.

They wanted a heavier bullet, up from fifty-five grains to sixty-three. Here too, the idea was to give the projectile more momentum and hence a greater facility to "ride the wind." The muzzle velocity of the M-16 was high, which allowed for an equally high rate of fire and, at close range, the hellacious wounds that Cuddy had seen. But the light bullet it shot tended to run out of gas and wobble.

"The misconception about gunfire that people have," says Cuddy, "is that a bullet goes straight from a gun to a target and all you have to do is put the cross hairs on a guy's chest or, at the worst, lead a moving target, and then pull the trigger. But that's not what happens.

"A bullet interacts with its environment just like everything else. Bullets hit the air and begin to do all the things that other airborne objects do. They hook and slice like golf balls. They wobble and sail like footballs. They surf on air currents."

The thrust of these first three ideas was to help the round overcome all these nasty impediments to a clean hit.

"Then," says Willis, "we wanted to get rid of the big-burst automatic weapons thing. We wanted it rigged to fire a single shot."

Returning to a single shot would mean returning to the days of the Civil War. It bothered Willis and the rest of the Marines not a bit.

"Everything you put on a gun that's extra just takes more and more accuracy away from the pure, straight-line performance of the old-time, bolt-action rifle. We wanted to get back as close as we could to that pure kind of performance."

The Army didn't. "The Army is the executive agent for all

small arms," says Cuddy. "That's by congressional charter. So the task of changing the gun ultimately fell to the Army, but of course they didn't see any need to."

But Colt, which had produced the M-16, and was stung by the mountain of negative response it had received, and was reeling from its sagging sales, was willing to meet with the Marines to discuss how to improve its performance. They agreed with almost everything the Marines suggested, except reducing the M-16 to a single-shot capability.

This new interest by the weapon's own maker eventually led to the JSAP, the Joint Small Arms Program, in which the Army, and the other services, reinvolved themselves in a second round of study on the potential redesign problem. The Marines had made their point, and suddenly everyone was excited about the new weapon.

JSAP went well for the Corps. Except for the single-shot capability, most of the research seemed to appeal to most of the members of the board. At the very least, they agreed, it looked like a good piece for the Marine rifle teams that Willis was always squawking about.

Budgetary constraints being what they are, it took time to convince the Department of Defense that the ideas coming out of the JSAP talks ought to be implemented and put into hard use.

"Oh, we had a hell of a time," Willis remembers. "Once we had an agreement on philosophy, our job became to convince everybody in the political end that this was the greatest invention ever for inflicting damage on their fellow man—while they were off getting all hot about advance reports about laser rockets and death rays and Stealth bombers!"

It wasn't until the early 1980s, Cuddy recalls, that "we got to make the changes, and even then, mostly because the stock of M-16's was so old and it was time to buy new ones."

It still rankles Willis. "We readily admit that one truck won't do for everything we need trucked. One plane won't do everything we need to do in the air. One ship? Ridiculous. But everybody thinks that one rifle is enough!"

In the end, the Marines received permission to proceed with the M-16 A2 program. That's when their real problems began. Reality set in.

"We got the heavier barrel," says Cuddy, "but we couldn't extend it as far back as we wanted because you wouldn't be able to hang a grenade launcher on it. You know how thick the current M-16 A2 barrel looks? Well, it's that thick only part of the way. But it was better than nothing.

"The stock was another problem. We wanted to make it a lot longer so that it would lay better in a shooter's grip. But we were only able to lengthen it three-eighths of an inch. If we had made it any longer it wouldn't have fit in the gun racks aboard our ships. And that would have been another zillion-dollar retooling job plus another two to five years to implement."

The single-shot feature also failed to make it past the JSAP committee. The Marines fell back to a two-shot version, in which a pulled trigger would squeeze off a pair of rounds, and then finally compromised on a three-shot pattern.

"This'll of course come as a disappointment to people who watch *Rambo* movies," says Willis. "You know when they fly by in the helo and they're firing their M-16's and their M-60's and you can see the rounds digging into the dirt?"

Willis jabs the table every three inches or so. "Bam, bam, bam, bam!"

"Well, bullshit." He laughs. "We tried that in an exercise back in 1965 in Okinawa, using machine guns up in an OH-34. We were putting one round thirty yards apart! I mean this sounds good and it looks good but it just ain't gonna work in the real world."

Willis still bangs away at his "one squeeze, one round" point of view. You can tell him that it is nothing but a romantic longing for a bygone era of Kentucky rifles and so on, but he keeps on coming back at you with arguments that make a lot of sense. Even the limited three-shot burst is anathema to the old sharpshooter.

"Lookit, I got a target set up down on range one with a computer set up to it. Now you fire off a three-round burst at it. You're stable. You've got your arm in the sling. Two hundred yards, okay? No problem. Nice pattern, right?

"Check it out. The first round will go right where you aim it. The second round, depending on the strength of your arms, will go up and away to eleven or one depending on your handedness, and the third will go only God knows where. It won't show up on the target at all.

"To the naked eye it all happens so fast that it appears that all three rounds just have to go into the body of the target, but in reality, the jump angle of the weapon comes into play and once the first round is going down there and it's igniting the next round and the barrel's jumping, there is nothing you can do about it.

"Our argument was, forget about the *Rambo* stuff; if the three-shot burst is only putting one round on the target then you're carrying three times as much ammo into combat as you need. They didn't see it that way, though."

The final version of the Marines' M-16 has a switch that can be set for single-shot or three-shot. There is no switch for *Rambo*.

Although it is, like most weapons, a compromise of many differing points of view, the new M-16 is, according to Willis, "a very serviceable field piece for Marines." He is proud of it, even if he is uncomfortable being thought of as its inventor.

"I'm not an inventor," he says with a grin. "In fact, I'm just the opposite. I'm the guy who says this won't work or that won't work.

"I don't see into the future. But there's not many men can do what I can do, because they don't spend as much time at it as I do. That's why the Army has failed. Because they never kept anybody in this weapons training job long enough to fully understand it. I been here forever and with the good Lord's help I'll continue on here for another forever.

"There's no magic in me. I just know a lot of stuff, that's all. I'm a plugger. I'm in charge of plugging holes in people's thinking. A lot of people dislike me for that. They send up all these whiz-bang ideas about riflery and I shoot them down."

Remember Big Sig Jensen, commander of the Battalion Landing Team? Well, Jensen had his own ideas about Colonel Willis. "He's an old water buffalo," Jensen said, that night in the muck of Camp Lejeune. "They ought to thank him for a job well done and move into the twentieth century."

Willis laughs when he hears this. "There are people who move too fast. They got too many ideas. They blow hot and cold. But these people wind up having to come to me to see if this thing they're onto is going to fit into the sequence of events, if it can be trained, if it makes sense in the overall picture. It may be a tremendous idea but while you're testing it out they come up with two more ideas. They never stop. Jensen is one of those guys."

What those guys don't realize, according to Willis, is that "people have been playing this game of war for a very long time and they've come up with and discarded a whole bunch of bad ideas because they don't work. You're not gonna get some flash of insight that's gonna change the battlefield. You're gonna work on stuff and improve stuff and get there bit by bit. The M-16 A2 started in Vietnam, really, and you're first up here talking to me about it now!"

Willis knows where he sits with his critics. "Anybody who says to them, 'That's bullshit,' or 'That was tried two hundred years ago and failed,' well, you're the enemy, you're not on board. You're not in with the clique. Well, I'm the guy who people keep telling, 'It ain't right what you're doing,' or 'You ought to do it this way or that way,' and I say to them, Why don't you come out here and help us design the training? Why don't you come out and see what's going on, not on some training simulator but right out here on the rifle range? In the rain. With callouses on your hands from shooting. They won't come. They won't help no kids in the pits. They'll just sit around and bitch and come up with schemes and ideas. You think to yourself somebody has to do something about this, somebody has to keep weapons training moving ahead without having the works all gummed up by people with an idea. Well, one day you wake up and you realize you are that somebody."

The next day Willis was out on the firing range again. The rat-a-tat-tat of the M-16 A2's filled the air with the sound of the firefight. To Colonel Willis the song of the 16's conjured no visions of glory; it just sounded like another day's work in the fields of Quantico.

"The important thing isn't so much a weapon, and who did what to it and when. It's about a whole program. It's about a weapon and a man together as a unit. This is what's important. Right out here. Making it work, bit by bit, no matter what

kind of weapons you got, and no matter who you got to shoot
them.

"We're dealing with human lives. We're dealing with a kid
out of Iowa who's got a father and a mother, and they think that
we're highly capable of training him and putting him into
combat.

"We can't make any mistakes. We can look at all the new
ideas you want to throw at us but we can't make any mistakes
in an overall program that has served us so well for a hundred
years. If we screw up we can't just put another piece of paper
in the computer and work it out a different way. We got to bury
a lot of good young people. If what we're doing is right now and
was right yesterday, it's probably going to be right tomorrow.
We don't want to make any quick moves."

He pulls the ear plugs out, as if to be heard better, and
says, "Look at the mistake the Army made. Simulators—they
regret it now.

"Oh yeah, they said, we'll bring in all these computers and
all these systems. Well, they're a diagnostic tool and they're
okay for support, I guess, but they ain't the grace and salvation
of what it takes to produce a man.

"But seven years ago the Army comes to me with all these
ideas and they say, guess what, we can now go direct from
snapping in right out to the field maneuvers and we can shoot
pop-up targets, right away, just like that, because of the simulators. And I ask them, but what about judging distance, sight
alignment, trigger squeeze? I said, you're moving too fast. They
say, we can do it all on the simulator. Willis, they say, you're
standing in the way of civilization. Well, it didn't work.

"And you know it came to pass. They paved over all their
known-distance ranges and turned them into motor pools and
their rates went straight down. They got soldiers who can't hit
a stationary target at a hundred yards. Can't bracket by kicking
up dirt. And now they are coming back to me, right down here.
We got three hundred Army people coming in this weekend to
shoot on our known-distance ranges.

"See, whether you're shooting an M-16 or an M-16 A2 or
an M-14 or an M-1 Garand, eventually you have to lay out there
and sweat and stink. You don't get that from something that

hums and buzzes. Nothing I've ever found is better than actually getting out there on the ground and doing it."

Proud as he may be of the M-16 A2, Willis feels his real claim to fame will be in the new course he calls "transition fire." For Willis, this new program represents the zenith of the man and weapon complex, the creation of the twentieth-century Marine marksman.

"We knew for years we were doing extremely well in the 'snapping in,' getting them familiar with their weapons. We knew we did well at known-distance firing. We'd been doing that well for many years in the Corps. Where we were letting down was in the next step, the advanced schools of infantry." Willis decided they were missing a step, that some course had to be given that more successfully moved the Marine trainees from programmed fire to running around in the mud.

Inventing the TRC, the Transition Rifle Course, was, like the reinventing of the M-16 A2, a long, arduous, and very political process. With the advent of Commandant Al Gray and his policies of "warrior training" and "every man a rifleman," Willis finally found a willing ear and an open cash drawer of support.

"After all these years of pushing this thing, I get the right commandant and bingo. And I've got them by the nuts now. Now I can take these would-be leathernecks from grass week to known distance to transition fire to the school of infantry to combat, and nobody misses a step."

The transition course comes after all the static range programs, the firing line "lock and load" programs, and it works something like this.

"First, the Marine has to fire with the helmet, and the flak jacket, all his gear. Forty rounds brought to bear on targets that are only exposed for seconds. He loads a weapon, moves forward, fires on targets.

"No longer does he lay there for sixty seconds before he shoots. No longer is he comfortable. No longer does the coach come by and say, 'Come one left.' He has to mentally calculate his offset, just like in combat.

"And the helmet slips forward so he can't see. And the sweat is dripping down because he had to run a little. And his heart is beating because he had to jump a little. And the flak jacket digs him here and so he can't see the sight too good. And there's guys firing on either side of him and the shock is messing with his mental pattern. And he's laying on top of his canteen. And that's right, Marine, you better figure out how to adjust to that and still get your score because that's the same heartaches that are gonna happen to you in combat. And you don't even have anybody shooting at you.

"Now you see Marine marksmanship starting to come together." Willis smiles. "From the very beginning when he steps on the yellow footprints as a private until one day when he marches off to defend his country."

The M-16's fall silent. The voice of an instructor barks from the range tower. New shooters take the place of those who've fired. Willis scans their faces. In a few minutes he will scan their scores. He puts the plugs back in his ears. The voice barks from the control tower. Men assume positions to fire. Rat-a-tat-tat! Rat-a-tat-tat!

And so Colonel D. J. Willis, smooth domed and whipcord thin, stands athwart the gates of weapons training. In an age of big-ticket, high-whiz battlefield gadgetry, of guided this and that and electro-countermeasures that would baffle Edison, he stands fast on the concept of "one well-aimed round."

The Marine Security Guard is training men to shoot the 9-mm pistol largely because Willis found a way to let the guards walk their posts with chambered rounds. Gunny Ski, the recruiter who hasn't fired a weapon in many years, is able to tell his customers, in all honesty, "The Marines will teach you to shoot straight."

Private Watson, who stood outside Big Sig Jensen's tent and allowed that the sword is the best part of a Marine uniform, wears his M-16 marksmanship medal with a very justifiable pride.

"You say that Colonel Jensen called me an old water buffalo?" Willis smiles. He returns the plugs to his ears and shouts, "You be sure to tell him what I think of him." Then he turns to the firing line without bothering to articulate it. It isn't necessary. He just winks.

The colonel may chafe a bit at being called the father of the Marine M-16, but as Commandant Al Gray's warriors march out to meet their destinies, Willis is happy as a clam to be the guardian of the sharpshooter's reputation won by the "Devil Dogs" of Belleau Wood.

An Ice Cream Social at Sea

———————————★———————————

I t is autumn now, as the wheel takes one more turn toward a destiny in the desert. You receive a note from Lance Corporal John Hess, the New Yorker from the 2/4 Battalion Landing Team, with whom you had once slogged all night through the mud of Camp Lejeune on his unit's trek to their SOC qualification. He's a warrior now, one of Commandant Al Gray's best. He has pumped. The envelope is postmarked Spain, where Hess's troop ship has paused for a few nights on its Mediterranean float. The letter contains an invitation to the Marine Corps Birthday on November 10, a day dear to the hearts of all jarheads.

You call Marine HQ and inquire about following up on the invite. The chance, after a year of Marine watching, to spend the Marine Corps Birthday with the men of the 2/4, who were your initiation into Marine life, is just too good to pass up. But HQ isn't exactly sure how to get you there.

For one thing, they aren't exactly sure where the 2/4 will be on the tenth of November. The 24th MEU, of which Hess's BLT is the strike unit, is on active patrol.

Floats, as Hess explained to you that night of the long march, are what the Marines are all about. Here they pack themselves shoulder to shoulder into troop transports, move off to responsibility sectors like the Indian Ocean or the Mediterranean, and they wait, fully armed and ready to go, for deployment orders to go into battle, or to land in support of some ally, or to show the flag in a hostile area, or to rise to whatever the Department of Defense deems cause to "send in the Marines."

Of course, the Marines don't float around twiddling their thumbs. Floats are also key training periods and the Corps uses them not only to implement its best hands-on shipboard and landing training, but also to cross-train with corollary military units of other nations. By the time of his letter, Hess had already been on maneuvers with the Israeli Defense Force and taken part in a major "force on force" war game with the crack Turkish Naval Infantry.

The problem is that owing to the schizophrenic nature of the float's operations-training mix, HQ isn't sure that a recent detour to cruise off the Lebanese coast, suddenly hot again, won't have knocked the 24th MEU's little task force off its training schedule; and if it has, pinpointing Hess on the tenth, which is still two weeks away, would be a chancy proposition at best. They say they'll see what they can do.

About a week later you get a message, through HQ, from Maj. Dan Conway of the 24th MEU. Conway is the S2 of the MEU, the intelligence chief. He ran the war game that you and Hess played in the mud. Now Major Conway has taken his operations post as head of what he calls "the intel shop." In addition to processing crypto-secret movement orders and such, Conway also has the less enviable task of dealing with the press.

His cheery telex indicates his pleasure at your request to attend the birthday and offers a better than fifty-fifty chance that the USS *Guam*, which houses both Hess and the intel shop, will be floating somewhere off the coast of Tarquinia on the tenth.

You go to the world atlas and find that Tarquinia is a tiny Italian coastal town a couple of highway hours north of Rome. Indeed, the next message from HQ comes in the form of a telephone call that says, "We can't guarantee it, but if you can get yourself to Leonardo Da Vinci Airport early in the morning of the ninth, Major Conway says he will have two drivers there to meet you."

You buy a round-trip ticket with a return on the eleventh

and set out for Italy. You have come to respect the can-do attitude you have found everywhere in the Corps, but you're just a little concerned about the hookup.

Before Hess, your entire experience with the military life has instructed you that not a lot of operations go as smoothly as you need this one to go. You have had firsthand knowledge of the dreaded snafu and the still more irritating FUBAR. You have been in more than a few of both.

So, despite your growing fondness for the Corps and the "Marine way" of ensuring that things get done, you have pretty much written off the airplane ticket money and have drawn up an alternative plan for covering a Marine Corps birthday bash.

It is with surprise bordering on shock that among the throngs of Italian cabbies waiting at the flight gate in Rome, there are two young men who, though in civvies, are wearing their hair unmistakably "high and tight."

"Yo, devil dogs," you say. They both laugh.

"You the writer?" the tall one asks.

You nod, you shake hands, and you move off to a white Renault van they have rented. "Welcome aboard the Twenty-fourth MEU's white ball express," says the shorter one as you stow your bag in the back. "The trick now," says the taller one, "is to find the Twenty-fourth MEU."

You head out of the airport and take the autostrada north. The white ball express, named for the van they have rented, is composed of the slender Staff Sergeant Jerry Toche of Biloxi, Mississippi, and Corporal Timothy Swank, the shorter one, who grew up in Manchester, Missouri. They both wear jeans and work shirts. Their job is to run up and down the coast road carrying packages and people, mostly the Italian press, back and forth between training areas and helo drop points. They have been as far south as Naples and as far north as Milan. They are averaging, they swear, over five hundred miles a day.

As you drive north through Rome's winding traffic, the two Marines talk mostly about their white ball—they are glad to get off the boats for a while but the Renault, they agree, is "getting old." Then you talk about girls, their own and the ones they have encountered in Italy, and about the float.

It had started out great, they agree, but for the past thirty days they've been without milk or "good meat."

"The last couple of weeks," says Swank, "we've had nothing but hot dogs." Then he rolls down his window and spits a chaw of Red Man out into the Italian countryside. They have also run out of toilet paper.

They turn off the main road onto a narrow one that runs first along an ancient aqueduct and then down to the coast.

The "Med" is breathtaking in the morning, especially in this section of the country, where climate and economics prevent the narrow tidal sands from becoming a posh lido development. Here it is just the land, the ocean and sky, along with a few old houses dotted here and there, swathed in mosaics of patched mortar, where people live out lives ordinary to themselves but incredibly evocative to the passing observer.

"We're looking for Monte Romano," Sergeant Toche says, and Swank answers, "I don't have the map." They pull into a gas station. As Swank fills up the Renault, Toche buys three Cokes and the local atlas.

Monte Romano is a very small town, a village really, on a hill about thirty miles from Tarquinia. According to the sergeant, you will find the main element of the 2/4 engaged in a training exercise somewhere up there.

You get back on the road. You find a sign. You start climbing the hills toward Monte Romano. You find it at the end of a long pull. It is a tiny village indeed, little more than a square with a few side streets entering and leaving it.

The outdoor trattorias are just beginning to open. An old man at one waves a linen cloth across a table and places a bottle of red wine on it in a single motion. It is suggested the "white ball" might stop for a bite.

"Let's find the MEU," Sergeant Toche says. He had expected to run into it on the way into Monte Romano. Now that he hasn't, he is a little concerned. You are a package he has to deliver. He cannot just leave you in the road.

You stop in the little town square to ask if anybody knows of any soldiers who might have been seen around the area, but no one speaks English and your Italian is limited to several kinds of pasta.

The best you can get out of anybody is that there is an

Alpini base on the hill just behind the town. The Alpini are crack units that, like the Marines, specialize in quick, expeditionary combat. You get the idea that the townspeople don't care for the soldiers of the Alpini unit on the hill. You move on in search of your own crack troops.

They are nowhere. You try every road out of town. You take every dirt lane. You wind up at three different farmhouses. At first Toche and Swank laugh at the predicament. Now they are concerned. It is becoming afternoon. That's when you hear the wacka-wacka-wacka of a Marine Huey.

"Just keep your eye on it," Toche yells to Swank, "and let's hope to hell that helo's landing somewhere." You begin chasing the Huey across the countryside. But when you see it is headed for the sea, and probably back to the task force, you stop and make a U-turn that takes you right up to the sign the Alpini have set up for visitors.

"Maybe we should ask them?" Toche offers.

"How would we know what they're saying?" says Swank. He is really into the Red Man now. An Italian jeep pulls up alongside the white ball. Three men in dark Alpini berets eyeball you for a moment and then one says, in perfect English, "Hey jarheads, you lost? The sign's right there." He points to the Alpini sign and the arrow pointing up the hill. Then he says something in Italian to his friends in the Alpini jeep and then, to us: "I'll ride with you guys."

As you bounce along the winding goat path up to his base camp, Passarella, the Alpini, tells you about how he was born and raised in Brooklyn, New York. "Always wanted to be a Marine," he says. But when his father died, his mother decided to move back to the ancestral home in Naples where her family runs a textile business. "So I joined the Italian Army and went Alpini," he says with a shrug. "But when I'm twenty-one I'm moving back to the States."

"What are you gonna do?" Swank asks.

"Join the Marines!" Passarella laughs.

A phalanx of men in caps like Passarella's meet you at the front gate of the small compound. They are all armed with automatic weapons and hard faces. Passarella, who is apparently the equivalent of a pfc., is barked at just a bit. His smile fades.

He explains to you that the main element of the BLT is on a training mission in the hills beyond but that the base camp hadn't been told about any press coverage. "They're a little tighter here than they are in America," he explains, and then he is relieved of assisting you by a senior Alpini. He shrugs as he is walked off in the company of two more Alpini, then half-turns and waves. "See you in New York," he calls out to you.

Your papers are checked twice and a jeep is brought up. You are firmly, but politely, motioned to get inside. You roar off, bouncing across the dry, rocky terrain. You climb several steep hills and race through a couple of draws, and then you come upon a large concrete slab on which sits a small motor pool and a fairly large amphitheater.

The jeep screeches to a stop at a suite of slapdash offices that are tucked beneath the bleachers. "S2," the Italian driver says, and he pulls away in a hailstorm of small stones.

Major Dan Conway comes out to meet you wearing the big college grin you remember from Camp Lejeune. "Gonna be a fabulous birthday," he says.

Toche and Swank check into HQ on the field phone inside the makeshift office and learn they have a run that will take them all the way back down to Naples. They say goodbye with weary smiles and remind you that you will rendezvous with them again on the morning of the eleventh for a run back down to Da Vinci Airport. You're starting to feel good about this expedition.

When they leave, Conway puts an arm on your shoulder and tells you Hess isn't here. He's been delayed on a field exercise, but, Conway assures you, you'll be getting together tonight in time for the long march.

"What long march?" you ask.

Conway begins to giggle. "We're marching the whole unit back down to the beach in Tarquinia."

"That's thirty miles!" you say.

"Well, that's where the helos are gonna land, so if you want a lift back to the *Guam*, you better go inside and get yourself some boots."

A uniform is waiting for you; so is Lt. Col. Sigurd "Big Sig" Jensen. "Hey, hey, hey," he says when he sees you. "I hear we're gonna take another walk together. We'll have to talk about the Turks and how I beat their ass this trip.''

Conway laughs. "He only came for the birthday."

"Great!" Jensen says in his gruff but courtly manner. "Then you'll be dining with us on the *Guam*."

"Excuse me," says a gray-haired Alpini, a liaison man of senior rank, "but exactly whose birthday is it?"

"Everybody's," says Jensen.

You go outside into the sunshine and sit down at the edge of the bleachers, and Conway and Jensen conjure up for you some memorable birthdays past.

Conway remembers the one during Grenada. "We were at work twenty-four hours a day processing information in the intel shop, but when it was time to perform the ceremony, my people ran it off like they'd been nothing but rehearsing."

Jensen remembers several. He had commanded the Marine Drill Team and had attended a few of the Washington affairs. "They were all like a living history of the Corps," he says. "The concentration of former heroes and legends and past or present commandants was just extraordinary. On the ship of course it'll be much different, but a birthday on a float is special in its own way. You're in for a hell of a time."

It is getting on into late afternoon when you hike with Jensen back to his BLT area. You find a sleeping bag and a ground cover waiting. "We'll be eating and sleeping alfresco," Jensen says.

Dinner is the typical chicken parts and mashed potatoes served from a steaming insulated tub. You eat beneath a bent pear tree on a gentle hill and talk about the float.

"It's a lot of things really," Jensen says. "It gives us a chance to make inroads in high-visibility places. I guess you could call it showing the flag. Yes, I see it as a geopolitical thing, I see it as a strategic thing, I also see it as an opportunity to use different training areas to keep up our skills. The end result is that the ships are in better shape, we're in better shape, the Navy-Marine team is in better shape. And when we leave, our allies are in better shape for having maneuvered with us. Just ask the Turks and see if they learned anything about the United States Marines. We went force on force. Our guys against theirs. Our plan against theirs." He is interrupted by a sergeant who needs to confer with him about the line of the night march.

It has grown dark. Some of the men are already asleep. A single fire is lit a little further down the hill and far off you can hear the whine of a gasoline generator. Jensen says goodnight and walks off with the sergeant. So you spread out your bag and climb in and zip up against the gathering chill.

Dampness is the bane of comfort and the death of sleep. A chilly dew is all around you. You wonder if you will sleep at all. A shooting star passes through the belt of Orion.

The next thing you remember is a kick in the ribs from some helpful leatherneck. Then you hear the voices of the men in the dark.

"Get up!" they call.

"Wake up!" says the Marine who nudged you.

"March or die!" shouts another you cannot see.

Major Conway is up and about and dispensing his doses of rah-rah. "It's real," he is saying, "it isn't a dream. It isn't a fantasy." You ask him where Jensen is sleeping and he says that the colonel is up and long gone.

There are three or four fires burning now and several of the vehicles have cranked up. People are up and moving all around you. Some are dressing or brushing their teeth in the shrouded glare of the vehicle night lights. It is now one o'clock in the morning and the march is shaping up. The night belongs to the Marines.

You are stiff all over. It is cold. You brush off the dew and walk down to one of the fires to warm yourself. You introduce yourself around until one of the Marines from the intel shop finds you and tells you where you'll be in the line of march. You've stumbled upon the right fire.

MREs are handed out. These packets of mostly freeze-dried food are semipalatable when stirred into hot water, but you have to acquire a taste for them dry. You remove the wafer and the chocolate bar from yours and pass the rest to a man beside you. An order is barked in the dark. You line up and check the man in front of you for any loose gear.

"Forwaaaaaad!" a voice calls, and you move out.

You mentally calculate the time and distance. Since it is

now two o'clock in the morning and you will be walking thirty miles, if you march at a rate of, say, five miles per hour, you will arrive at the beach at eight. It seems a depressingly long way off, any way you look at it.

Unburdened by a pack like the rest you shuffle up and back in the line looking for Lance Corporal Hess, the man who invited you to this party. You find Major Conway instead.

"He didn't make it," Conway says. "They came in all beat up from their operation with the Alpini, so we gave them the night off."

The word is that Hess's company will helo in to the beach and be there to meet you when you march in. Hess's people have drawn the duty of setting up the seaside birthday ceremony that the 24th MEU had planned for the arrival of its marching troops. It will be the first of several ceremonies.

"We'll have the ceremony on the beach," Conway huffs and puffs as he walks, "and then a cake cutting on the *Guam*, and then at night you have the party in the officers' mess, and I think Jensen is cooking up something. He's been very secretive about it but something's on the brew for after the party."

You walk with Conway awhile and then fall back. Logic dictates that the inland must be higher than the coast but you seem to be marching uphill all the time. Well, up and down.

First the shins go. They begin to burn at the top of the ankle. Then the feet become sore, first in the toes and then all over. Then the lower back. The pace isn't killing but it is relentless. Up hills and down. Down hills and up. You observe no particular tactical silence, but after a couple of hours of this you get pretty quiet anyway.

You get to know your body during a long march like this one. Unlike the year before's stroll through the swamp, you find no gullies or brambles or snakes to engage your mind. You have no objective to think about, no aggressors to watch out for, no armored vehicles to duck in the dark. You begin to dwell on things that are better left undwelled upon.

That click in your elbow, for instance. You've had it for years but suddenly it becomes a loud snapping sound, each time you swing your arms. It's so loud you wonder if the others hear it. Or maybe it's just that you're so aware of it. You've become so aware of lots of things: the joints that don't quite mesh, the shoes that don't quite fit, the hand that swings too close to the thigh, the sound you make when you breathe and how it differs on the uphills and the down.

Up and down, up and down, your footsteps rattle up your thighs, vibrate in your spine, thunder in your ears. You search the sky for signs of lightening. It's impossible to gauge the distance any other way. If it's light, you're almost there, you hope.

Someone calls your name in the dark, or else you are just dreaming, sleepwalking. No, he calls it again. It is Lance Corporal Watson, the blond Oklahoman, the one you met outside the tent of Colonel Jensen the night of the big raid, the one who had just come into the Corps, the one who thought the sword was the coolest part of the uniform.

"How you doing?" he chirps, as cheerful as he seemed a year ago.

"Doing it," you answer. "How you doing?"

"My feet hurt," he says, "otherwise I'm great. I never walked this far, though. Not even in boot camp. S2 better have some beer on the other end of this."

The last part, about the beer, is something you didn't think Watson would have been caught dead saying a year ago. You rib him about it. "I'm not the same person," he says.

He asks you if you knew there was going to be a party for the birthday. You tell him that's why you're here, humping it in the dark. You tell him you're going to go aboard the *Guam*, if you make it to the beach.

"You'll make it," he says. Then he invites you to spend the birthday with him. "We're having steaks in the enlisted mess," he says with some pride and also some anticipation.

You've already accepted the invitation to the officer's mess so you feel a little awkward. "I eat on the early shift so there's no problem eating with me and then going to the officers' party," he says. Then he smiles. "I'm in the intel shop," he reminds you with a wink. "Everything Major Conway plans up, I get to read."

You tell him you would be glad to have a steak with him and he falls back into the ranks. First light is breaking over the

Mediterranean, a cerulean blue so pure and fine and as welcome to the eye as to the foot. You have to be halfway there now. You have to be.

Up ahead, on a deserted stretch of beach just north of the town of Tarquinia, three AAVS have been pulled into a line. A sound system is being rigged, and a podium is being erected on the center vehicle.

Behind them the beach is alive with Navy people. At first light they had begun securing materiel for transport back to the ships. By dawn the helo flights and the back and forth ferries of the landing ships had begun removing the stuff of the 2/4 from the beach. Pallets of canvas-wrapped cargo went onto the helos. Trucks and tracks were loaded onto the landing boats.

It is into this scene of ceremonial preparedness and beehive activity that you march, looking sharp and singing a bawdy song, at about nine o'clock.

You turn off the road at a dirt path and head into the beach area. You march past the ruins of an old farmhouse and follow the winding path until it stops at the big green expanse of dune grass. You can see the Med now and hear the gentle lapping of its breakers against the shore. You can see the helos. Hello, helos.

Colonel Jensen is up front leading the column. He snaps off a jaunty salute as you pass by the men who are standing at the three amphibious vehicles. Then, gilding the lily just a bit, Big Sig orders his march-tired BLT to "double time" in a large circle.

Sailors shout their welcomes as the marchers pass by. Marines on duty at the pallets stop and salute no one in particular. Then, double-timing full circle on the beach, the BLT forms into its constituent companies and stands at attention facing the three AAVS.

Several officers now mount the podium to make droning speeches about the Navy-Marine team and the need to keep it sharp. Then a tape is played in which Commandant Al Gray praises the U.S. Marines for being: "The best disciplined, particularly *self*-disciplined, fighting force in the world." Then a bugle plays and the morning's ceremony is over.

The marching and the standing at attention is at an end.

You retire, in ranks, to positions on the broad flat grassland where you will wait in "sticks" for the arrival of the helos. Men lean their heads on their backpacks or fall asleep flat on the ground. MRES are traded along with tired wisecracks about the march. Everybody feels pretty good.

Watson comes over and sits down. He is eating the chocolate from his MREs. "Been through a lot since I saw you last," he says.

For one thing, he'd lost his fiancée in the first month of the float. "But it's okay." He smiles, undimmed. "I met the sweetest American girl when we were in Israel."

Watson didn't care for Spain, which he likened to the camp towns he'd seen in the States—"all bars and whores." He liked Palma de Mallorca a little better, "especially the topless beaches." He'd gotten sick a couple of times on the *Guam* but said everybody did once or twice. By the time the "Dear John" letter arrived it had already proved a pretty poor pump, "and now what was a young, jilted Marine to do?" he asks with a wicked grin.

"It was really a strange thing but I just decided to go out and get drunk. I had never really partied before and I just thought, okay, this is it!"

He and some friends went out "to be rowdy in Haifa," and that's pretty much what they did. "It was the first time I ever got into a fight. First time I got totally smashed drunk. Matter of fact it's the only time," Watson says, thoughtfully.

"Anyway there was this waitress and we were giving her a bad time. I mean not really bad like grabbing her or sexual discrimination or anything like that, just teasing. And this girl invites us over to her house! Now I've got no respect at all for that but we went over anyway and she's got this cute friend named Sherry, little blond girl, from Pennsylvania. I spent the rest of my tour in Israel with her. We write now. She says she's going to visit me in the States this summer."

Watson has had some time to rethink his picture of the Corps as the knights-errant of the modern era. "When you first caught me, I was real wet behind the ears," he says, "and, to tell you the truth, I wasn't having such a good time. I mean it was my first time away from home and everything and I didn't have any friends I really liked and I was trying to fit in and everything. Now I've sort of learned what's going on.''

And what has he learned? "That there's no such thing as a poster-perfect Marine so you might as well stop trying to be one. I am a lot better than I was then. I'm a better man and I'm a better Marine, but I know that a lot of things I believe in, a lot of the chivalry and stuff, it's all for the posters, you know?''

Wacka-wacka-wacka. Helicopters are suddenly hovering overhead. Orders are being rasped through the swirling dust and men are lining up in their sticks. The operation goes smoothly and with tick-tock precision and in twenty minutes Watson and the rest of the staff contingent are touching down on the gently rolling USS *Guam*.

You are immediately hustled off the deck, Watson to the lower decks and you to the stateroom you're to share with Major Conway.

The *Guam* is not a new ship. It was built in the 1960s and began life as a lowly freighter. With boats as with most other materiel, the Marines are last in the funding line. When the order went out to build a 600-ship Navy, the admirals' thoughts immediately went to fast subs and big aircraft carriers and sophisticated missile cruisers rather than to barges for hauling around Marines.

Though eight brand new, high-tech, Whidbey Island class assault landers, and five aircraft carrier-like Wasp class assault ships were commissioned and are now on active duty, the bulk of the Marine floats are sailed on old war-horses like the *Guam*.

You walk through the narrow bulkheads, just wide enough for two men to pass, and knock on the door that says "S2." Major Conway lets you into a tiny room with a foldout desk, a small closet, and two narrow bunk beds.

"You're on top," he says.

You throw your stuff up on the bunk and realize with a shock that there is hardly room for yourself. Conway smiles and takes your bag and stashes it in a small cabinet beneath the desk. Then he briefs you on your day.

You can nap, he says, if you can sleep through the noise. "The number two helo landing pad is right above us," he twinkles. Then at 1430 you're to attend the birthday cake cutting ceremony on the hangar deck. Dinner with Lance Corporal Watson is in the enlisted mess at 1630. "You sure you want to go in there?" Conway asks, only half in jest.

You say you do, and that you also want to visit Colonel Jensen if you could. The major makes a note. Then he looks up with a peculiar expression on his face. "See if you can find out what he has planned for his men tonight after the mess, will you?" he asks.

"You're the intel chief," you say.

"I know." He frowns.

You sleep straight through the boom and clatter of the helo landings, as you suspect most of the marchers are sleeping through whatever is happening down on their decks, and you're awakened by Conway just in time to shower and shave for the cake cutting.

Showering on a troop ship is a unique experience. You run the water just enough to get wet. Then you soap up. Then you run the water again just enough to rinse. Singing is out. Any song you can think of is too long, and the line behind you is longer still. Shaving is the same drill, but in a sink.

At 1430, feeling a good deal better than you did at dawn, you take a place with the HHC contingent in the semicircle of men who line the walls of the huge hangar deck. Despite the events of the past few hours, each and every Marine looks ready to have his picture snapped for a recruiting poster. They come to attention in their ranks, and wait.

Off to the left of the hangar a Cobra gunship, broken down for repair, sits forlornly on the deck. Beyond the open hangar doors the Mediterranean Sea slowly rises and falls, accompanied by the low hum of naval machinery. A cool sea breeze blows through the ship.

Some of the sailors who have been working in this area of the ship stop and form themselves up into a work gang, at attention. A second group of spit-shined sailors walks in and stands in formation with the Marines.

A flag detachment composed of Marines and Navy men takes their post in the center of the hangar. The naval commander of the *Guam* is the first to speak. "I'm glad you guys are on our side" is the gist of it.

Then the cake is wheeled out, a big rectangular Marine flag, red on white, with an enormous gold eagle, globe, and anchor in its center. The cake's escort, four Marines in their dress khakis, cut sharp corners as they push and pull the enormous cake into position.

The oldest Marine on deck, a captain, and then the youngest, a pfc., are called out to have the first pieces of the cake. The ceremonial cutting is done with a shiny Marine sword. Lance Corporal Watson catches your eye and smiles.

The captain and the pfc. are given their small squares of cake. They take a bite and hand back the plates. They have rehearsed of course, and they know their roles. This cake cutting ceremony has its own page in the NCO manual. It's the same ceremony every year. This year it's in the Med. Next year it may be in the desolate sand dunes of Saudi Arabia. Every year, everywhere in the world that the Marines deploy, things stop on November 10 for the big birthday. It is one of the mysteries of the order.

Now the Marine commander of the 24th MEU speaks. "You may go to more memorable birthdays in terms of size or of ambience or of elegance or whatever," he says, plainly, "but I know you won't go to any one more memorable than this for being fitting. Here, on a hangar deck, with an amphibious attack force, and the Navy men that support it, this is what being a Marine is all about."

A bugle plays the "Marine Hymn." Hearts beat, chests heave, throats choke. When it is over, men shout. Then the assembly is dismissed. Within five minutes the hangar deck is empty of celebrants. The Navy men are back at their jobs. The Marine crewmen are crawling all over the lame Cobra. There is a new energy everywhere on the *Guam*.

"It recharges you," says Colonel Big Sig Jensen as he welcomes you into his tiny room. "It reaffirms the affiliation and the sense of brotherhood."

Jensen's room is smaller than Conway's, but he is the only one using it, and he has decorated it with some personal gear. A red Marine blanket he's carried since basic school is laid atop his issue blanket on the bed. A big insignia of the 2/4, "the magnificent bastards," is posted on one wall. A Turkish prayer blanket, picked up during the float, hangs on the other. Atop the locker, next to Jensen's several covers, is an Alpini beret. He explains the last.

"When we landed I was invited to a very nice dinner hosted by the commander of the Alpini training base here. So some of our drivers had already eaten their MREs and were sitting in their vehicles as security. But the commander of the Alpini was so gracious that he invited them all in for the dinner. We had some concerns about security but he said no problem. He'd put some of his men on it.

"When we returned to our vehicles, we found that two of our helmets had been stolen. By the next morning I had my helmet back and my driver had his back. I don't know how they did it but, whatever, they sent along some Alpini hats with them." The beret has already become one of Jensen's many treasures.

"The Alpini are fierce fighters," he says. "We've met a few good outfits on this float. The Portuguese marines are very good too. And the Italian San Marcos Brigade which we exercised with against the Turkish Naval Infantry. That was rich."

Jensen is burning to talk about his experience with the Turks. It had been, at least by his reckoning of it, another elegant Jensen attack. So, you ask him how it went.

"I cheated a bit," he smiles, "and sent my surveillance and target acquisition platoon well out forward, past where they were supposed to be, in order to eyeball the Turkish position. I had a lot of confidence in them not getting caught." He rips a piece of paper from a notebook and begins scribbling arrows and boxes depicting his landing against the Turks.

"With their information I drew up this plan that was based heavily on deception. My flanks were protected by the San Marcos people. We put two companies on the beach, and when they reacted to that, we sent a very deep heli-borne strike deep in their rear, way behind them, in a classic hammer and anvil. That forced them out this way," he draws an arrow. "They scooted to this position in the hills."

The second day, Jensen attacked the same way. Heavy artillery prepped a frontal assault by two companies, "and we sent another deep strike behind them and, right here, we got them again!" Again the Turks retreated.

On the third day, "After they'd seen how we were doing it, they said, aha, now we know how Jensen operates. So they figured out where the deep strike would land and they moved their armor over there to shoot our helicopters down as they came in, right here." He jabs a finger at a circle he's drawn amid the arrows.

"That's when we put together our decisive deception. We took a mechanized force and drove through the San Marcos area as if to flank them. At the same time we started our artillery to prepare the landing zone that they had already guessed at.

"So we ran a mock assault. We sent in empty helos under cover of smoke. Just go in and stay out of range. They said, here they come, they're doing it to us again. So they moved all their armor in and found—nobody. We had the high ground, we had them surrounded. They tried to back out and got jammed up against the river. It was all over. The umpires stopped the game."

Well-told battle stories weave a web that traps the sands of time, and by the time Jensen's Turkish opponents are well routed it is 1600 and you are late for your appointment with Lance Corporal Watson.

You hurry through the bulkheads and down the ladders of the *Guam*. You get lost on one deck and cut back through the open hangar. You had set it up to meet Watson at the intel shop and when you finally hook up there—he is out looking for you— the program is fifteen minutes behind schedule.

"No problem," he says, "I allowed for it, and besides," he smiles, "I thought you'd want to see where I live."

You do. And he's got plenty of time for the tour he'd planned to take you on. You plunge down into the lower decks of the *Guam*. The deeper you go, the more crowded it becomes, and the more stiflingly humid.

"This is it," says Watson, as you pick your way around some sea bags and arrive at a rack of three bunks stacked one upon the other. "I'm the middle bunk."

Lance Corporal Watson is spending his float in a thirty-six-inch space with a two-foot-square locker at his feet. And next to his rack is another and another and another, like stacks in a library. Between fifty and seventy-five men are living in an area about the size of a suburban living room.

"It's pretty compact," Watson understates. "We got these little mirrors at the end of each bunk, and a TV over there."

In a cramped corner of this overheated area a wall-mounted television is playing one of the twelve currently available video-cassettes to about a dozen Marines who lounge bare-chested or in T-shirts on the sea bags and each other.

"You're supposed to keep your bags under the bunks, but there's no room and it's hard to get to them there anyway so we just leave them around most of the time for furniture. The locker you use mainly for your watch and your money."

He squirrels sideways into his bunk to show me how it is done. "My home away from home," he says. Pinned above him is a picture of the girl he'd met in Israel. He pops back out of the bed and surveys the area. "It's really not as bad as it looks. We play a lot of cards."

Indeed there are card games going everywhere: on the bunks, in the TV area, even in the bathroom, whose three show-ers and six stainless steel sinks are otherwise pretty constantly in use.

"Come here and I'll show you my special place," Watson says. He takes you past a bulkhead to a door that is left ajar. You feel a thin breeze. "In here," he says, and slips inside the door.

On the other side is a small spare room with a torn-up couch, three folding chairs, a large eyewash dispenser and a Coke ma-chine. It isn't much, but it is cooler than the bunks and the air is fresh. "That's not air conditioning," Watson says. "It's where the Navy guys who work on the helo deck come in for their breaks. They have to leave the door open upstairs so it's always pretty nice. You can smell the ocean."

It doesn't readily occur to you that Marines at sea often go long, tedious stretches without even seeing the ocean, but the bulk of their time is spent in these rack areas. Watson has lucked into his special place. He has friends in the helo crew now who invite him in, share the Coke machine with him. "Other guys have it a lot worse."

You plunge even lower into the ship. Two decks down, and then three. The deeper you go, the more bunks there are to a rack. Four bunks per rack in the deck below your host's. Five per rack in the deck below that. It is like sleeping in a sock drawer. And the more bunks per rack, the more clutter you find, and the younger people you find, and the better bodies you find. These are the grunts, the line troops, the fundamental jarheads. They are literally shoulder to shoulder in their TV areas and their card games of gin, poker, and hearts. And it is beastly hot.

It is in a way a kind of nightmare hotel. Bare, dirty feet stick out from most bunks, none of them more than a yard from their neighbor. The overheated air is filled with a din of bad language pierced here and there by the blast of an unintelligible shout. Yet these are the men who marched thirty miles without a single Marine falling out, who sang as they double-timed around the beach site, and who snapped so smartly to attention at the cake cutting.

"It's all part of the program," Watson says, and looks slyly at you for your reaction. "Wanna go up and eat?"

The chow line has grown short while you sojourned and so you stroll straight into the mess hall. The noise and the aroma are an assault. There is steak, as had been promised, but served as it is in the steam-table style, it has the look and texture of boiled meat.

You walk the line and get your steak, your potatoes, your vegetables, your slice of cake, your bug juice—choice of pink or purple or else milk—and your slices of bread.

There are no spaces at the tables so you take your trays to a stack of cartons where several other latecomers to the feast are partaking of their festive meals. Happy birthday. Semper Fi.

Watson, who's been on hot dogs for a week, devours his thin steak with great relish. It is impossible to speak above the din but you don't have to. Words are no longer necessary. This lance corporal who had come into the Corps for its pretty sword has already, and very eloquently, shown you that what he had found instead was the arduous duty of the grunt.

Watson is right about what he said on the beach. He is not the same person. He has broadened his shoulders and winnowed some of his fairy-tale beliefs. But one thing has not changed. He is still proud to serve. You excuse yourself with some reluctance and head upstairs to the ward room and the officer's mess. As you leave an announcement comes across the loudspeaker of the enlisted mess hall.

"The Battalion Landing Team will present an ice cream social in the enlisted mess at twenty-two-thirty hours this evening."

There is a huge cheer that follows you all the way down the bulkheads and up the ladder to the next deck.

The officer's mess is dimly lit and martial music from a tape is playing softly. Most of the junior officers are already assembled. Some snap flash photos of their first birthday at sea.

Naval prints adorn the walls. There is linen on the tables. The places are set with paper party decorations and the champagne, prepoured, appears to have lost all its bubbles.

There are ten tables in all, each long enough to serve a dozen men. On a table to one side is an ice sculpture of an eagle, bathed in a blue spotlight. Next to it, a small table is set for the fallen. It is a full linen and silverware service, white gloves, a sword and a cover. An invitation to the party lies on the plate.

Jensen arrives with the MEU commander and the service begins. With the first toast to "our honored guests" the flattened bubbly is revealed to be not champagne at all, but apple juice.

Lieutenant Bolden, the officer to your left, says, "Oh, we never get alcohol. We're the only navy in the world that doesn't."

Lieutenant Grimaldi across from him says, "Whenever we pull up next to a British ship or a Danish ship or whatever, they'll come over here for a courtesy call but then it's always, let's go over there for a brandy and a cigar."

As the dinner is served the table for the fallen receives each course and is carefully cleaned in between. The toasts come faster now. The pilots are toasted for "either finding or stealing a pair of cami utilities to wear to the feast." The Navy is toasted by the Marines. The Marines are toasted by the Navy. The grunts are toasted by the airmen.

"You won't see the helicopter tonight, or the aircraft carrier," says Bolden. He means the rowdy party games that Marines play, lifting each other up and spinning each other around or "landing" each other with great running leaps on the tables; not just lieutenants but majors and colonels.

"This is too tight a group for that," says Bolden, "too buttoned up. And besides there's no booze so we all want to be in good shape for the ice cream social."

Jensen stands and turns to the single table and toasts the fallen. The room falls silent for a moment. Then the chatter rises again in time for the main course. The steak is the same thin slab of meat that was served belowdecks, but here, where only a hundred or so men have to be fed, it was grilled over a fire and tastes much better. The rest of the meal is identical right down to the piece of cake and the bug juice.

The table talk is mostly of other birthdays and other tours and other Corps topics. There are a few discouraging words. "I didn't join the Marines to be a staff officer," grumbles a lieutenant who probably needs a pep talk from the ebullient Major Conway.

"You'd change your mind if you were out in the field all the time," says the staff man's neighbor.

"I'm not married," says the staff man.

"Oh, that's different," says his friend. In fact, they both are dissatisfied and fall eventually to talking about opportunities outside the Corps, when their hitches are up.

Then the MEU commander stands and proposes the "Marine Hymn." These two men rise with the rest and sing "From the Halls of Montezuma . . . " in throat as full and heart as mighty as any of the men in the room.

Those who are in it for life share one thing in common with those who are in it for a hitch and those who are in it only for the Marine six-month reserves—love of the Corps. Every man here is a warrior and every warrior here is a Marine.

Jensen leaves early to prepare for his ice cream social but the party doesn't miss a beat. They are table hopping now and back patting. The disgruntled staff officer comes over and says, "You know, I've been living in a room with six guys and it's smaller than the bedroom I had when I was a kid. But we're having so much fun, so much silly damn fun. In the real world you wouldn't live like that because you're not forced to and the married guys are always at home with their wives. Some guys like to go out on a float and some guys don't, but I'll tell you, once you're out here, everyone has a hell of a time."

Four bells ring and someone announces, "the commander is leaving." All stand as the MEU commander takes his leave. Then someone shouts, "Let's party!" And someone else shouts back, "More apple juice!"

Belowdecks, in the enlisted mess, Jensen has rolled the sleeves of his impeccable utilities and is helping two Navy mess NCOs move three gallon drums of ice cream into place on a long table.

"They'll come in this way?" he asks one of the NCO's.

"Yes, sir," the man snaps, "and the officers can come in on this side so they can—"

"The officers will line up with the men," Jensen barks back. "Navy and Marine, the only guys jumping the line are the guys pulling duty."

Conway arrives. Jensen shows him the layout. "Nary too soon," Conway chuckles, "you got a line out there that goes halfway around the ship."

Jensen laughs. "Been saving this stuff all the way across," he said. "Got Israeli ice cream, and Spanish ice cream, and Turkish ice cream. We're gonna feed a thousand guys tonight. Let them in!"

The line hurries to the table. "What do we got here," says Jensen, and then he answers, "vanilla, strawberry and, well, mystery stuff. What's your pleasure, Devil Dog?"

The Marine says he'd like a scoop of each. Jensen digs in and delivers up three scoops. Music pours out of the mess hall speakers. Rodgers and Hart's "Victory at Sea." Jensen scoops out three more balls for the next Marine and then three more for a Navy lieutenant.

In ten minutes his three vats are exhausted and he calls for three more to be rolled into place. "Chocolate!" he cries as he opens the first one. Everyone begins to cheer and then, suddenly, the cheers cut out.

The "Marine Hymn" is being played on the speakers. "Oh, damn," Jensen mutters, "I told them not to get a tape with the hymn. This is the Boston Pops version; it could take twenty minutes!"

The Marines stand and wait. Jensen stands and waits. A few sailors in their denims sit and slop up their ice cream. Their chief yells out, "Hey, you yutzes! Get up and show some respect."

The sailors rise and smile awkwardly. The Marines are all smiles back at them. Jensen twirls the ice cream scoop in his hand. A thousand guys in a hundred armies would have dished the first few ceremonial scoops and then yielded the table to the mess crew. Jensen waits for the music to stop and then, before the cheers and bulldog barks die, he begins scooping again.

Watson walks up for his serving, reading a paperback novelization of *Rambo III*. He gets an enormous helping and moves off. He tells Conway that he just got a message from the intel shop that said Hess's unit had to miss the party and was being detoured to another one of the ships.

Conway apologizes to you for the foul-up, but it really doesn't matter anymore because you feel you've already seen and heard more than any outsider has a right to expect of the Marines.

It takes over two hours for Big Sig Jensen to exhaust the line of revelers. In all, he scoops out ice cream for a thousand men. His men. Three thousand balls.

"Anyone want seconds!" he shouts. It is, in its way, truly heroic.

The next morning is business as usual for the *Guam*, with the exception that they have to figure out a way to get you off the ship and back to Rome. They've gotten orders to move overnight so the landing zone on the beach has been struck. They say not to worry; everything's good to go.

At about five A.M. Toche and Swank call in to say they had finished their business in Naples and spent the night in a hotel in Rome. They are told to be at the abandoned farmhouse just up the beach off Tarquinia at 0730.

With the fleet already steaming away from shore, flank speed on the way to Palma, this is a very dubious hookup.

"We'll make it happen," says Conway.

At 0700 the helipad opens. Major Conway is waiting with

a mock salute. Over his shoulder, the Huey's blades are turning.

It is a twenty-minute flight back to the beach. But the pilot sees no sign of the white ball express. He circles the ruined farmhouse a few times. Radio chatter goes back and forth between the helo and the *Guam*.

It is decided that you'll be put down behind the farmhouse. Then, with a jaunty little wave, they take off and wheel for the sea.

A cool wind is blowing in off the breakers. The wind whistles through the swaying grass. The winding coast road is deserted; but only for a minute. Then here comes the white ball express, rolling around the bend and pulling to a stop in front of the old farmhouse. The Marines have made it happen. It is not a surprise.

As the white ball blasts down the coast road toward the autostrada and Rome, Toche and Swank tell about the private party they held for themselves in the little hotel room in Rome and how they'd sung the "Marine Hymn" together.

They were cut off from their unit; they were unwatched by their superiors. They made sure they had their Marine Corps Birthday just the same. Like Willis did at the party down in Quantico. Like Gunny Ski, the recruiter, did at his party in upstate New York. Like the commandant did at the Washington, D.C. ball. Like Lance Corporal Hess, who missed the *Guam* and partied on one of the other ships. Marines all.

The helicopter suddenly comes roaring back up along the road. It's checking on you. Spotting the little white ball express, it waggles itself in a Happy Birthday salute to the Marines in the truck. Then it flares and zooms off again to sea.

"Helo drivers," says Toche, "they think they're so cool."

"Tell you what," says Swank, as he spits another wad of brown tobacco juice out the window. "I don't care where the next war is gonna be, guaranteed those helo drivers are the boys that are gonna win it."

"Bullet" Bob, the Helo Driver

---★---

The Marines never say "chopper." They say "helo." They never say "pilot." They say "driver." So, if you're looking to train in a rotary-winged aircraft, and you want to be a Marine, then you want to be a "helo driver."

The Marines train lots of drivers for lots of different kinds of helos, but it's the guys with the "fighter pilot eyes" who all seem to fly the AH-1W, the Cobra Whiskey.

Made by Bell, this helo's shark-shaped basic airframe dates from the Vietnam War, but its constant upgrades in armament and in "smart" target acquisition have kept it the predator of the skies.

The flyability of the Cobra was the big appeal. The idea was to keep stuffing into the airframe increasingly heavy ordnance, more and more smart electronics, and bigger and more powerful engines in order to give it thrust and climb to carry all that stuff into combat.

The current product, then, is something like an old-time hot rod. It's a little rough around the edges, and a little touchy on the controls, but it goes like stink, and guaranteed, it'll get your attention.

When you ask the Marines for a demonstration drive in a helo, they recommend the Whiskey, and they invite you out to

Camp Pendleton, on the dusty shores of southern California below San Juan Capistrano.

You know you're almost there when the coastal highway starts offering up road signs that say, "Sudden Dust Clouds Next 17 Miles."

The turnoff to the training base leads to a two-lane blacktop. Five miles up that road is the first of several hangars housing the wide inventory of Marine Corps Aviation.

You pull past V-tailed FA-18 Hornets, air superiority fighters, and close air support bombers, which bristle with the latest fly-by-wire technology. You see A-6 Intruders that can carry tons of ordnance long distance from the most ragged airstrips. You see AV-8 Harrier "Jump Jets," which can provide close air support from no airfield at all. You see the heavy lifting helos and the big tankers and cargo jets. Then you come to HMLA 267.

The building has the words "Light Attack" painted across a wall. Behind the wall and up a stair is the ready room for a group of men who call themselves the "Spades." They are the Cobra pilots of HMLA 267, and their motto is "Anywhere. Anytime."

The room is long and narrow. Brown, fake leather seats line the walls like knight's hall chairs of old, now used for the pilots and their support crews.

Memorabilia hang from every hook. A twelve-foot-long "stinger" hangs on one wall. The stinger acts as the tail wheel of a helo. This one is comically bent. Below it is the plaque that says "Cherry Hop" and bears the name of the pilot who busted the piece on his first flight.

On another wall there is a helo skid with live fifty-caliber shells hanging from it. There is a plaque from the Israeli Defense Force commemorating a joint training operation, and another marks the 267's role in the Persian Gulf reflagging operation. "The Persian Excursion," it says across the top. Below, it lists the names of the drivers who flew that sea lane top to bottom. You are to meet one of them. He has been delayed.

You peruse the rest of the room. There's an award for having fired the very first smart TOW missile and the notation, "direct hit." There's another award for one-hundred-thousand miles of accident-free flying. Given your assignment for this day, you hope that record stays intact.

Right next to the safety award is a poster detailing the "Top Mishap Cause Factors."

Inadequate air crew coordination leads the list. It is underlined in yellow. Then, excessive sink rate. Then, failure to wave off. Then, power plant malfunctions. Then, gearbox failure. You go over this a couple of times.

Captain Cochrane shows you the name on the Persian Excursion plaque. There it is. "Bullet" Bob Brady. Right up there with "G-Man" Steele, and "Chemo" Reynolds, and "Crash" Wackola (glad we're not flying with him), and "Wart Boy" Cronin, and "Wonder Dawg" Pierce.

"You my crew?" Brady asks as he strides through the door and stands in something like an "at ease" position.

He's wearing a flight suit that betrays his slender build. He has fine red hair. He looks like a high school English teacher. But he has piercing pilot eyes, and the Cobra driver's grin.

"Hit the lockers," he says, "there's a flight suit and boots waiting for you by the showers."

Stepping into a flight suit is a bracing experience until you start trying to figure out what goes where. After a while, Brady comes in to help. As he tucks in this and that and attaches what has to be attached to wherever it has to go, you begin to catch on to something playful in his manner. Then you walk out into the ready room, robed as a Cobra driver, and someone says "good luck," and you realize what it is.

You are about to be indoctrinated into the mysteries of this band of men. There is the price of initiation to pay. They are going to play with you. That's why you drew good old red-haired Bullet Bob Brady for your maiden flight. Bullet Bob is cool.

He's from a Boston suburb, a graduate of the University of Massachusetts. He went into the Corps as an infantry officer back in 1978 because he had been in the Marine Platoon Leader Program."

A couple of years later he signed up for a full burst at Navy Aviation in Pensacola for pretty much the same reason.

He walks you out to the HMLA 267 hangar and then pauses to explain what he means by that.

"I'm thirty-two. I'm flying. I'm having a hell of a time."

By the hangar door, backlit by the southern California sun, a stripped-down Cobra squats malevolently on its pad. It is long and sleek, all motor and rotor. It's about the length of a Korean War–era Sabre Jet, but it delivers a whole lot more punch. With half its body panels off, this particular Cobra makes a splendid teaching tool. Brady smacks it on its tail and launches into the lesson.

"I volunteered for Cobras," he says. "You get picked based on your grades. If you get good grades, you get what you want. If you get bad grades, you get what you get. I got what I wanted. This is it."

He rubs his hands along the nose of the airframe, where the rotating cannon has had two of its barrels removed for work.

"I wanted to fly something that fought. Put it this way: I like the Cobra's mission."

Out on the tarmac another Cobra begins to turn. Brady raises his voice above its rotors.

"I flew the Cobra-J for four years," he shouts. "It had only half the power of this baby. And the Whiskey is significantly heavier. But the big difference in the Cobra Whiskey is that it can carry Hellfire laser-guided missiles. It'll also carry air-to-air missiles. You get into an air threat situation and you can defend yourself like crazy."

He starts pointing out the main points of interest. "Gas turbine jets," he yells, "two of them, 1,690 horsepower each. This little box here, under the ordnance pod, this is the brain. It controls the engine electronics. Just this little box costs three hundred thousand dollars, and like most of these other boxes, it's a swap-out technology. You don't really work on these things, you just plug stuff in and out. You get it all plugged in and this helo will run you about nine million!"

Brady glances at his watch and indicates that we have only a half hour to flight time. We go back up to the ready room.

"Sit down," Brady says. "I have to brief you on the flight."

"What do you mean, brief me?" you say, taking a seat on one of the brown, fake leather couches.

"It's a two-seater helo and each seat has a job to do. It's no real problem to fly it from the back, where I'm going to be sitting, but it'd be a lot easier if you perform some of the jobs my co-pilot usually does."

"Okay," you say, although you wonder what he could possibly want you to do.

Brady goes into his briefing. "This is a NATOPS brief, that's Navy Training Operations brief, and you are being briefed as a co-pilot for this mission."

Your head is swimming already.

"We will be carrying thirteen thousand pounds gross weight, with no weapons on board. The mission primary is an AH-1W familiarization flight. Our op area will be the Las Pulgas TERF, that's terrain flight area. We will finish up with a GCA, that's a radar landing, and we are good to go for a "practice auto rotation," a simulated two-engine flameout landing with a dead stick. Do you know what that is?"

"No."

"Well, don't worry about it yet. We're cleared to op anywhere in the Camp Pendleton area. Your radio call sign is Stinger two-zero, but don't take any calls. I'll do that."

Fine.

"Obstacles." Brady gives this a special emphasis. "There are high-tension wires all over this place. If you see any just tell me in my headset. Don't assume I see them! Same with any other aircraft. You are my co-pilot. Don't assume I see the obvious!"

The briefing is over. "Let's fly," he says. As we leave the ready room, a group of Cobra drivers are coming back from a training mission, talking with their hands in the way that pilots do. They toss off some jaunty salutes at Captain Brady and he salutes back.

"Anytime. Anywhere," says one of the lieutenants. Brady just smiles.

A crew chief is waiting at Brady's Cobra. He snaps off a very stylish salute which Brady returns just as stylishly.

We take our seats in the helo. The moment you put on the helmet, Brady is in your ear.

"Can you hear me?"

"Yes sir."

"Okay, basically don't touch anything unless I tell you to, okay?"

He explains that a helicopter is balanced in the air by three different controls that both complement and oppose one another. It's a little like starting a manual shift car on a steep hill, using three clutches at the same time. The better you balance them, the better you fly.

"This thing on your left. It'll move when I move mine; see it?"

"Yes."

"Especially don't play with that. The rest of your stuff, like the rudder pedals on the floor and so on, they shouldn't work but leave them alone anyway."

"Roger."

Brady laughs. Then he says, "Familiarize yourself with your cockpit."

Piece by amazing piece he walks you through it. It has a kind of whiz-bang video game feel. Gauges and lights for everything: fuel, rounds, engine out. Whoa.

"There is no ejection mechanism in a helo," he says in the headset. "You'd get sliced up by the rotor. Instead we have a system that blows out the window. It is right down by your hand. Yellow and black stripes. Unless we crash, don't mess with it."

Okay.

"Now we're gonna fire up. All your warning lights will go on and a lady will come onto your headset telling you about all the things that are gonna kill you if you don't correct them this instant. She's kind of annoying, but I guess she's supposed to be. Don't pay any attention to it. Everything's okay."

The Cobra coughs into life and begins to vibrate. All the warning lights go on! The lady whispers her warnings in your ear. "Rotor RPMs are low, single-engine fire, dual-engine fire, rotor brake engaged . . ."

Brady overrides her to say, "She'll run through all the warnings to make sure they're working. Believe me, this is the only time you want to hear them."

The crew chief down on the tarmac sends some hand signals Brady's way and he increases the RPMs. The warning lights wink out one by one. The Cobra starts to shake.

As the lady in your helmet calls off one system after another, Brady goes through a lengthy systems check. It all seems good to go.

"Any warning lights stay on up there?" he asks.

"No."

"Well, that's a good sign. I want to give you a last briefing on possible problems so you know what I'm doing if we run into trouble. I don't want you having a heart attack up there."

"Go ahead."

"Okay, if you see the fire light come on, I will not shut down and fight the fire unless I can confirm it in some other way. Unless I have secondary indications I'll just land and sort it out on the ground."

"Got it."

"If we have a single-engine failure, that's no problem. This is a strong engine pack and we can fly okay on one engine. However, it's hard to hover that way so we'll be doing a no-hover landing, straight in."

The Cobra starts to nibble at the air now, not lifting but skittering about on its skids. It wants to go.

"If we have a dual-engine failure," Brady says, "or a main drive shaft failure, I will enter into a rotation, take the pitch out of the blades. We'll drop like a rock but at the bottom I'll go into a real hard flare, nose up, to bleed off some speed. Then I'll rock it over to square ourselves and pull pitch to cushion the landing."

The idea of a dual-engine flameout is the kind of thing that puts sweat marks on the back of your flight suit.

The Cobra leaps up into the air and hovers at about twenty feet. Then, with the go-ahead from the control tower, Brady tilts the beast forward and roars off down the runway.

We rise into the sky at a steep angle, quickly leaving the safety of the ground behind. Once up at two hundred feet, you can appreciate the TERF area. It is a warren of hills and ravines and deep canyons. It is a playground for a Cobra driver.

"Stinger two-zero," says a voice in the headset, "you are clear for carrier landings."

The air is full of chatter that goes back and forth between the tower and the various "stingers" and "vipers" and "gun-fighters" and whatnot. There are several Cobra units working this TERF.

"I got those high-tension wires down there to your left," Brady says.

You look down. Son of a gun. You clear the wires by an easy 150 feet, but you never saw them.

"Keep alert up there," Brady says. A mental picture of what happens when a helo skid catches a high-tension wire zaps through your brain like a shock treatment. You're alert.

"See that cement deck over there on the beach?" Brady asks. Up ahead there is a concrete slab painted to look like the deck of a Marine troop ship. "We're gonna land on it."

The helo roars and we rise up and over, pulling a very surprising 2.5 g's. Just enough to make you uncomfortable.

"You like that?" Brady asks. "Let's try a dive."

He rolls the thing over in the other direction. We slice down through the sky, sideways, a roller coaster without tracks.

"This's about as fast as she'll dive," he says as you hurtle to earth. "You don't want to get into a negative g situation because the rotors will hang down and snap the mast. We're limited to a sixty-degree angle bank. We were right at that."

"Wires dead ahead!" you call out.

"I got them," Brady says. "Relax."

He clears them and heads out to the "carrier." Brady makes three landings and three takeoffs. "It's a little harder," he says, "when the deck is going up and down, and a lot harder when it's rolling side to side." He climbs off the deck and you resume cruising.

As you cross back across the coast road, a convoy of military vehicles is working its way south to the Las Pulgas gate. Brady points them out. Target of opportunity. "This is how you want to hit them."

Brady launches into a rocket run. He climbs a little higher, crests at the "perch," and just as it feels like he will come to a complete standstill, he slides off to the left and banks into a dive: 2.5 g's again, yet diving all the time. Body parts are being pulled in two directions at once. And you're homing straight in on the convoy. He pulls back with a roar.

"I'm gonna have to show you how to work that TSU unit," Brady says. The Telescopic Sighting Unit puts the gunner's eye right on the target for the TOW missile system. "We had that sucker, bad."

We climb steeply again and then roll off toward the hills. "We'll go up the canyon," Brady says. "That's where the fun is."

In two minutes you're over the hills and the ravines. Then you dive at the ground and pull up. Brady does some last-minute engine checks at ten feet, and then twenty-five feet, and then at fifty feet. These rough hilly passes are a bad place to have an engine failure.

"Then we'll just pop up here to see who else is working the area."

He rises straight up over the razorbacks and the ridge lines. "Don't want to come roaring around some rocky ledge and have a meeting of the minds with some other Cobra driver. Okay. Here we go."

The Cobra races off through the winding ravines. Dirt and detritus and general "ground effect" pound away at us, peppering the canopy and leaking in through the seals. It gets in your teeth. You're clearing some of these ravines with only a foot or two to spare!

"You want to keep your head on a swivel in here," Brady yells, and he blasts through a winding gully at a hundred miles an hour. "And you want to keep your tail following you as straight as you can. You hang it out in the wrong spot and you can come out the other side without your tail rotor."

You fly past the walls of dirt and rock. Bushes and trees flash by you on either side as you charge through your own dust cloud. At the end of a long hillock you rise above a ridge and come upon a tank unit.

Brady flares and dips back below the hill—it's called terrain masking—and offers up a quick burst of instruction on the TSU. "Okay," he says, "we're gonna sneak up and pop up."

We slowly pull around the hillside that gives us cover and

then pop up over the hill. You sight in on the tanks and let go a missile. In the real world of battle you would follow your laser spot until the missile hit its target, but this time out all you get is Bullet Bob's sound effect in your helmet. "Blammo!" Then, whammo! Brady's blasting off through the very bottoms of the gullies again, keeping out of sight.

"That beep-beep sound is only the low-level warning. I have it set for fifty feet," Brady says. "If it bothers you, I could reset it. Oh, hell, let's go for it."

He takes another turn through the passes, even lower! When you emerge at the other side of the canyon the feeling is that of being shot from a cannon.

We rise into the hard blue sky. The sun flares off the canopy and strobes through the rotors. Suddenly you realize that your flight suit is soaked through with sweat.

"We'll go for that simulated dual flameout now," says Brady. He falls silent awhile as we peregrinate back to the airfield. This takes a little concentration.

He talks to the tower. Tells them what he's going to do. They give him the go-ahead. He backs about fifty feet off the airstrip, over into the grass, so that if he fails he takes no one with him—except you. Then he climbs to 1,000 feet and cuts the power.

For a heartbeat the world goes silent. Then you start to fall. Not like a rock, as you had thought, more like a pinwheel. You are rotating a bit. The wind is whistling up through the rotors. Actually, it's sickening.

The lady with the warnings is all over your headset.

We know, we know. As the ground rushes up we flair, nose high, like a duck coming in on a pond, then we touch down with a bump.

"You okay?" Brady asks.

"Good one," you answer.

A quick shower washes away the sweat but not the tingly feeling. Bullet Bob himself seems a little bouncier in step as you leave the hangar for the parking lot.

"It was a good run." He smiles and ducks down into his silver Camaro, the one with the golf clubs in the back.

We decide to go out for hamburgers. A book is lying on the

front seat. It is yellow and bound in white plastic. It is a publication of MAWTS-1, the Marine Aviation Weapons and Tactics Squadron, down in Yuma. It is titled *Helicopter ACM Guide.*

ACM means Air Combat Maneuver. Dogfighting. It is something Brady alluded to earlier on in his briefing for the Cobra flight. You've never heard of helicopter dogfights so you ask him about it. He lights up.

As you drive downtown to a favorite burger joint, Brady explains this relatively new concern of helo drivers.

"MAWTS is our version of *Top Gun*," says Brady. "We started teaching air-to-air for helos there back in the mid-seventies." In fact, Brady has been a student. Air-to-air is something he believes in.

The air-to-air scenario is a main reason for the Cobra Whiskey. It is why, when the Army went for the new Apache, the Marines did not. Though the main mission of both helicopters is the killing of tanks, the Marines, according to Brady, sensed, in their war gaming, a potential for helos pitted against powerful Russian Hinds in deadly low-level dogfights above the battlefields of the future. The Cobra, with its strength and maneuverability, and its ability to carry air-to-air missiles along with the rest of the load, is far more able to handle the challenge of ACM than the Army's Apache.

For Brady, the advent of air-to-air helo fights is all but inevitable. "Look at it this way. Our tanks will be going this way. Their tanks will be going that way. Our helos will be trying to kill their tanks. Their helos will be trying to kill our tanks. It's only natural that we'll start shooting at each other just to clear the air for our tanks. One week into the next war," he says, "helo drivers will only be talking about their helo kills."

There hasn't actually been a sustained helicopter dogfight yet, although Brady alludes to certain classified information he has about Iraqi-Iranian encounters and how they turned out.

"It's just human nature to go after your counterparts, to go after the Hinds. Mind against mind. Skill against skill. Air to air. It'd be great to get into the 'six' [to get behind] of one of those babies and blow it out of the sky. You want to paint that little Hind silhouette below your cockpit. The kill."

But it's not going to look like the Battle of Britain or Midway or MiG Alley, Brady says; helo ACM will be different.

"True dogfighting, in the fighter community, is now shoot before you see. Our dogfights are gonna be like two blind dogs in a meat locker. Up close and personal. Like biplane warfare in World War One. In fact, it's not gonna be a dogfight at all. It's gonna be more like a catfight. Short and lethal. Encounters at four hundred yards. Even closer in areas where you can terrain-mask, like the TERF. Imagine an air-to-air shoot-out in there!"

You're joined by three of Brady's fellow Cobra drivers, Red Redding, Gus Gabbo, and Fist Faber. Fist is a tall, almost pale, intense-looking guy with an overactive Adam's apple. Red is short and squat and built like a power tool. Gus is a beach boy. They all have Cobra driver's eyes, and they're ready for fun.

"Fightertown!" says Red. Brady begs off. The rest pile into Gabbo's car for a lady run.

Wednesday night is ladies night at the officers club over in Miramar, as was well publicized in the movie *Top Gun*. According to the grinning Redding, "It's gotten way worse!" He means, of course, better.

As you roll through the parking lot looking for an empty space, attractive women, both young and formerly young, flow toward the neon entrance like fish on the way to spawn.

You pass several open parking spaces and when you ask why, Fist tells you, "We're looking for a commander so we can break his balls."

It's something of a Marine Cobra driver tradition. Find some Navy brass's private spot and take it. They find one, a spot with a checkered tail emblem and a squad number. "This is it!" yells Redding. You take the commander's spot and go inside.

It is noisy and packed and horny. "There's about fifteen hundred drivers here and maybe fifty of them are Marines," says Gabbo, meaning to watch yourself.

The truth about Fightertown is that, with very few exceptions, the only guys with a guaranteed ticket to heaven are the ones wearing the flight suits with the F-14 patches. The women gravitate to these guys like they have magnets in their undershorts. All of the rest have to shift for themselves.

Being an F-18 driver is okay. Being a Marine is less than okay. "The girls mostly think the Marines are a bunch of wild-eyed lunatics," says Fist Faber. "It is a hard-earned and mostly accurate reputation."

Huge models of Navy planes hang from the ceilings, big bright neon sculpture glares from the walls. A live band is playing in the main bar. But it is too jammed to move.

The little Cobra band goes out into the garden, where a deejay is spinning hits in front of a roaring bonfire. A pretty girl in a red dress slinks by.

"Boy I'd like to get into her six," says Faber. By the "clock" of dogfighting, twelve o'clock is straight ahead and six is your behind. Everyone laughs at getting into the "six" of the girl in the red dress, but when she turns round to scope out the source, the general agreement is that "she's a skank." So goes the mating ritual of Fightertown.

Faber explains, "You got basically three kinds of women here. You have your marry-ups looking out for a husband. Remember that a Navy or Marine pilot clears about forty thousand dollars a year and the prospects for good civilian work are good. You have your Westpac widows whose husbands are away on duty and you always have to keep an eye out for the husband's best friend. And you have your hard cases who are here for the thrill, every week with a different guy. Kissing one of those babes is like giving a blowjob to a hundred sailors."

A pretty waitress comes by and Redding hustles her very gently. "You married?" he asks.

"No," she says.

"Wanna ball?" he asks.

"Hey," she says, "what do you want to be when you grow up, tall?"

She takes our order and wiggles off. Red shrugs. "Happens," he says, and talk turns to great nights on the town in former hot spots like Subic Bay, the Philippines.

It's a strange room. Almost everywhere else in the service wearing your uniform while off duty is the mark of the jerk. Here it's a ticket to paradise.

Just make sure you're not tabbed a "backseater" by the faithful. It's the ultimate put-down.

"What do you fly?" a pretty blonde in pink jeans asks Fist Faber. "Cobras, babe," he says. "Merchant of Death."

"These guys are Marines!" she calls out as if to warn her friends about the table of men in civvies. Red pounds his beer bottle on the table. "Damn right—Semper Fi!"

Gabbo saves his drink, a vodka and grapefruit juice, from the pounding bottle and talk turns to ACM. Redding has just come back from Yuma.

"Been shadow shooting," he says. That's where one helo flies evasive patterns and his wing man shoots at the shadow on the desert floor. "It's a lot of fun."

Redding is real bullish on the subject. "Hell, a Cobra will go after the MiG's if it has to. We have the same kind of air-to-air missile as he has, why not? He's got all the speed but you've got all the maneuverability. You prevent him from getting a shot at you by turning tighter—hell, man, we can spin a Cobra! Then if he pops up and spreads out against the sky"—he shows this with his hands—"you have a hell of a Sidewinder shot!"

Fist argues that the jet would make only one pass at the helo and then make his turn well out of range.

Gabbo doesn't even consider this a dogfight. "This is an encounter. A helo dogfight is a helo dogfight when everyone's come to play.

"Let's say we're flying cover for some transport helos and the Hinds come in. Our job is to cover those transports because they've got riflemen in there and the Marine Air job is to support the riflemen.

"But the Hinds want those transports. Their job is to kill our riflemen. How do we protect our riflemen? We kill those Hinds."

Now Gabbo starts talking with his hands. "I engage at maximum effective range. I use the Sidewinders. The Hind probably uses its antitank missile at me. Similar kind of weapon, but mine's dedicated. Okay we miss. We're still closing. I can see a face now. I mean we're not flying at the speed of heat. We're doing one hundred fifty miles an hour. I try to get into his six. I climb. I want to get above him. He can't shoot through his rotors. But he climbs too. I wheel around. I must keep up my air speed. Energy is life. And I nail Him!"

The table erupts in applause. "You know what I mean," says Gabbo.

At about one in the morning you realize that F-14 drivers have gotten all the pretty girls.

The Cobra gang drags itself out of Fightertown. There will be other Wednesdays.

The Widow of Paradise

---★---

The Marines rarely use it in their promotionals, but a pervasive underlying reason to "join up," in this or any of America's armed forces, is to see the world. There are few spots in the world to see that are prettier than the valley leading to the gates of the Kaneohe MCAS, directly across the narrow, mountainous end of Oahu from Pearl Harbor.

The sun is a ball. The mist hangs in the mountaintops. The air is so clear that you can usually see the ubiquitous Hawaiian rainbow touching the ground at both ends. It is a United States Marine outpost that almost no one wants to go to.

"We have families on food stamps," says Yolanda as she jogs along Heleloa Beach on the Pond Road, at the northern edge of the MCAS housing area. She's in her early thirties, the wife of an NCO, a maintenance chief for the big CH-53 heavy-lift helicopters. Of all the fifteen thousand Marines, sailors, and dependents who live or work at the base, she is that most curious of beasts, what Fist Faber of Fightertown called a "Westpac widow," now four weeks into her husband's latest six-month tour of duty at sea.

This is Yolanda's second tour in Hawaii, so she is well acquainted with the problems, "but it's a shock," she says, "for the new families who come here."

Land is scarce here and the waiting period for a two-bedroom house on post for an NCO is fourteen to seventeen months. Living off post will run him more than $1,000 a month in rent. If there is no space in the school on post, private school for his children (a welcome brochure warns, "It is important to note that the quality of schools here varies...") will cost him $2,000 to $6,000 per child. If he buys a car, he pays more than he is used to at home, and his loan will have a provision that he pays a "balloon" sum or even pays it all off completely before he is allowed to ship it off the island for a transfer home. His car is subject to insurance rates running twice that of most states in the continental U.S. Even his pets, to make their way through the Hawaiian quarantine (the state has no rabies and wants to keep it that way), will run him almost $500 a head. All this on the paltry salary of a military man.

One way Marines make it in Hawaii is by sending their wives out to work. The official "Ten Pointers for Military Families Transferring to Hawaii" says, "Fill out SF171 for federal civil service employment of spouse prior to arrival (however, do not expect employment)." Work "on the economy" is almost as difficult to find and a lot harder to get to and from. Most of it is in Honolulu, and rush hour traffic back and forth over the pretty mountains is as daunting as the idea of buying a second car.

"I got divorced here," says Yolanda as she turns down the road that runs along the golf course. It is midmorning and the links are almost empty of players. Yolanda smiles at nothing in particular. She has an attractive, open face and dark hair, ungathered, that cascades to the towel around her neck. She wears a blue jogging suit and white sneakers. She is not slender, but well toned. The maintenance NCO is her second marriage.

"My first husband was a Marine, too," she says. "We were both from Texas. We got here and, I don't know, he was away and I was working as a sales clerk on the other side, and, you know how it is. We got married when we were nineteen and all of a sudden we looked around and realized we'd grown up different. When he transferred out I stayed here with the children."

In the intervening years Yolanda's ex-husband, Gunnery Sergeant Robert Orosco, has put in two tours in Hawaii. "He and my Henry get along great," Yolanda says. "They're together a lot. They sit around and drink beer and talk about the Marines—what's good, what's bad, what they should change. They are both in the air wing. Robert maintains FA-18's." Divorce is quite common in the Marines, as it is in all military service, and the good relationship shared by the husband and the ex-husband is not uncommon.

"The two children are both Robert's," Yolanda points out, and even though "Henry is a good and loving father to them, they spend a lot of time with Robert. In fact, both of the kids are in the arts—one's a dancer and the other is an actor—and very often me and Henry and Robert go to their performances together."

Despite the hardships, Yolanda loves Hawaii. "And my kids do, too. I don't want to move them."

A formation of helicopters flies overhead and Yolanda points and identifies them. They are not the kind her husband Henry works with. But all helo people are blood under the skin.

"We had a wreck here just a few weeks ago, right out in the shallows where the windsurfers go in Kailua. And all the wives run out to hear what kind of helo it was and what the squadron was. And it was the kind like my husband flies but it wasn't him. The man who died was a captain who was a bachelor. So the families can't help but breathe a sigh of relief, but it was horrible, you know? We watched them try to save people and pull them out of the water. They were just coming back from a mission at night and they went down.

"My son, my youngest, wouldn't go in the water for weeks after that. My husband, he just shakes that kind of thing off. Helo accidents happen all the time. You worry. First you say, 'I don't want to know when he's flying.' Then you get used to it and you want to know everything, so you can be prepared for whatever might happen. But still you worry."

The route of Yolanda's morning run takes her away from the golf course and down a road lined with white clapboard buildings. She passes the housing office and a small post exchange, then the veterinarian's block.

"Some of the wives are very superstitious. They make the same breakfast or they fold the socks the same way or they do all kinds of crazy things. My only superstition is not to be superstitious. He doesn't have any so I won't let myself have any. Robert didn't have any either. We say if you're gonna go, you're gonna go, and someday I'll catch up with you up there. It's kind of morbid." She laughs. "We never talk in front of the kids that way."

At the bowling alley two women wave from the front door. Yolanda waves back. "Henry doesn't like to bowl. I do. I go bowling a lot when he's not here. I need to." Not today. Today she needs to talk.

"Lebanon was the worst," she says. Her husband was in the area when the Marine barracks was bombed. "He flew the people in and out. I don't really know. We have sort of an agreement not to talk about things like that. But I know he was going back and forth and back and forth, seven hours a day; and I know about the Stinger [surface-to-air missile] and all that. What can I say? He loves his job and I just have to back off.

"A lot of wives talk to husbands about transferring to safer jobs. There's a little jealousy of wives who've got desk-job husbands. But almost everybody pulls the sea duty.

"We were married in a January and in that March he was gone to Okinawa for a year or so. If you count up all the nine years we've been married, I've had him home for about maybe a third of them."

She jogs past the mini-gym. "I go there a lot, too. You learn to keep busy. They try to give you a lot to do on the post. It's not that they don't want you going into town or anything," she says, and then pauses to think that maybe it is.

At the fire station several men watch her jog by. She is not hard on the eyes but they don't call out to her. It isn't the thing to do. "While on duty." She laughs.

One of the things Yolanda does is serve as ombudsman for the squadron. It is a nonpaying job attached to the post Family Service Center. Yolanda helps the squadron's many dependents in their dealings with the family service. She may get someone in for Navy Relief, or meet someone at the airport with a lei and some help in locating housing. "The hardest part is just to get people to come out of their own houses and away from their television sets," she says.

The letters *FSC* have a negative connotation on post. "If

you have to go to family service," Yolanda explains, "then there must be something wrong with your family. A lot of the men, when they go away, they don't want their wives going to the FSC. They want them to sit in their houses and button up."

So Yolanda helps organize picnics and softball games and activities that "at least coax some of these people out of their hiding places so maybe they can get some help. I'm a big believer in softball and picnics," she says. "That's how I met my Henry." Perhaps that is precisely what Marines away on sea duty are afraid will happen.

She jogs in silence along First Street. Military hardware is everywhere. Cami on steel. At the Flightline Snackbar Yolanda hangs a right and heads up B Street toward the base's main drag.

"You have to be very careful here," she says, finally. "The gossip and the rumors are unreal. You may not be doing anything wrong and someone comes in to fix something, some guy you and your husband know for months, and you even have the children there, but somebody says something and, wow, it is like a little Peyton Place.

"You try to tell people the truth and they become monsters; it goes in one ear and out the other head. Some people got nothing better to do than watch each other's back doors. Heaven forbid you meet a male friend at the bowling alley and roll a few frames with him."

She runs in silence for a while, brow knit, shoulders square. She runs by the commissary and then the senior NCO bachelor's quarters. Marines live a hard life, and that hardness is visited upon their dependents in many ways. "We have less dependent services than the Navy," Yolanda says, "and we have longer separations and more of that 'do it for the Corps' kind of sensibility about sacrifices. But we're not really in the Corps. We're just married to it; so maybe that's the hardest part."

Again she falls silent. Her feet rise and fall in a steady, rhythmic pace. She turns onto Mokapu Road and shambles to a loose walk.

"You can't get over it once it starts," says Yolanda, returning to the subject of the gossip. "If you go back and argue, you're guilty. You have to leave well enough alone and hope it will die out."

She stops. "When I was new, I let a guy into the house to change a light bulb. I mean, literally change the light. I didn't want to call in post maintenance for that. It got back to my husband. This one. So for getting the light bulb changed I had two months of heartache. But look," she says, starting into her jog again, "as long as I know I'm all right, then I'm all right."

It is getting into the earliest part of lunch now and the road begins filling up with trim Marines in their red shorts and yellow T-shirts, eschewing mess for a go at their conditioning. Men and women are out laying tracks. A spray sweeper has come by recently and steam rises from the road as the joggers flash past. A lot of things still aren't clear to Yolanda, including the motives of the man who came by to fix her light bulb.

"There are very strong regulations against adultery in the Marine Corps and they police it very hard. Marines can go to jail for it. But when your husband goes away, the men come around, one way or another. They find ways to make themselves available. Sometimes even it's your husband's friends. I never confront guys on that. I just pretend that I don't get it, whatever it is they are trying to do. And maybe sometimes I really don't get it.

"I don't hide, though. I still dress up. I still put on makeup. But if you get too dressed up while he's gone, wow, people will talk. Hey, I like to look pretty for me. I tell them, 'My husband's gone; but he's not dead!' I'm not going to wear black. I try to do the same things as if he were here. I'm not going to go roll over and hibernate for six months. Some wives do; they button up.

"Some other wives come alive. I don't mean they fool around, I mean they really start to look good. And why not? Now they can go shopping for themselves. They can wear what they want to wear. A lot of wives look better when hubby is gone.

"And I think about him, too, my husband, away, all alone in some place, liberty. I think, jeez, just don't bring back anything." She laughs. "Seriously, that's a problem, even though they're pulling in their horns a little these days. More and more when the deployments come back home you see a lot less cases of herpes and syphilis and whatnot. Look, it's a dangerous world now. My husband knows that it's not worth the agony. It's not morality that keeps him faithful, it's common sense. Before, it was 'You're no Marine if you don't fool around.' Now it's 'You're a fool if you do!' I guess it's like the flying thing. I really don't want to know what he does when he's away and he really doesn't want to tell me. So it all works out. You can get used to anything if you try."

This is one of the things that Yolanda tries to give back to the new wives, a calming sense that you'll get used to it.

"I try to tell them that it's okay to be lonely. It's not a bad thing. It doesn't mean you're a sucker. You know you didn't make a life mistake. It all works out if you just keep your love strong and don't be afraid to give more than you get.

"But it's hard to learn that when you're eighteen and you're a newlywed and you're away from Mom and Dad and your friends and your new husband is away. You know some of these girls got married because their guy was a Marine, and something special. And now they're here and everybody's a Marine and they realize that their guy maybe isn't so special. He's just a guy with a lousy, dangerous job, who's going away most of the time. But you have to learn to cope with that.

"Especially you have to learn to cope with the going away part. I'm a pro but even for me, boy, the last couple of weeks before he goes out on a pump, that's rough.

"His way of coping with not wanting to go and my way of expressing my not wanting him to go is the same, we fight with each other, over everything. I pack for him. I get his gear. There's so much to do that you're on edge anyway. Everything you say or do is wrong. Is the insurance paid? Is the car lubed? All the things I take care of without him even knowing, anyway. I just bite my tongue. And there's no romance. You're breaking away before you break away. I actually prefer it that way. It's easier on both of us. So then he has to give the teenager the speech: 'You're gonna be the man of the house, now.' "

Yolanda laughs grimly. "When he's finally gone, I'll be honest with you, I heave a sigh of relief, but, you know, then he comes back." Her face warms to the thought. "It's like sleeping with a new man. Not that there's no problem with the coming back, too.

"He's been away for six months and I've been the chief

cook and bottle washer and now he wants to just step back into his role as the boss and it just isn't that easy. The kids have changed and I've changed, sometimes he's changed too. And then you go drive off from somewhere, the movies, and leave him because you're not used to having him around. That happens! You can really psych yourself out. It's a period of adjustment. But the romance is great, as long as one of you don't do something in bed that you didn't do before. Nobody wants anyone to change. Nobody wants to think of what that might mean.

"I lost fifty-eight pounds on one deployment," she says, and grins. "I used to be fat. But I didn't have to cook for him for six months so I decided to go on a diet and I looked great! When he came back, he was astounded. He didn't like it."

According to Yolanda, the very first words out of her husband's mouth were "Why'd you wanna go change?"

He was jealous, she says. "I told him I did it for him. Actually I did it for me, but I did it for him, too. He wouldn't buy it. He wanted to know, who was the man?

"It took a lot of convincing on my part, a lot of making him feel secure. He thought, now he's going to lose me. I said, 'Baby, the easiest time to leave you is when you are away. I can do that with a letter.' That didn't work either. But eventually he came around. I think, when he saw all the other guys flirting with me, which they did, and me not flirting back, I think he just needed to see that and to know I was still there for him."

Back at the house, a modest little three-bedroom in the NCO area, Yolanda putters around putting things away and then takes a shower. Then she comes out in a sweatshirt and shorts.

She apologizes for the state of the decorating. "There really isn't much you're allowed to do in these places. You just keep them neat and hang a few things. In one corner is a collection of military stuff that can be described only as a shrine to her deployed husband. Her day's plan includes a stint at FSC, some bowling at the lanes, and tonight she may go to the NCO Club with some of her girlfriends. She sits down on a small couch and smooths a pillow as she talks.

"The club is tricky," she admits. "You got a lot of single guys and some married guys who come to the club all alone. Some of these people won't even talk to you the whole time you're there with your husband, but when he's gone, here they come. And it's funny because there is another bunch of guys where it's just the other way around. They'll flirt with you in front of your husband, like one of their Marine macho games, but as soon as your husband is gone, they don't want any trouble, any gossip or rumors.

"I go down with the girls to have a few drinks and to unwind. Some of them dance. I don't. Well, I have but not a lot. You dance with someone, even an old friend, and they all think, she's here to get picked up. They're on you in a second. They want to buy you a drink, you know? But that's just part of a ritual that goes you know where."

In the meantime the men are out being Marines, their days consumed with the pride and the passion that the job entails. Whatever they miss of home can be subsumed in the rocket run of the helo or the clang of the tank or the crisp footfalls of the line of march. What the women miss cannot be so easily replaced. Yolanda rises and walks to a window and looks out over a rather splendid Hawaiian sunset.

"Dancing is walking a tightrope," says she without a trace of guilt or guile. "Fast dancing, maybe okay. Slow dancing is a big no-no. A lot of the other wives will dance the slow dances with guys. But I don't know. What can they get out of it? A little closeness? And then they go home and dream about it, or else about who it is that they are missing." She lets out a sigh.

In a year's time she would be standing at the same window watching the same sun go down, and the TV would be broadcasting the bulletin that Iraq had just invaded Kuwait. She wouldn't have to wait long to find out what the U.S. response would be. She would get that over her personal phone.

"Robert called from Nellis [AFB in Nevada] about an hour later to say he was on his way. You remember those Marine FA-18's you saw landing on CNN, right at the start? Those were some of Robert's planes. They were the first to go and he only had time to make a couple of calls.

"I called the children down and they talked to their dad awhile. He told them how much he loved them. He told them that he knew it was going to be a war and that it was a just one and that if something bad happened to him that it was all right for them to be sad but they shouldn't be angry. He really didn't know if he'd be coming back."

Henry didn't go. "He had just gotten out and he started calling everybody up hoping to get a recall, but all he got was a lot of encouragement; nobody ever called. He paced around here for the longest time. We watched CNN. The night the bombing started I think was the hardest. He'd been a Marine so long and he really wanted to be a part of this. He was bitter, no question about it, he was bitter. But I was glad."

Being There

──────── ★ ────────

Lance Corporal Hess didn't go to Desert Storm, either. He had gotten himself into a study program and was enrolled in classes at a large midwestern university.

The helo drivers Gus Gabbo, "Red" Redding, "Fist" Faber, and "Bullet" Bob Brady, now a major, were stuck on a pump to Okinawa.

Gunny Ski fought the war as he'd fought Grenada and Panama, from a desk in a recruiting office. "When Iraq invaded Kuwait," he says, "I was in my office with a couple of other recruiters and no recruits," but the phone began ringing almost immediately.

"A lot of prior-service Marines wanted back in," he says. Like Yolanda's Henry, "They wanted to get to their units. Everyone wanted to get out to the fleet. Heck, *I* wanted to go! A recruiter. That stuff comes to haunt you at a time like this. But, you know, my wife, God bless her, she said to me that if I hadn't been doing the job I'd been doing then we wouldn't have the men we have that were out there for the buildup and we wouldn't be good to go the way we were. That made me feel good."

And there was more than enough to do at the office to keep Gunny Ski's mind off dreams of glory. "We also got a lot of calls from parents who already had kids in," he says. "They were worried. They wanted someone to talk to, maybe to get something off their chest, or hear a good word. Then we heard from a lot of poolies, the people we'd signed up for a later entry date. Some of them were scared and needed to be calmed down; some of them were hot to go and they were volunteering to come in. I tell you what; one way or the other, we didn't lose one. Yeah, the phones really lit up, here and at home."

At home, Mrs. Chelstowski was taking the same calls. "She handles a lot of moms. A recruiter's wife has to roll with the punches. She's real good at it. She talked to a lot of the parents. Most of them just want a kind word, really, and no matter where their kids are in the Corps or no matter where they've gotten to, the parents always seem to think we're their best connection to their kids."

In Wilburton, Oklahoma, D. L. Watson, a district superintendent for a local gas company, got the connection by mail. It came about three weeks into the bombing of Iraq. It was a letter from his son, Cpl. Daniel Watson, the one who had pulled midnight guard duty outside the command center during the raid on Carteret; who spent the time spinning dreams of sword-carrying knights on horseback; the one who sat on the beach at Tarquinia and waited for the helos to pick him up and allowed as to how he had "grown up about a lot of things" in the Corps; the one who had made it all the way to Desert Storm:

Dear Dad,

What's up? Not much here, just your average everyday fool. Things are all right. We are hearing about massive amounts of bombs being dropped across the border over in Iraq. I fear that many people will die. The ground war has not begun yet. So far so good. All my pilots have returned safely home [Watson was working intel for an artillery spotters unit], knock on wood. Things aren't bad here. I do PT a lot plus stand watch a lot and sleep some. There's not much else to tell other than I love you and miss you very much. Things are going pretty fast. I been writing my brother a lot but he never writes me. So far I have gotten letters from

grand dad and some friends and some guy in the Marine reserves
so how about you writing me soon before I think there's something
wrong. Or maybe I'm getting all excited for nothing and you've
written me and I just haven't got it yet. Things are starting to
warm up around here. In a couple of months the heat will be
almost unbelieveable. I hope I'll be home by then. I don't know
what else to write because this place is pretty boring and I really
can't write about the work I do so why don't you write me. I love
you. Best luck to us all.

"I'm not much of a writer," the elder Watson says. "I guess
that's why he was ribbing me about not getting any mail from
me." He smooths out the letter, refolds it, and replaces it in the
envelope.

"When he got the call to go over there, I was out checking
on some people in the field. He called me at work. So coming
into the office I started thinking, what in the world does a dad
tell a son that's fixing to go to war and he may never see him
again? I mean all you can do is tell him to trust in God and that
you love him and that he'll be okay.

"And it turned out my son did most of the talking. He
wanted me to know that he loved me and that any differences
that we may have had in the past didn't mean anything. And of
course I already knew that. And I was thinking, what if he died
over there? It's really something having a talk like this. So I just
told him I loved him and to be careful.

"I talked it over with my boss, later. He's an ex-Marine
himself and he said there isn't much else you can say. He asked
me if I was proud. I said, yeah."

Watson stops in his reminiscence. He smooths out the envelope. Then his hands go to his eyes in a futile effort to push
back a tear. "But I can't be proud of anything," he blurts out,
"until I have him back in these arms again."

Three months later young Daniel Watson, Marine veteran
of Desert Storm, was indeed back in his father's arms. They
laughed, and they partied, and they had all their friends and
relatives over for a series of dinners. There was nothing unique
or special about the celebrations; they resonated with that heart-
strong feeling of millions of similar affairs that have taken place

since the first time man took up arms against man. The war is over!

Daniel Watson, now dressed in a pair of shorts and a Marine Corps T-shirt, sits in his dad's big beige recliner in the living room and tells his first war stories.

"We didn't know which units were going to go and which weren't. Certain units went and others didn't. You just had to wonder. I always wanted to do my job, you know? I always wanted to know what it would be like when everything was on the line. I didn't want to go. I didn't want the war to start. But I wanted to be there if we were going to fight. Not that I wanted to be glorious in battle or like that. Just, if something was going on, I wanted to be a part of it, too. There were a lot of different attitudes in my unit. Some guys were excited, some were scared. But morale was good. We were ready.

"Being in intel section we heard to the positive effect that we were going, no question, but we weren't positive until about three hours later when the colonel called a formation and told us it was real. He said, 'Marines, we've been given the order to deploy to Operation Desert Shield,' and that was about it. It wasn't an in-depth talk and it wasn't a pep talk. It was just, 'Go!'

"I wasn't scared and I wasn't gung ho. I used to get scared when I went out on pumps before. I was always afraid that I'd go away and never see America again. But, then, I also used to get a little gung ho too. But for Desert Storm I wasn't either of those. I was just—ready. I don't know if you call that growing up or good training or just getting used to it or what. But I was good to go."

In January, just before bombing commenced, Corporal Watson walked across the tarmac at the airport, loaded his gear into a big green C-5 transport, and took off for what to him seemed like the end of the world, the wrong end.

"I remember I was on my way to the plane and looking at the grass and the trees and I really thought, hey, this could be the last time I ever see green stuff. And it really bothered me that any one person anywhere can cause so much harm that we would have to take as many people away from their homes as we did to deal with Saddam Hussein. It just amazes me how people can be going along, living their life and being happy, and somebody can just come along and screw it all up."

The C-5 landed in Jubayl Airport in Saudi Arabia, a town which would become Watson's home for the next five months.

"Saudi Arabia is the most desolate country I have ever been to. There are no trees. Sand as far as the eye can see. Of course there are some palm trees, but, gee. I'm a small town boy from Oklahoma. Where was the grass and the cats and dogs, and the people, and the pastures with cows? Sand, miles and miles of sand. I don't mean to be unkind to a whole country, but it was depressing.

"We had billets in the Jubayl soccer stadium. Tents on the field. Offices in the stadium itself. This way you could look out over the airfield. I could see our OV-10's taking off and landing. We fixed it up as best we could. We built shelving and desks and tables and whatnot. We had a TV table for CNN. One of the guys who was a carpenter back in the real world built a rocking chair out of packing scrap. That was a pretty popular item."

Watson was on station only a week or so when the bombs began to fall.

"Again, like back in North Carolina, being in intel meant I knew the bombing was about to start a little bit before everyone else. A couple of hours at least. So we are in the ready room, you know, getting ready, and I'm getting real tired, so I tell one of the corporals that I'm gonna catch a little nap before the war starts.

"So, here I am in my rack and the guy wakes me and he says 'Hey Watson, they're bombing,' and I say, 'Okay,' and I go back to sleep. About ten, fifteen minutes later the same guy is shaking me awake and the lights are out and everyone is yelling and he shouts at me to get up because we are under a Scud attack and they think it's chemical weapons!

"I leap out of bed and start putting on my gear. But there's this woman Marine who's lost a contact lens; someone has kicked over her little jar in the dark. So picture this scene in pitch blackness with flashlights on trying to find a contact lens and get our gear on at the same time and here come the Scuds. I about shit a brick. But we got it all done. You'd be amazed how the Marine Corps boot camp really prepares you for hurrying up without screwing up."

The Scuds flew overhead and on to Riyadh. "We were never actually hit by any Scuds, and, as we know now, none of the Scuds carried any chemical or biological weapons. But I'll tell you what; that first night's alarm sure got your attention."

The next morning it was strictly business as usual in the military trade. Watson's job is partly classified, but if you summon up a picture of the briefing tents in the old World War II films about "bomber command" and such, then you might sketch Corporal Watson into it as one of the guys with the charts and the pointers.

"What I was doing in the OV-10 unit was mostly briefing the pilots. I briefed them on air threats in their area and missile system threats and triple-A [antiaircraft] systems. You wait for the message traffic to come in from the field and you mark up the maps before the pilot gets ready to go on his flight to tell him where the activity is. Tell him where it's really dangerous. Try to figure out the patterns of the missiles and the air defense. I can't tell you much more about how we do it, but you really do get close to the pilots. You're the last person they see before they go up."

From Watson's point of view, the Iraqi air defenses were "a joke." But they were not without effect. "Even jokesters make a lucky hit now and again. So when your guys are out, you check their ETAs and you scan the sky."

One day one of Watson's two-seater OV-10's didn't come back. "It was the second day of the ground war. I had told the crew that there wasn't a lot of defensive stuff left out there but we still had some lone shooters around who'd try to kill them if they got the chance. I told them to be careful about this and that and then they took off.

"When my watch was over I checked the board to see who I still had out and it was them. Okay, I got relieved by a gunny and I went down to do some PT. And I'm running around a track when I hear a WM say we've lost a crew. I had a bad feeling about it.

"I ran off the track. I ran to the stadium. I ran up three

flights of steps to our office. Well, the gunny had the face on already. He said we'd lost my guys. Just north of the border. One chute. That meant that one was most likely still alive and the other was dead. And that's just how it turned out. One guy was captured and released after the war, the other guy, well. . . I didn't sleep that night. I briefed them. I missed something. Maybe it was something I didn't know about, who knows? I wished it was me instead of them."

Watson is still dealing with the responsibility he feels over losing a team he had briefed. His guess is that he will deal with it for some time. Casualties of war come in all shapes and sizes. Some wounds aren't visible to the naked eye.

"I still believe in the Marine Corps myth," Cpl. Daniel Watson says, "the sword and the shield thing. But I know some things now I didn't know before. I don't think the Marine Corps is for everybody. I mean I came in to be the world's greatest Marine, but I'm not going to reenlist. I'm getting out. I've seen the business of killing. I'm going to go to college for premed and I'm going to be a doctor. I'll always be a Marine. But this chapter of my life has come to a close.

"But there'll be other guys to take my place. There will always be a Marine Corps. You know why? Because we are something different. We are the elite of the elite. There is something about a Marine. We do more things with less money. We go further. We do everything we're asked to do and we do it now and we don't complain. There's just too much honor and too much tradition here to throw away. That kind of stuff should never be allowed to die. The Army does a lot of things very well, but we're always overseas doing something. People take a lot of comfort knowing that there are Marines. People like to see us coming ashore."

In his Connecticut office, Gunny Ski ruminates about this. "But did we come ashore?" he asks. It's that malaise again. That feeling of not being wanted. "Waiting for that amphibious assault was like dropping your shoes and not hearing them hit the floor. Marines have a certain amount of pride in the amphibious operation. It's what we are. I was a little scared about what might happen in a shore raid. The Iraqis had a lot of firepower on that beach. But when it didn't happen, hey, I was down."

Herbert Newman, the "former" of Iwo Jima, disagrees. "That beach was too heavily defended to attack," he says. "It would have been crazy to go in that way. Yeah, Iwo Jima was a heavily defended beach, too, but that was the only way we could get in there! In Kuwait we had better options.

"All those people who weep and wail about amphibious operations, they just don't understand," Newman cries. "We're not going to raid Gallipoli! You probably couldn't do it anyway, but the point is the Marine Corps isn't going to be called on to do it!"

They were called on for something very different in Desert Storm, and they did it very well. "Yeah, I felt a lot better when I heard General Schwarzkopf's briefing after the war," says Gunny Ski. "It feels good to hear an Army guy saying things like that about the Marines."

In describing the first hours of battle against the dug-in forces of the Iraqi army, what General Schwarzkopf told the press in Riyadh was this:

> At four o'clock in the morning, the Marines, the First Marine Division and the Second Marine Division, launched attacks through the barrier system . . . I can't say enough about the two Marine divisions. If I use words like *brilliant* it would really be an underdescription of the absolutely superb job they did in breaching the so-called impenetrable barrier. It was a classic, absolutely classic, military breaching of a very, very tough minefield, barbed wire, fire trenches type area. They went through the first barrier like it was water. They went across into the second barrier line even though they were under artillery fire. They continued to open up that breach until they had both divisions streaming through. Absolutely superb operation, textbook, and I think it will be studied for many, many years to come.

The Marines may not have come from the sea as Gunny Ski had wanted, as they had come in other wars. They may not have stormed the beaches. But in Desert Storm they were, as always, "first to fight."

The first artillery exchanges with Iraqi gunners were Marine artillery exchanges. The first wounded were Marine wounded. The first major ground battle, for the small town of Khafji, was a Marine operation. The first American force into Kuwait City was a Marine force. The first Purple Heart was won by a Navy Medical Corpsman—for a wound he received while tending a fallen Marine. And then there's this story General Schwarzkopf did *not* relate in his briefing.

There were many small-unit probes, perimeter-scouting and commando-recon probes in the days before the ground war, but there was one that made all the difference. Using their "mission pull" style of combat, the commander of the Marine Corps' 1st Division, Maj. Gen. Mike Myatt, interpreted General Schwarzkopf's recon orders loosely enough to send two task forces, three thousand strong, twenty kilometers inside Kuwait, two full days before the launching of the ground war!

When Schwarzkopf, at a briefing on G-Day (which was the name given to the commencement of the ground campaign), gave instructions to commanders to conduct their recon so as to "do nothing that is irreversible," Myatt had to laugh.

"I had Task Force Grizzly and Task Force Taro sitting twelve miles behind the enemy lines."

When you think of the Marines and the cami and the rope ladders over the sides of ships and the storming of the sand wall beaches of the South Pacific, you may not think about the Marines as also being "sappers" and engineers. But then you would also not be thinking about the Marines in the way Al Gray was thinking about them. You would not be thinking about flexibility.

But it was the three thousand Marines of Grizzly and Taro who fanned out along the two great Iraqi barriers, who cleared the minefields, plotted the fire, planted the explosives, and even captured an Iraqi battalion which just happened to have in its van a company that had laid a new minefield the coalition had not known about.

It was these Marines of Grizzly and Taro who opened up the seams through which the "textbook" Marine attack sped that glorious morning. It was these three thousand Marines who opened the gates to Kuwait City.

"The mission was to defeat the Iraqis, not to destroy them," General Myatt said in a postwar briefing. "There is quite a difference. If we were there to destroy them, we would probably still be there trying to root out every Iraqi position." The casualties, on both sides, would have been considerably higher. On the Marine side, they would have been unacceptably higher. "But we can defeat [the enemy] by getting in behind him, causing him to collapse, and moving quickly to unhinge him. Speed was very important."

Some two months after Desert Storm, the House Armed Services Committee held extended hearings on the subject of military reform in the wake of lessons learned in the Gulf.

One of the first experts called upon to speak to the committee was ex-senator Gary Hart, whose article in *The Wall Street Journal* a decade before is still held as the watershed point for the military reformists.

Hart told the committee that in the Marine plan, "everything was geared to the mind of the enemy commander and the will of his men to fight. This is classic reform theory. Going through as fast as we did made every action they took irrelevant. Commander of the Marine First Division General Mike Myatt used 'mission orders,' which are also central to reform theory. He told subordinate commanders what he wanted and gave them maximum latitude in deciding how to accomplish the mission. It worked. Much of the credit for the Marines' outstanding performance, of course, goes to their commandant, General Al Gray. He in fact adopted maneuver warfare for the Corps and has been personally active in seeing it implemented. From the military perspective . . . this is the most important lesson of the Gulf War."

So, in the end, the memory returns to that brief snatch of conversation noted a couple of years before at the garden party during the commandant's trip to The Citadel.

"Yes, we are the raiders from the sea," Gray said to the young cadets, "but we're also the ski troops of NATO and we're desert troops and we are the Marine Security Guards in your embassies, too. We are all that stuff and more because we are ready and we are able."

Follow the Marines around for three years and a thing like that begins to stick in your mind. You come to believe in it yourself.

It's not like I had bought the whole program. After all of my walking and talking I found myself left with many of the same questions about the Corps that I had originally set out to answer.

It was still hard for me to justify, for all of Jensen's elegance and Willis's doggedness, and Mahler's recklessness and Watson's faithfulness, any combat role for the Marines that couldn't be handled by the Army or the Navy or the Air Force. I still wondered why the Marines needed an air arm when the Navy had such a good one. I still wondered, with Gunny Ski and others, about the uniqueness of their amphibious mission.

The amphibious landing is, after all, not exclusively a Marine specialty. The greatest landing of all, D day, was an Army show.

Nor is the very highly touted "low intensity combat" a role uniquely suited to the Marine Corps. The Army may have blundered around in Grenada and Panama, but it performed mightily in Desert Storm.

So what does America do with its Marine Corps? Let's face it, the truth is we just don't "send in the Marines" anymore, or at least not the way we used to, not for a long time.

And so you return to the hard question of the Brookings Institute, and you ask, after all, does America really need a Marine Corps, and you find yourself wondering if all these military and quasi-military considerations of expertise and role uniqueness are really what matters most.

The Marine Corps is an excellent force of men-at-arms, far superior to the force it was in the seventies with its high AWOL rate and the rumors of decommission and of being folded into the Army.

Riding a tide of military technology, it is a corps of dedicated marksmen moving into an era of "smart" weaponry that will find the footsoldier armed not just with dead-ball bullets, but with shoulder-fired, precision-guided, explosive munitions.

The military mind contemplating the lessons of history and the promise of twenty-first-century ordnance can scarcely help tracing a straight line from the longbowmen of Agincourt through the sharpshooting Devil Dogs of Belleau Wood, and extrapolating a picture of the "one shot, one kill" Marine, armed with the ballistics of tomorrow, standing toe to toe against the heavy tank and the strafing helo and the other "knights" of the contemporary battlefield.

However, this too is refutable. The Army's marksmen are justly proud of their own abilities. And if military history is any guide they will be the first to get the gear. And the Marines, as ever, will have to make do.

No, the best reason for having a Marine Corps has not a thing to do with weaponry or battlefield utility. It has to do with pride.

The Marine Corps is a relatively small group of men and women who still believe in themselves; this is no small accomplishment in a time of lingering self-doubt. It is a force that has retained its pride in an era that too easily lets slip the lion's share of that virtue. It seems to me necessary to keep that belief and that pride alive in some meaningful way.

The Marines were and are and will be a part of the American myth. Like the cowboy, the baseball hero, and the movie star, they inform in some magical way our sense of ourselves; in fact, in many ways, they are a reminder of our better selves: strong, dedicated, confident, all the things that first attracted young Daniel Watson to "a pair of blue pants with red stripes."

Do the Marines have a role to play in the modern defense posture? Yes, they do. Truman thought them among the most highly propagandized outfits on the face of the earth. I have found that to be as true now as it ever was. But I think of the sappers of Kuwait, and I am convinced that people who really believe they are ready for anything are the ones most likely to be so. And there's always a role to be found for people like that.